N. B. R. Local Charge 1/6
ONE BICYCLE (Accompanied by Passenger At Company's Limited risk
EDINBURGH Way. Stn. (No. 1
TO
DUNDEE (Tay Bridge)
Via Forth Bridge and Cupar
This Ticket which is available for a single Journey only, must be given up at destination Station. For Conditions SEE BACK.

Days Out: *Edinburgh Castle*

THE STONE OF DESTINY is the original stone on which Scottish Monarchs were crowned. It was taken from Scone Palace by King Edward I of England in 1296 to Westminster Abbey in London, where it remained for 700 years.

In 1996 it was returned to Scotland by Her Majesty Queen Elizabeth.

St Margaret's Chapel sits near the top of the castle rock. It was built by St Margaret's son King David about the year 1130, and is the oldest building in Edinburgh.

The Crown Room of the Royal Palace contains the crown jewels of Scotland (called "The Honours of Scotland") – the crown, the sceptre and the sword, all about 500 years old. They were used at the coronation of Mary, Queen of Scots in 1543.

The National War Memorial was opened at the castle in July 1927 by the Prince of Wales and Field Marshal Earl Haig.

THE EDINBURGH MILITARY TATTOO 1963

A. E. HASWELL MILLER 1963

Boom!

ⓘ Edinburgh Military Tattoo, EH1 1QB
Tel: 0131 225 1188
www.edintattoo.co.uk

Edinburgh: The Royal Mile

The Scotch Whisky Experience
EH1 2NE
Tel: 0131 220 0441
www.whisky-heritage.co.uk

STEPPIN' OOT DOON THE ROYAL MILE
by The Broons "Royal" Family

Maw Broon

We're a' writing this doon in oor family diary as we step oot DOON the Royal Mile in Edinburgh. We're haein' a wee flask on the Castle Esplanade afore we set aff for oor day. It mak's real sense tae "do" the mile goin' doonhill. Wid ye no' agree? And wid ye believe it, ane o' Edinburgh's traffic wardens is already booking folks' cars and it's no' yet nine o'clock. Come by train!!

Joe Broon

Exactly 57 steps take us fae the wee sentry kiosk at the exit o' the esplanade past the CAMERA OBSCURA AND WORLD OF ILLUSIONS tae the SCOTCH WHISKY EXPERIENCE visitor attraction. Nae further explanation required. In we go! Had tae keep Granpaw in check here. Ootside again, it's only 110 gentle strides mair tae reach THE HUB, Edinburgh's Festival Centre. It's in an auld converted kirk. Pit ae foot in front o' anither 18 times fae here and ye're passin' the ENSIGN EWART pub. Ensign Charles Ewart was the famous Scots Grey wha captured the French standard at the Battle of Waterloo. There's a memorial tae him back up on the Castle Esplanade. The captured eagle standard is in the castle.

Camera Obscura and World of Illusions, Edinburgh, EH1 2ND
Tel: 0131 226 3709, www.camera-obscura.co.uk
From inside a Victorian rooftop chamber, you can see live moving images of Edinburgh projected onto a viewing table through a giant periscope. Amazing!

Daphne Broon

It's 140 paces now, doon tae the George IV Bridge crossroads and ye pass mair woollen and tartan shops than even I can visit. Kilts, skirts, tartan souvenirs, jumpers, cashmeres, Jimmy hats and anything ye can think o' that visitors like. On yer left at George IV Bridge there's DEACON BRODIE'S tavern. Brodie was the 18th-century rogue said to hae been the inspiration for Robert Louis Stevenson's "Dr Jekyll and Mr Hyde". Jist behind is the WRITERS' MUSEUM in Lady Stair's Close.

Ye jist must mak' a diversion here an' turn right alang North Bridge till ye see the statue o' wee GREYFRIARS BOBBY on Candlemaker Row. He was the Skye Terrier that guarded the grave o' his master John Gray in Greyfriars Cemetery for years. The story was made intae a Walt Disney film. Back up to the crossroads on the Royal Mile it's 98 steps tae the HEART O' MIDLOTHIAN. A prison once stood on this site and it was the site of public executions. It's laid oot in cobbles richt beside ST GILES CATHEDRAL, the High Kirk o' Edinburgh. Ye've a problem here . . . dae ye visit St Giles or the ROYAL MILE WHISKIES shop across the road? Go tae baith. We did.

Hen Broon

I hae tae count everybody else's steps cos I only tak' half as many. 114 easy strides and we're doon at MERCAT CROSS opposite City Chambers. It's a kick-off point for guided walking tours tae auld underground streets and ghost tours. They're great fun, especially if ye hae a lassie wi' ye that needs a wee cuddle in the dark. 20 more steps now and we're passing the statue o' ADAM SMITH, the lad that wrote "The Wealth of Nations". I wonder what he'd say aboot a' the bank disasters here of late? Or maybe he'd change his book tae "The Debts of Nations". Time for me to stride on doon tae South Bridge at THE TRON. Maggie tells me it was 150 paces fae Adam Smith on his plinth. Lots o' shops and cafés aboot here.

STATUE OF GREYFRIARS BOBBY

St Giles Cathedral, EH1 1RE
Tel: 0131 225 9442
www.stgilescathedral.org.uk FREE
Royal Mile Whiskies EH1 1PW.
Tel: 0131 524 9380
www.royalmilewhiskies.com

The Writers' Museum, EH1 2PA
Tel: 0131 529 4901
www.edinburghmuseums.co.uk
FREE
Greyfriars Tobooth and Highland Kirk, EH1 2QQ
Tel: 0131 226 5429
www.greyfriarskirk.com FREE

Visit The
Scotch Whisky
Visitor Experience
NEXT TO EDINBURGH CASTLE
ENJOY AN EXCITING JOURNEY OF DISCOVERY THROUGH THE STORY OF SCOTCH WHISKY
THE
MAKING
THE SMELL
THE TASTE
THE SECRETS

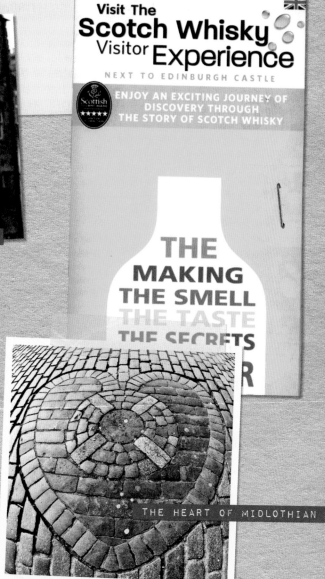

THE HEART OF MIDLOTHIAN

Edinburgh: The Royal Mile – continued

The Museum of Childhood, EH1 1
Tel: 0131 529 4142
www.cac.org.uk FREE

Maw Broon

We take 175 paces in ma guid shoes past pubs and folk eatin' an' shoppin' till we arrive at the MUSEUM OF CHILDHOOD. The Bairn is fair lookin' forward tae this as she's ta'en three times as many steps as the rest o' us wi' her wee leggies, the wee lamb. Opposite is the BRASS RUBBING CENTRE.

We're fair birlin' doon the High Street now and left, right, left, right 42 times and we're at JOHN KNOX'S HOUSE. It's a lovely auld building an' worth a nosey inside. Ootside there's a lump o' a thing ca'd the Netherbow Wellhead, a relic fae 1675 o' the drinking water system o' auld Edinburgh, "Auld Reekie" as my father kent it. Take 28 strides mair and it's the SCOTTISH STORYTELLING CENTRE next. I have tae say there's nae end o' things in this street.

Horace Broon

This counting steps is getting silly, but I have tae join in. Another 48 steps now and we've arrived at the World's End crossroads. At the Battle of Flodden in 1513, King James IV and maist o' the nobles o' Scotland and hunners o' Scottish fighting men ("the flowers o' the forest") were slaughtered. Folk thought it was the end o' the world and hastily built a wall roond Edinburgh Toon tae protect it. The WORLD'S END pub on the corner is built on the foundations of the old wall.

MAW

Brass Rubbing Centre,
EH1 1SS
Tel: 0131 556 4364
www.edinburghmuseums.co.uk
FREE

John Knox House and Scottish Storytelling Centre, EH1 1SR
Tel: 0131 556 9579
www.scottishstorytellingcentre.co.uk

JOHN KNOX'S HOUSE

Granpaw

Aff we go again, me oot in front. The Royal Mile is ca'd the Canongate at this point and it's quieter doon here, an' I'm showing the family a clean pair o' heels as I canter through 320 steps (there's nae haudin' me back here!) to the green-and-white frontage o' ma favourite shop, CADENHEAD'S WHISKY SHOP. I've been in twa whisky shops already the day and it's third time lucky for me. A rare cask-strength Ardbeg stowed awa' in ma jaicket afore ye can say "Jings, Crivvens, Help ma Boab". Anither 42 strides tak's me tae the CANONGATE TOLBOOTH as the family catch up.

We're a' together again for 52 mair steps tae the CANONGATE KIRK. Edinburgh's past celebrities are buried in the graveyard here, including "Clarinda" (Mrs MacLehose), described as the "sweetheart of Robert Burns". ANE o' his sweethearts I'd say. It's a fair bet Rabbie had a rare time o' it, up and doon this street in his day. There's a statue of poet ROBERT FERGUSSON by sculptor David Annand on the pavement here. Fergusson was much admired by Rabbie Burns. The puir lad died aged 24 in the Bedlam Asylum.

Maggie Broon

Time tae call a halt for the day and it's only 190 steps tae CLARINDA'S TEAROOM. An Edinburgh institution and a welcome ane at that for us . . . tea time. Ye'll be hard pushed tae find better hame cookin' in Edinburgh. It's usually busy, an' it certainly was when oor gang descended upon them. What a rare end tae a rare day oot in the Capital. Cheers, everybody!

The Twins

We coonted the day as 1410 steps fae the castle tae here. There's still a wee bit tae the parliament at the bottom o' the street, but we'll go there anither day. We're no' movin'.

CANONGATE KIRK

The People's Story,
Canongate Tolbooth,
EH8 8BN
Tel: 0131 529 4057
www.edinburghmuseums.co.uk
FREE

Cadenhead's Whisky Shop,
EH8 8BN
Tel: 0131 556 5864
edinburgh.wmcadenhead.com
Clarinda's Tearoom, EH8 8BS
Tel: 0131 557 1888

Edinburgh: Holyrood

AT THE BOTTOM O' THE HIGH STREET
by Maggie Broon

Sometimes it's hard for me tae tear masel' away fae the braw shops in Edinburgh, but there are some things that just can't be missed . . . like oor new Parliament building, its royal neighbour Holyrood Palace and Arthur's Seat, which for me is a funny name for a hill. First stop just has tae be the PALACE OF HOLYROODHOUSE.

And it's only a hop an' skip ower the road tae the next FREE port of call, the new SCOTTISH PARLIAMENT building. Me and Daphne thought it looked real cool, but Granpaw and Paw thought it looked like a pund o' mince. Whatever ye think o' it, it's oor Parliament and it's worth a look.

Efter a' the politics and intrigue o' "The Holyroods" ye'll be raring for a bit o' fresh air and Edinburgh's rightly popular Arthur's Seat is jist across the road. ARTHUR'S SEAT is the main peak o' a wee group o' hills right in the middle o' the city in Holyrood Park. The hill itsel' is aboot 823 ft high. It's an extinct volcano aboot 350 million years old. I'm aye suspicious o' "extinct" volcanos, but if this ane erupts when ye're here on yer day oot, ye'd hae tae say ye've been awfy unlucky. There are so many different ways tae reach the top, the best advice is jist tae pick oot ony path and follow it. If it's still goin' up, ye've no' reached the summit . . . keep walkin'! Local tip is that the easiest way up is fae Dunsapie Loch on the wee road that goes richt roond the hill.

Here's a guid wee tip tae end yer day oot here. Jist east o' Holyrood Palace at the foot o' the hills ye can tak' YOUR seat, no' Arthur's, and watch the maist overfed swans in Scotland glidin' aboot on a wee loch. Awfy bonnie.

EDINBURGH.

NISI DOMINUS FRUSTRA

Holyrood Park, EH8 8HG
Tel: 0131 652 8150
(Rangers)
www.historic-scotland.gov.uk/ranger

THE SCOTTISH PARLIAMENT

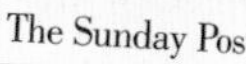

Days Out: *Holyrood*

THE PALACE OF HOLYROODHOUSE

IT'S RIGHT at the very bottom of The Royal Mile and is Her Majesty the Queen's official residence in Scotland. Originally the site of an abbey founded by King David I in 1128 (the ruins of which are attached to the palace), the building of the palace started around 1500. The oldest surviving section is the north-west tower. The Palace has been associated with Mary, Queen of Scots more than any other monarch. It was in the tower, in one of Mary, Queen of Scots "private rooms" that her jealous second husband, Lord Darnley, murdered Mary's Italian secretary, David Rizzio (for a long time afterwards people said that blood stains could still be seen on the floor). Charles II had built most of the palace we see today. The work was finished in the 1670s, but he never visited it. Bonnie Prince Charlie stayed here briefly in 1745, when the soldiers at the castle refused to let him in.

The Queen has a big garden party here every year, when people who have done good work are invited. About 8,000 people come and they work their way through 27,000 cups of tea, 20,000 sandwiches and 20,000 slices of cake!

THE SCOTTISH PARLIAMENT

CREATED by world-famous architect Enric Miralles, the design is supposed to look like upturned boats on a shore. It's not really one building but a collection of buildings. Some have likened it to a village. It's not going to be like anything else you will have ever seen. Probably the costliest building of recent times, its construction caused controversy. On non-parliamentary-business days guided tours are available and free but they are popular so book in advance. It is possible to hear the Scottish government in action in the debating chamber or in the committee rooms but it is advised to book in advance.

Palace of Holyroodhouse, EH8 8DX
Tel: 0131 556 5100
www.royalcollection.org.uk

The Scottish Parliament, EH99 1SP FREE
Tel: 0131 348 5200
www.scottish.parliament.uk

Edinburgh: Holyrood

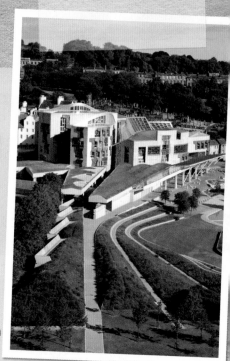

HORACE GOES TO HOLYROOD

The Chess Club's outing this year was to the Scottish Parliament. I had heard a lot aboot it – I had also heard a lot o' mumping fae my Paw and Granpaw about how much it cost to build, but I kept an open mind.

From the outside it is mair impressive than it looks on the telly. Very unusual shapes and curves. It's unique – and why would you build a building that looks the same as a' the others?

First place you go to is the MAIN HALL, that's where we met to take the tour. Even that is quite something. There are crosses carved into the vaulted ceiling which are an abstract version of the Scottish saltire cross. There's art on the wall that looks like the slats fae a boat. I was imagining it made up as a boat. There are a lot of curved shapes inside and outside the building that remind you of boats. Very boaty.

The first route on the tour was up the public stairs to the PUBLIC GALLERY of the debating chamber. The guide said the chamber has 131 seats and desks. They are all set out in a semi-circle facing the Presiding Officer's desk (that's the person that keeps all the MSPs in order) and it's angled so the MSPs can all see each other. I bet that's so they can argue better. The gallery has seats for 227 members of the public, 16 invited guests and 37 members of the media. It was a' very impressive. Parliament usually meets in the debating chamber on Wednesdays and Thursdays.

I asked the man: "Does that mean the MSPs aren't busy the rest o' the time?" "No," he said, "one of the other places parliamentary business takes place is in the six COMMITTEE ROOMS in the building." The tour took us to ane of the committee rooms. Each room has seating for the public and journalists and is wired up so a'thing inside can be filmed. I like the thought that we can keep an eye on our MSPs if we want to.

ANE O' THE COMMITTEE ROOMS

The committee room I saw had a boaty-shaped vaulted ceiling and interestingly angled wooden panels. There's been a lot of attention to detail in this building.

"Committees are important in the Scottish Parliament," said the guide. "They conduct inquiries and scrutinise legislation. Most meet on Tuesdays or on Wednesday mornings."

Next we were off to the GARDEN LOBBY. It has the staircase you always see on the telly when they interview MSPs. Those stairs are the MSPs' route to the debating chamber. This lobby joins up a' the areas o' the Scottish Parliament. The light in there was really bonny. I looked up and I could see the shape of boats in the curved ceiling again. And there's a shiny Aberdeen granite floor.

Next we went to see where the MSPS' OFFICES are. We had a wee keek into an actual office. I love the window seats. The MSPs are lucky to have such a nice space to work in. I have to do my homework at the dinner table.

Next we saw the DONALD DEWAR ROOM. Donald Dewar was the first First Minister o' the Scottish Parliament and the room contains some belongings o' his that his family have gifted to the parliament. This is a room where the MSPs can come to study.

Then they took us out to a lovely garden outside the garden lobby. The whole outside of the complex is landscaped and of course they have grand views all round of Arthur's Seat and the Salisbury Crags. Last stop was the gift shop, and even that had an amazing boaty ceiling.

I was really impressed by my visit to the Scottish Parliament. It is a building that is as impressive inside as it is outside. I think it is a worthy location for the Parliament of Scotland.

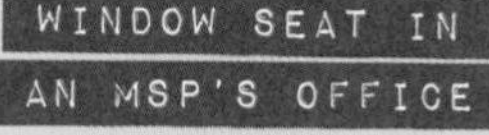

WINDOW SEAT IN
AN MSP'S OFFICE

THE GARDEN LOBBY

More tae do in Edinburgh

There are hunners o' things tae do in Edinburgh, but ye'd expect that, seeing as it is a UNESCO City o' Literature and a World Heritage Site and is known as the Athens o' the North.

The Royal Yacht Britannia
EH6 6JJ. Tel: 0131 555 5566
www.royalyachtbritannia.co.uk
Edinburgh Zoo EH12 6TS.
Tel: 0131 334 9171
www.edinburghzoo.org.uk
Rosslyn Chapel EH25 9PU.
Tel: 0131 440 2159
www.rosslynchapel.com

Royal Yacht *Britannia*

Once it was used by the Queen and the Royal family as a floating palace to travel the around the world. Now it is moored at the Ocean Terminal in Leith, just to the north of the centre of Edinburgh and you can make a royal tour of the boat. Visit the Royal Deck Tea Room for stunning views.

Edinburgh Zoo

Edinburgh Zoo is the largest and most exciting wildlife attraction in Scotland, committed to the highest standards of animal welfare, conservation and environmental education. In just one day, you can meet over 1,000 wonderful animals in a beautiful parkland setting on the outskirts of Edinburgh. There are some wonderful attractions for you to experience, plus you can also enjoy a wide range of visitor facilities and masses of events and activities throughout the year.

Rosslyn Chapel

This church, a few miles south of Edinburgh at Roslin, was founded in 1446 by William St Clair, the third and last Prince of Orkney, and is noted for the beauty and intricacy of its carvings as well as its lack of conformity with fashion or contemporary architecture. The church has a wealth of carvings, including the Apprentice Pillar. In the carvings there are references to the Knights Templar, Biblical stories, pagan symbols and the largest number of 'green men' that have ever been found in a medieval building. There are also carvings of plants from the New World, which are said to have been carved before Columbus discovered it. It played an important role in the book *The Da Vinci Code* and is one of the strangest buildings you will ever visit.

CITY OF LITERATURE

Edinburgh is the world's first UNESCO City of Literature, a pioneer in a new international network of creative cities.

The Edinburgh UNESCO City of Literature Trust was established to promote book culture in Edinburgh, encourage involvement with Scotland's literature and develop literary partnerships around the world.

edinburgh (edɪnbʌrə) *n.* UNESCO City of Literature

Find out what else is going on in literary Edinburgh.
Visit www.cityofliterature.com

IT'S THE DAY OF THE GLEBE STREET OUTING TO THE ZOO
ZOO
ORGANISED TOURS
HURRY ALONG NOW!
HURRY, PAW! ME WANT TO SEE A' THE BEASTIES!

NOW FIRST OF ALL WE HAVE THE THE CAT FAMILY— LIONS AN' TIGERS!
LISTEN TO THAT BLETHER! WE ALL KNOW LIONS AN' TIGERS ARE THE CAT FAMILY!
SH-SH, PAW!

AND HERE WE HAVE THE REPTILE FAMILY—THE SNAKES, CROCODILES, LIZARDS—
ACH, COME ON, YOU LOT! THAT GUIDE'S A BLETHER! CAT FAMILY! REPTILE FAMILY! I'LL SHOW YOU ROUND BETTER MYSEL'!
BUT, PAW—

ELEPHANT HOUSE
KEEP OUT
I'LL SHOW YE THE ELEPHANTS, AN' DINNA MIND THAT NOTICE—ELEPHANTS ARE ALWAYS TIED UP— I KNOW!
BUT, PAW, IT SAYS, 'KEEP OUT'!

INSIDE
HELP! AN ELEPHANT! I THOUGHT YE SAID THEY WERE TIED UP!
RUN!
QUICK! THROUGH THIS DOOR! IT CANNA GET THROUGH HERE!

MEANWHILE-
—AND NOW, FROM THE FISH FAMILY, WE WILL MOVE ON TO—

—THE BROONS FAMILY! HA-HA-HA!
!
DUDLEY D. WATKINS

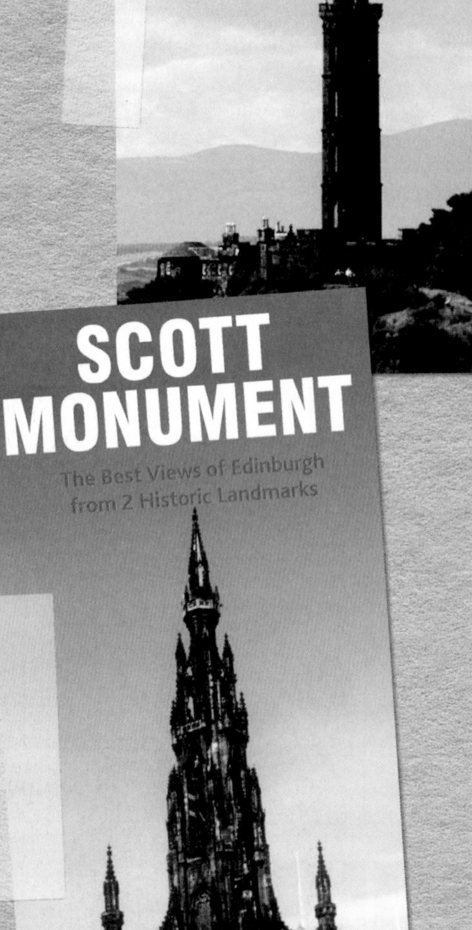

The Best Views of Edinburgh
from 2 Historic Landmarks
SCOTT
MONUMENT
The Best Views of Edinburgh
from 2 Historic Landmarks

Scott Monument

This monument, containing a marble statue of the novelist Sir Walter Scott, was completed in 1844. It stands 200 ft high and is a confection of neo-Gothic spires, crockets, gargoyles and niches, looking like a medieval rocket. The monument has many statues of characters from Scott's novels, including Rob Roy, Ivanhoe and John Knox. There are 287 steps to the top. Climb up the internal stairway for fantastic views from the heart of Edinburgh's historic Old and New Towns and over Princes Street Gardens which provide a beautiful green island between the two.

Calton Hill

Perched high on Calton Hill in the heart of Edinburgh sits a monument to Admiral Lord Nelson, and it looks like an up-turned telescope! The top of the monument is the best place to experience breathtaking views of Edinburgh's Old and New Towns, Arthur's Seat and the distant Forth rail and road bridges. There are other monuments on Calton Hill as well. The strangest is the National Monument, originally designed to be like the Parthenon in Athens, only the money ran out and just twelve columns were built – less a National Monument, more Edinburgh's Folly. It was meant to be a monument to those who died in the Napoleonic Wars.

Museums and Art Galleries

There are lots of Museums and Art Galleries in Edinburgh, especially the National Gallery of Scotland and the National Museum of Scotland. They may be museums full of old things but they do keep changing. The National Portrait Gallery is completely closed until 2012 and the old part of the National Museum of Scotland is closed until 2011 while they are refurbished.

ⓘ The Scott Monument and the Nelson Monument
www.edinburghmuseums.org.uk

The Georgian House EH2 4DR.
Tel: 0844 493 2118
www.nts.org.uk

The Georgian House

Find out what is was like to live in Edinburgh's New Town – an inspired creation of sweeping crescents, broad streets and gracious squares. It offered wealthy citizens in the late 18th century a means of escape from the overcrowded tenements of the Old Town, around the Royal Mile. The Georgian House, with its elegant furnished interior, is located at No. 7 Charlotte Square. The Square was conceived by the architect Robert Adam as a vision of the Georgian ideal in the centre of Edinburgh. The Georgian House has been magnificently restored to show a typical Edinburgh New Town house of the late 18th and early 19th century. The fine collection of period furniture, porcelain, silver and glass, reflect the lifestyle and social and economic conditions of the time. The house also features the 'Below Stairs' life of the servants who made the elegant lifestyle possible.

The Firth of Forth

FORTH RAIL BRIDGE

FORTH ROAD BRIDGE

20 *The Scots Magazine*

FACT FILE

FORTH RAIL BRIDGE

- The first proposed railway bridge was designed by Thomas Bouch and was to be a suspension bridge. Work was stopped when his other bridge, the Tay Bridge, collapsed.
- The present bridge was designed by John Fowler and Benjamin Baker.
- Building commenced in 1883 and it took 7 years to build. It opened on 4 March 1890.
- It was the first major bridge in the world to be made of steel.
- It is 1.5 miles long. The two main spans are each 1,710 ft long.
- It used 54,000 tons of steel.
- The railway line is 158 ft above the Forth.
- 6,500,000 rivets were used in its construction.
- There are 45 acres of metal surface to paint. The new paint being used today should last 25 years.
- Nearly 200 trains cross the bridge every day.
- It cost around £3.2 million (about £235 million at today's prices).

FORTH ROAD BRIDGE

- It was opened on 4 September 1964. It was the longest suspension bridge in Europe when it opened.
- The same company, Sir William Arrol & Co., built both the rail and the road bridges.
- It is 1.5 miles long. The central span is 3,298 ft.
- It used 39,000 tons of steel.
- The suspension cable is 2 ft in diameter and contains 11,618 individual wires.
- It cost £19.5 million (around £250 million at today's prices).
- A second Forth Road Bridge is planned for 2016.

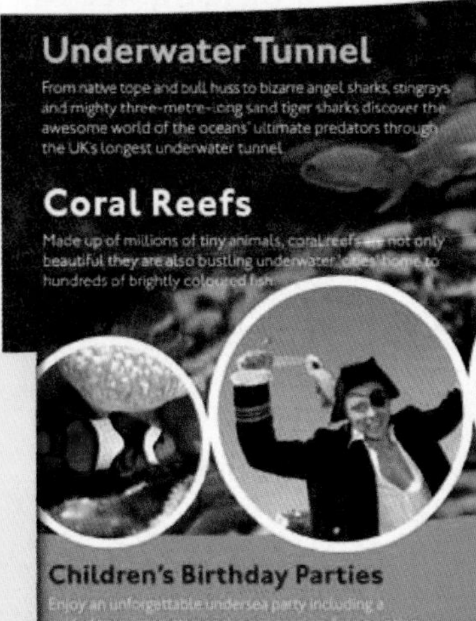

Underwater Tunnel
From native tope and bull huss to bizarre angel sharks, stingrays and mighty three-metre-long sand tiger sharks discover the awesome world of the oceans' ultimate predators through the UK's longest underwater tunnel.
Coral Reefs
Children's Birthday Parties
Enjoy an unforgettable undersea party including a guided tour, interactive rock pool session, face painting and birthday lunch.
www.deepseaworld.com

ⓘ For information about the bridges:

www.forthbridges.org.uk

Deep Sea World KY11 1JR

Tel: 01383 411880

www.deepseaworld.com

DEEP SEA WORLD
SCOTLAND'S NATIONAL AQUARIUM

The Firth of Forth – continued

PAW

THE FIRTH OF FORTH
by Paw Broon

The most photographed bridge in the world, I reckon. Certainly, ye'd be hard pushed tae find somebody that disnae recognise it, the world-famous FORTH RAIL BRIDGE, a colossal and beautiful monument tae Victorian engineering.

But afore I go on aboot the bonnie bridge, I must tell you aboot the place on the north side of the River Forth that the bairns jist love tae visit. The DEEP SEA WORLD. It's aboot 20 minutes in a car fae Edinburgh. But ye wid surely want tae come here on the train and cross the Forth Rail Bridge itself, unless ye're comin' fae Dundee, that is, when ye need tae get aff AFORE ye cross. Clear?

Deep Sea World is doon fae North Queensferry station (steep doon!) and it nestles richt under the mighty bridge. It jist towers ower the aquarium like a giant red spider wi' a' its girders. It's "awesome", as the bairns put it. It's got the largest collection of sand tiger sharks in Europe and conger eels and stingrays (if that lot got oot, I wouldna fancy Aberdour beach's chances o' stayin' in the Blue Flag safe beach list!!). There's also thoosands o' weird and wonderful sea creatures tae look at through the glass. And ye can even watch divers feeding the sharks by hand. Gies me the heebie-jeebies, but the bairns loved every minute. Here's anither thing. If ye want tae jump intae a tank full o' sharks, ye can dae just that here. I kid ye not. If ye're no' feart, ye can get full training and a' the necessary equipment, and in ye go! Can ye believe it?? I'd want a suit of armour and my ain cage. I'll stick tae watchin' the sharkies through the glass.

Back oot under the bridge now in North Queensferry. It's a bonnie wee place itsel' an' there's a wee cafe richt doon there that I aye visit. Their home baking is braw.

Then it's on the train for us and over tae South Queensferry or Dalmeny as the station's ca'd. Back doon the path tae the famous HAWES INN under the south side o' the bridge. This inn featured in Robert Louis Stevenson's "Kidnapped". Ye can get boats here oot tae the islands in the Firth itsel'. . . and ye can watch the big boats heading doon the river. Try and come back at nicht if ye can and see the bridge a' lit up. It's like a big Christmas tree!

ⓘ Hawes Inn,
EH30 9TA
www.vintageinn.co.uk/thehawesinnsouthqueensferry

THIS IS A' GRAN'PAW'S IDEA! FANCY US GOIN' TAE THE FIRTH OF FORTH FOR THE WEEK-END. I'D RAITHER HAE HAD A TRIP DOON THE WATER.
OH! BUT THIS IS A RARE CHANGE—AN' WE'RE GETTIN' THE USE O' AUNTIE JEANNIE'S COTTAGE WHILE SHE'S AWA' THE WEEK-END!
AN' I'M GOIN' FISHIN'. I'VE GOT MA GEAR A' READY IN THIS PARCEL. A' I NEED IS A FEW LANG POLES.
HUH! YE'LL NO' CATCH ONYTHING.

OH, AUNTIE JEANNIE'S COTTAGE IS IN A RARE SITUATION, RIGHT BESIDE THE FORTH BRIG.
I'M GOIN' FISHIN'!

ON THE BEACH
I'VE GOT A' THE FISHIN' GEAR WE NEED—AN' YOU TWA CAN COME WI' ME AN' ROW THE BOAT!
BUT SURELY THAT'S A BUNDLE O' SHEETS YE'VE GOT THERE. YE CANNA FISH WI' SHEETS.
AYE, WE'D BETTER GO WI' YE, OR YE'LL GET YERSEL' DROONED!

ON THE RIVER
NOW TIE THE SHEETS TAE THAE POLES—THEN WE'LL STICK THEM OWER THE SIDE O' THE BOAT.
OH, MICHTY ME! WHIT A QUEER WAY O' FISHIN'.
THIS IS MAIR LIKE A SAIL YE'RE FITTIN' UP.

HOURS LATER
LAST CALL FOR DINNER!
OH, LOOK AT THE GREAT BIG GIRDERS ON THE BRIDGE!
TICKETS, PLEASE!
WE'LL SOON BE IN EDINBURGH NOW.
IT'S HIGH TIME GRAN'PAW AN' THEM CAM' ASHORE. IT'S NEAR BED-TIME.
THERE THEY ARE AWA' OOT UNDER THE BRIDGE.

AW! THAT'S ABOOT THE LAST PASSENGER TRAIN FOR THE DAY AWA' BY. WE MIGHT AS WELL GANG HAME NOW.
AYE, IT'S CAULD OOT HERE. SOME FISHIN' TRIP THIS HAS BEEN.

IT'S ABOOT TIME YOU ANES CAM' ASHORE.
WELL, WHIT DID YE CATCH WI' THAE DAFT NETS?
ACH! HE WISNA CATCHIN' FISH AT A', HE WIS UNDER THE BRIG A' THE TIME WAITIN' FOR THE TRAINS GOIN' BY.
AYE!—AN' I CAUGHT £1·12·3 IN PENNIES THAT PASSENGERS THREW OOT O' THE TRAINS FOR LUCK!
DUDLEY D. WATKINS

LOOK AT A' THE PENNIES!
JINGS! YE'RE NO' SO DAFT EFTER A'!

The Royal Highland Show

THE ROYAL HIGHLAND SHOW
by Maw Broon

This is a real day oot. I never miss it. I don't think any o' the family would willingly miss a day oot at the fair. This is the show, where there honestly is something for everybody. The first show was held on the site near Holyrood Palace now occupied by the new Parliament building. Some wid argue that the smell o' "horse manure" lingers to this very day!! For many years, the show travelled around from one place to another but since aboot 1960 it's been near Edinburgh.

I'm told there are generally aboot 4,000 animals at the show in various classes and competitions. The Twins and the Bairn jist canna get enough o' things like sheep shearing, show jumpin' an' things like bees and what they dae . . . an' we never miss the Scottish Wildlife Trust stand wi' help on how tae look efter the birds in yer garden. Granpaw and Paw like tae get dressed up in their tweed suits and wander roond lookin' like gentlemen farmers.

Ye'll see horses fae Shetland ponies tae Clydesdales, falconry displays, ferrets, sheepdog trials and fly fishin' exhibitions (oor twa auld rogues are richt "fly" fishers). Then there's things like how tae mak' bagpipes, drystane dyking, basket weaving and . . . och, I could go on a' day.

And it's no' just a' farmin' stuff like coos an' ducks either . . . there's FABULOUS food an' drink. Jist ask oor Daphne, if ye can catch her withoot something in her moo'. There's aye plenty o' stuff tae taste, smoked salmon and shortie bein' my favourites. Daph says it's "taste and tipple", that's taste for Daphne and tipple for oor lads. There's whisky and beer and wines, sometimes mair like the New Year than June. Musical entertainment as weel, bagpipe bands of course, but pop bands, ceilidh bands, jazz and somethin' ca'd salsa. I love lookin' at the arts and crafts, the jewellery, the ceramics, the handmade bags, cashmere, tweeds, tartans, outdoor clothing. Jings, I canna wait tae get there again.

When oor lads are no' in the beer tents, ye'll maist likely find them at the biggest outdoor motor show in Scotland. There's everything fae the latest motor car tae bewilderin' displays o' modern farm machinery, tractors, harvesters an' things that look mair like science fiction than tattie howkin'. It's a' changed since my schooldays at the tattie-howkin' holidays.

moo moo
heiland
coo!

ⓘ

Royal Highland Show,
EH28 8NB
Tel: 0131 335 6200
www.royalhighlandshow.org

26 The Sunday Post

Out & About: *The Royal Highland Show*

- Where: The Ingliston showground, eight miles west of Edinburgh, near the airport.

  How to get there: the entrance to the showground is off the main A8 dual carriageway in the direction of Edinburgh. It is a busy road used by people working in Edinburgh and going to the airport, so leave plenty of time in case of traffic jams.

- When: the show is held on Thursday to Sunday towards the end of June.
- Car parking: there is space for 25,000 vehicles on 150 acres of land – Scotland's biggest car park.
- Attendance: 2010 attendance was 187,660
- Children under 16 accompanied by an adult get in free

East Lothian

There's lots tae do in East Lothian. My favourite is the Museum o' Flight at East Fortune. There are real planes tae see, including "Concorde" and what a sight it makes. Here's some information aboot things ye can do.

The Scottish Mining Museum

Housed in the former Lady Victoria Colliery at Newtongrange, you can find out all about the mining of coal and what it was like to be a miner – there is even a re-created roadway and coalface to give you a feeling of what it would have been like underground in the mine when it was working.

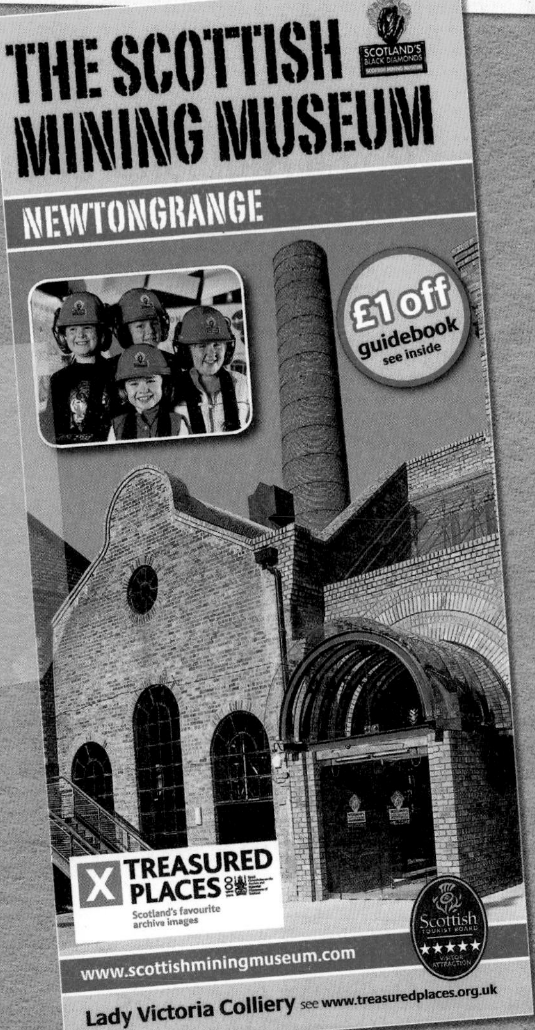

THE SCOTTISH MINING MUSEUM
SCOTLAND'S BLACK DIAMONDS
NEWTONGRANGE
£1 off
guidebook
see inside
TREASURED PLACES
Scotland's favourite archive images
Scottish
TOURIST BOARD
VISITOR ATTRACTION
www.scottishminingmuseum.com
Lady Victoria Colliery see www.treasuredplaces.org.uk

National Museum of Flight, East Fortune

EAST FORTUNE played an important role as an airfield during two World Wars. Now the National Museum of Flight hangars are packed with aircraft that reveal how flight developed from the Wright brothers to Concorde. The East Fortune site itself is steeped in history. In 1919 the R34 Airship took off from East Fortune to make the first east–west transatlantic flight. Now, Hangar 4 is home to Concorde G-BOAA, the first of the British Airways Concorde fleet to fly commercially. You can visit the "Concorde Experience" and follow the story of supersonic passenger flight. The other hangars display lots of civil and military aircraft, including a Spitfire and a rocket-powered Messerschmitt Me 163 Komet from the Second World War and some Scottish-made planes.

Concorde Facts

- **Only 20 Concordes were ever built.**
- **The pointed nose helped Concorde speed through the air. It was tilted down at take-off and landing to allow the pilots to see the runway.**
- **Concorde used a staggering 5,637 gallons of fuel per hour.**
- **The top speed Concorde achieved was 1,490 miles per hour.**
- **There have been more US astronauts than British Airways Concorde pilots.**
- **Concorde carried 100 passengers and 2.5 tons of cargo.**
- **The standard return fare from London to New York was £6,636.**

National Museum of Flight,
EH39 5LF
Tel: 0131 247 4238
www.nms.ac.uk/flight
Scottish Mining Museum,
EH22 4QN
Tel: 0131 663 7519
www.scottishminingmuseum.com

The Scottish Seabird Centre, North Berwick

THE CENTRE sits on a rocky outcrop at North Berwick Harbour, overlooking the islands of the Firth of Forth and sandy beaches of East Lothian. It has live cameras on the Bass Rock and other islands in the Firth and you can remotely watch the birds, zooming in to see the tiniest details (like the ID ring on a bird's foot). Look out for puffins and gannets, and if you're lucky, dolphins and seals! The centre also contains interactive displays and a Kids' Zone. It organises guided bird walks along the beach and boat trips around the islands, giving you a chance to get close to the Bass Rock and the amazing wildlife.

ⓘ The Scottish Seabird Centre, EH39 4SS
Tel: 01620 890202
www.seabird.org

Tantallon Castle, EH39 5PN
Tel: 01620 892727
www.historic-scotland.gov.uk/places

Dirleton Castle, EH39 5ER
Tel: 01620 850330
www.historic-scotland.gov.uk/places

Bass Rock

Off the coast by North Berwick is an enormous lump of rock – the Bass Rock. It is rises steeply out of the sea to reach the height of 350 ft and is a volcanic plug (like the rock Edinburgh Castle sits on). It is now home to over 150,000 gannets, our largest seabird, with a wingspan of around 6 ft, and lots of other seabirds. It was once used by the Christian hermit, St Baldred, in the 8th century and as a prison for religious and political prisoners in the 17th century. Some Jacobite prisoners in 1691 captured the rock from their guards and held it for four years, supported by the French and resisting all attempts to recapture it. They settled on 'most honourable terms' in 1694. In *Catriona*, Robert Louis Stevenson's sequel to *Kidnapped*, David Balfour is imprisoned on the Bass Rock. (*'It was an unco place by night, unco by day; and there were unco sounds; of the calling of the solans [another name for gannets], and the plash of the sea, and the rock echoes that hung continually in our ears.'*)

Gannet on Bass Rock

Tantallon Castle

Mighty Tantallon Castle was built in the 1350s by the Earl of Douglas. In the 1380s the house of Douglas split into two branches, known as the 'Black' and the 'Red'. Tantallon passed to the junior line, the 'Red Douglases', Earls of Angus. For the next 300 years, the Earls of Angus held sway at the castle, acting out their role as one of the most powerful baronial families in Scotland. During that time, it endured three great sieges, in 1491, 1528 and 1651. The last, by Oliver Cromwell's army, resulted in such devastating destruction that the mighty medieval fortress was abandoned to the birds.

Tantallon was the last truly great castle built in Scotland. This remarkable fortification is built on a promontory looking out to the Bass Rock and has earthwork defences and a massive 14th-century curtain wall with three towers in which the mighty Earls of Angus and their henchmen lived. The castle was further strengthened during the 16th century to try and protect it from the new weapon of the day – the cannon. It could not resist Cromwell's attack, however.

Dirleton Castle

Dirleton Castle has graced the heart of Dirleton since the 13th century. The impressive cluster of towers – including the imposing keep at the south-west corner – is among the oldest castle architecture surviving in Scotland. The castle suffered badly during the Wars of Independence with England that erupted in 1296. Dirleton was captured in 1298, on the specific orders of King Edward I of England, "the Hammer of the Scots". By 1356 Dirleton had a new lord, John Haliburton. He rebuilt the battered castle, adding a new residential tower and great hall along the east side of the courtyard. Although largely ruined, the surviving storage cellars, family chapel and grim pit-prison convey a wonderful impression of lordly life in the later Middle Ages. Further buildings were added in the 16th century. The siege by Oliver Cromwell's soldiers in 1650 rendered it militarily unserviceable.

The wonderful castle gardens date from the late 19th and early 20th centuries.

Robert Smail's Printing Works,
EH44 6HA
Tel: 0844 493 2259
www.nts.org.uk

HORACE

Me!

By Horace Broon

You would think that with us Broons bein' printed every week in "The Sunday Post" that we would know somethin' about it - printin' I mean. We jist kind of tak it a' for granted, don't we? Did you ever stop and imagine how it's a' done? How ye actually do printin'? We went jist a wee bit further than Peebles tae find oot. Here's ma report . . .

Robert Smail's Printing Works, Innerleithen

The office at Smail's is piled high with invoices, ledgers, old newspapers and all sorts of stuff that they printed over the years. You can see even the records of the passages booked by local folk who emigrated from Scotland with Robert Cowan Smail's shipping agency.

You can see all kinds of examples of printed work from way back in 1877 right up to the present day. The "St. Ronan's Standard and Effective Advertiser" (printed here from 1893 to 1916) made us laugh - advertisements for the best place to buy your "high class artificial teeth" and a "vacuum clothes washer". When it was first published it said it "would not be merely a medium for claptrap and gossip", unlike some papers I can think of.

We had a visit to the Composing Room and learned about a way of printing which lasted over 500 years. The room is filled with rack upon rack of wee pieces of type. Each rack was called a case. The "Upper Case" contained capital letters; the "Lower Case" contained ordinary letters. Computers still use those terms today! We were allowed to pick up the letters and put them in a line on what they call a "stick" and see our names in print - I didn't get it quite right!

Hoarce Broom

The Machine Room contains several printing presses that go back over a hundred years. The printing machines were powered by a waterwheel until as recently as 1930. Part of the works was built over a river, and they just lowered the waterwheel into the river when they needed some power for the machines.

The printing machines have funny names - the Arab Clamshell Platen, the Wharfedale Reliance, the Original Heidelberg and the Columbian Eagle. They still work today and we were given demonstrations of how they worked.

SAMPLE OF SMAIL'S PRINTING

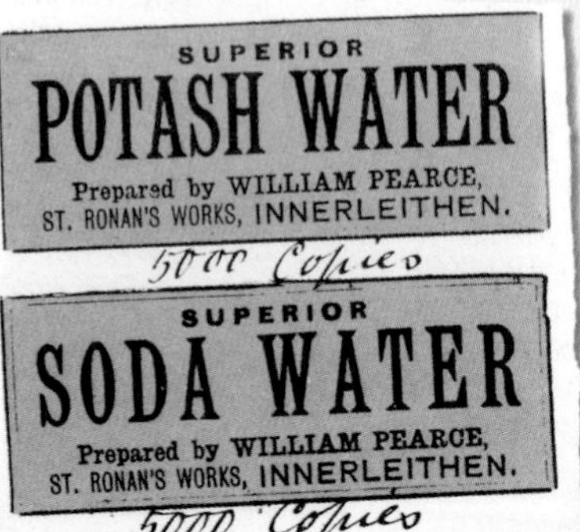

SUPERIOR
POTASH WATER
Prepared by WILLIAM PEARCE,
ST. RONAN'S WORKS, INNERLEITHEN.
5000 Copies
SUPERIOR
SODA WATER
Prepared by WILLIAM PEARCE,
ST. RONAN'S WORKS, INNERLEITHEN.
5000 Copies

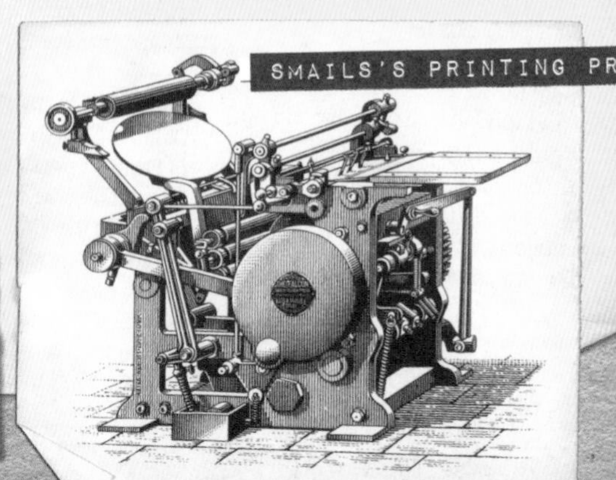

SMAILS'S PRINTING PRE

The Scots Magazine 34

The Borders: places to visit

Abbotsford House

On the banks of the Tweed, Abbotsford was built by Sir Walter Scott, the 19th-century author of classics such as *Waverley*, *Rob Roy* and *Ivanhoe*. It contains an impressive collection of historic relics, weapons and armour (including Rob Roy's gun and Montrose's sword), and a library containing over 9,000 rare volumes.

Country Houses

The Borders contains many grand country houses still lived in by the families that built them. They are open to the public, but check opening times: Floors Castle, Kelso (it's not a castle, but much grander); Manderston House, near Duns; Mellerstain, near Kelso; Paxton House, near Berwick; Thirlestane Castle, near Lauder.

Dryburgh Abbey (near Melrose)

The ruins of this 12th-century abbey are well preserved. The abbey was sacked by English invaders in the 14th and 16th centuries. Sir Walter Scott and Field Marshal Sir Douglas Haig are buried in the abbey.

Flodden Field (in England across the border from Coldstream)

A tall cross in a field marks the site of the 1513 Battle of Flodden when the Scots were routed by the English. King James IV and many Scottish nobles ('the flowers o' the forest") were killed in the battle, along with about 10,000 others, many of whom are buried in St Paul's Church at Branxton, nearby.

Dryburgh Abbey

Smailholm Tower (near Smailholm)

This small rectangular tower is set within a barmkin wall (a stout defensive wall) on a rocky outcrop and is five storeys high with 7-ft thick walls.

Traquair House (near Peebles)

Dating from the 10th century, this is one of Scotland's oldest inhabited houses. At the end of one of Traquair House's parallel drives is a set of gates that are permanently closed. They were closed behind Bonnie Prince Charlie after he left the house in the autumn of 1745 as the fifth Earl wished him luck and vowed never to open the gates again until a Stuart was on the throne. It also has its own brewery dating from the 18th century. It stopped being used in the early 19th century and its equipment remained untouched until it was rediscovered in 1965, when brewing started again.

(i)

Traquair House, EH44 6PW
Tel: 01896 830323
www.traquair.co.uk

Abbotsford House, TD6 9BQ
Tel: 01896 752043
www.scottsabbotsford.co.uk

26 The Sunday Post

Out & About: *The Eildon Hills*

JUST SOUTH of Melrose are the triple peaks of the Eildon Hills. This place is full of history and mystery. There was a fort at the top of North Eildon over 3,000 years ago and the Romans built a very large fort at the bottom of the hills, called Trimontium (three peaks). But then it is said that Thomas the Rhymer met the Fairy Queen here and the hills are the entrance to the Fairy Kingdom, that King Arthur and his Court are asleep under the hill, and that the 13th-century Borders wizard Michael Scott split the original hill into three peaks.

You can walk up the Eildons from Melrose. It will take around 2 hours.

Oor Favourite Museums

There are quite a number of museums mentioned on other pages but I have selected a few that I especially like and put them here. Lots of toons and villages have museums aboot their history – find oot aboot the ones where you stay.

SOME GREAT MUSEUMS – by Horace

ABERDEEN MARITIME MUSEUM

This award-winning museum tells the story of Aberdeen's relationship with the sea, covering ship-building, fishing and the North Sea oil industry. The museum is on Shiprow, overlooking the harbour and incorporating one of Aberdeen's oldest houses, Provost Ross's House, built in 1593.
Aberdeen Maritime Museum, AB11 5BY
Tel: 01224 337700
www.aagm.co.uk FREE

CREETOWN GEM ROCK MUSEUM

This museum displays one of the finest private collections of gemstones, crystals, minerals, rocks and fossils in Great Britain.
Gem Rock Museum, DG8 7HJ
Tel: 01671 820357
www.gemrock.net
Admission charge

DENNY TANK, DUMBARTON

Discover the world's first commercial ship model experiment tank, the length of a football pitch, and see the ship model mechanism running. Experience the working environment of the model makers, clay moulders and carpenters in 1882. Make a real wax hull model.
Denny Tank, Dumbarton, G82 1QS
Tel: 01389 763444
www.scottishmaritimemuseum.org.
Admission charge

ABBOT HOUSE HERITAGE CENTRE, DUNFERMLINE

Situated in Dunfermline's historic Maygate, Abbot House, with its pink walls, is one of its most distinctive buildings. With two floors of display rooms, volunteer guides are available to conduct you through 1000 years of Scottish history. Why not have some great coffee in the Abbot House Café.
Abbot House Heritage Centre, KY12 7NE
Tel: 01383 733266
www.abbothouse.co.uk
Admission charge

OUR DYNAMIC EARTH, EDINBURGH

Thundering tropical storms, icy winds from the North Pole and moving tectonic plates bring the extremes of our planet to life at Our Dynamic Earth. An all-encompassing adventure for both adults and children, Dynamic Earth is the only centre of its kind in the UK dedicated to telling the story of our planet Earth.
Our Dynamic Earth, EH8 8AS
Tel: 0131 550 7800
www.dynamicearth.co.uk
Admission charge

MUSEUM OF SCOTTISH LIGHTHOUSES, FRASERBURGH, ABERDEENSHIRE

This museum is based around Scotland's first mainland lighthouse, built in 1797 for the Commissioners of Northern Lights and built on top of the 16th-century Kinnaird Castle. The museum tells the story of how lighthouses work, how they were used, and the people that used to work in them.
Museum of Scottish Lighthouses, AB43 9DU
Tel: 01346 511022
www.lighthousemuseum.org.uk
Admission charge

HUNTERIAN MUSEUM, GLASGOW

Part of the University of Glasgow, this museum, recently modernised, contains an outstanding collection of fossils, archaeological remains, and much on the history of science and medicine.
Hunterian Museum, G12 8QQ
Tel: 0141 330 5431
www.glasgow.ac.uk/hunterian
FREE

SUMMERLEE HERITAGE PARK, MONKLANDS

A museum that looks at the industrial heritage of Central Scotland, with exhibits of industrial machinery, Scotland's only working electric tramway, and a re-created underground mine and miners' cottages from 1840 to 1960.
Summerlee Heritage Park, ML5 1QD
Tel: 01236 431261
www.northlan.gov.uk
FREE

MUSEUM
COME ON, MAW, LETS GO ROOND THE MUSEUM!
NA! IT'S OWER LATE–TIME YE WERE BEDDED!
OCH! WE COULD LOOK IN FOR 10 MINUTES, ONYWAY, MAW!
WEEL, I'LL GREET IF YE DINNA LET US GO IN!
BUS STOP

INSIDE
SAY, MAW, IS THAT STATUE OF A WIFIE BEGGIN' FOR MONEY?
AYE, AN' SHE'S GOT NAE BOOTS ON, PUIR SOUL!
JINGS! FANCY JUIST WEARIN' A TOWEL IN THIS WEATHER! NAE WONDER HE LOOKS CAULD!

HEY MAW! LOOK WHIT I'VE FOUND–A BONNY STUFFED BIRDIE,–I'M TAKIN' IT HAME!
OH MY!–PIT THAT BACK WHAUR YE FOUND IT–YE'LL GET ME IN THE JAIL!
JINGS! THAT'S A DINGER O' A FISH, EH?
LOOK! ME AN' YOU'LL GO OOT ON SATURDAY WI' OOR FISHIN' NETS, AN' CATCH A FISH JUIST LIKE THAT YIN!
NA! NA! YE'D MAYBE HAE TAE WAIT HOURS AFORE YE GOT ANE THAT SIZE!

TOTAL DARKNESS
OW!! THE LICHTS HAVE GONE OOT!–WHAUR ARE YE, PAW!
'SA'RICHT MAW–DINNA WORRY! IT'S MAYBE A FUSE OR SOMETHIN'!
I'LL TELL YE WHIT IT IS–IT'S A BLACK OUT!
THE LICHT SWITCH DISNA WORK!
OOH! MAW!
STRIKE A LICHT SOMEBODY!
I'VE GOT A TORCH IN MA BAG!

OOH! MAGGIE! LOOK AT THAT!
MAW! MAW!
COME AWA, MAW, WE'LL HAE TAE GET OOT O' HERE!

MICHTY ME! I CANNA OPEN THE DOOR!–WE'RE LOCKED IN!!
OH DEAR, OH DEAR!!
YELL! SO'S SOMEONE'LL HEAR US!
HELP! HELP
HI! THERE!!
OI!
HEY! POLIS!

AN HOUR LATER
WE'LL MAYBE HAVE TAE STAY HERE TILL THE MORNIN' OR TILL SOMEBODY HEARS US AN' LETS US OOT!

2.A.M
HEY! WHIT ARE YOU FOWK DAEIN' HERE? I DIDNA SEE YE WHEN I LOCKED UP LAST NICHT!
I HEARD SNORES AN' I THOCHT IT WIS BURGLARS!
SNOOZE
SNORE
OH! WHAUR AM I? WHIT'S THIS BIG TIGER DAEIN' IN MA BED?
SNORE
JINGS! LOOK WHA I'VE BEEN SLEEPIN' WI? –IF I'D ONLY KENT!
AULD CAULDRON USED BY THE WITCHES OF MACBETH
EGYPTIAN MUMMY OF PHAROAH SOWPSUDDS III

Dumfries and Galloway

This bit o' Scotland should be better known cos whether it's weddings or wildlife, Burns or beautiful clothes, there's somethin' for ye – and there's ice cream for the Bairn.

Ice Cream!

Enjoying some ice-cream

The Cream o' Galloway visitor centre has an ice cream parlour, a tearoom and shop, as well as a fabulous adventure playground that includes the indoor 'Smugglers' Warren' with its underground tunnels and climbing towers, miles of nature trails and cycle tracks. What about having a go at creating your own ice cream flavour? Make your own ice cream starting from the basic ingredients of milk, cream and sugar, then add your choice from a range of ingredients. The 'Ready Steady Freeze' activity runs during July and August from Monday to Thursday starting at 4 p.m. You get to eat the ice cream that you make!

THE TIDE OOT ON THE SOLWAY FIRTH

Wild country

WITH OVER 200 miles of coastline, rolling hills, moorland, forest, mountains and rivers, there is plenty to choose from. The long coastline of the Solway Firth welcomes over 120,000 wildfowl and waders each winter and places such as Caerlaverock and Mersehead Nature Reserve make it easy to get close to flocks of birds.

Galloway Forest Park is the largest forest park in Britain covering over 300 square miles of forest, moorland and lochs rising towards the mountains. It teems with wildlife – red deer, wild goats and red squirrels. Birds of prey also make the forest their home, with buzzards a common sight, golden eagles more elusive and rare red kites, successfully introduced in 2001. Follow the Red Kite Trail and visit the Feeding Station.

red kite

Robert Burns

ROBERT BURNS spent much of his adult life in and around Dumfries, dying here aged just 37. While his most famous works such as "Auld Lang Syne" and "Ae Fond Kiss" were written with a romantic and timeless grace in and around Dumfries, he also wrote some of his most politically scathing work here, frustrated by his work as an exciseman and critical of the establishment of the day. You can visit his farm at Ellisland, his house in Dumfries where he died or his favourite howff, The Globe.

For information about Dumfries and Galloway:
www.visitdumfriesandgalloway.co.uk
For information about Burns in Dumfries and Galloway:
www.burnshowffclub.org
Cream o' Galloway, DG7 2DR
Tel: 01557 814040
www.creamogalloway.co.uk

National Museum of Costume

Whether you are interested in exploring the house and learning about the costumes or having a picnic on the lawn, there's plenty to see and do at this splendid country house museum set in beautiful wooded grounds. Shambellie House near New Abbey in Dumfries and Galloway presents a fascinating look at fashion and social etiquette from the 1850s to the 1950s. Wonderful room settings with accessories, furniture and paintings complete a graceful Victorian and Edwardian environment of well-to-do living, from parasols to party dresses, linen to lavender bags and samplers to shoes. Leave time to visit Sweetheart Abbey, which is close by.

Sweetheart Abbey

In 1268, Lord John Balliol died. His grieving widow, Lady Dervorgilla of Galloway, had his heart embalmed and placed in an ivory casket. She carried it with her everywhere. She undertook many charitable acts in his memory. These included the founding of the Cistercian abbey of Dulce Cor (Latin for Sweet Heart) in 1273. When she too died in 1289, she was laid to rest in front of the abbey church's high altar, clutching her husband's heart to her bosom. Sweetheart Abbey's conception as a shrine to human and divine love is deeply appealing. So too is its attractive setting. The graceful ruin nestles between the grey bulk of Criffel and the shimmering waters of the Solway Firth, whilst its blood-red sandstone walls contrast with the lush green grass at their feet. Despite the prolonged wars with England, and the vicissitudes of time, the beautiful abbey church of St Mary the Virgin survives almost entire but the monks' cloister to the south has almost entirely gone.

Kirkcudbright

The pretty harbour town of Kirkcudbright is the most well known haven for artists in the region and has acquired the title of Artist's Town for its historical artistic connections. At the turn of the last century it became the focus of an artist's colony which included E A Hornel, who introduced several of the "Glasgow Boys" to the town and eventually settled there permanently in 1895, with his home and garden, Broughton House is now managed by the National Trust for Scotland. As the reputation of the Kirkcudbright School grew it attracted other artists including the distinguished illustrator Jessie M King.

National Museum of Costume, DG2 8HQ
Tel: 0131 2474030
www.nms.ac.uk/costume

Sweetheart Abbey, DG2 8BU
Tel: 01387 850397
www.historic-scotland.gov.uk/places

Broughton House, Kirkcudbright, DG6 4JX. Tel: 0844 493 2246
www.nts.org.uk

Gretna Green

WHEN A law was passed in England saying that no one under the age of 21 could marry without their parents' consent, a new cross Border trade started, for, until 1940, a legal marriage in Scotland could take place in front of two witnesses with no clergy involved. Gretna Green, being the first place over the Border, quickly became a centre for runaway marriages. The local blacksmith soon dominated the trade – and so marriage "over the anvil" at Gretna became established. It is still a very popular place for weddings and for the number of people who visit the Old Blacksmith's shop there.

A few things you dinnae ken aboot Dumfries and Galloway

Dundrennan Abbey is where Mary, Queen of Scots spent her last night in Scotland in May 1568.

Ruthwell Cross from the end of the 7th century is considered to be one of the major monuments of Europe in the Dark Ages.

Sanquhar is home to Britain's oldest Post Office, which was first opened in 1763 and operates to this day.

Whithorn is the cradle of Christianity in Scotland and was first founded in the 5th century by St Ninian.

Ayrshire

Ayrshire is the "Land o' Burns" an' its streams, hills, valleys and villages are touched wi' the magic of a poetry that has made their names famous the world over. Ye can find oot more on Robert Burns on page 38. There's more to Ayrshire, however, than Burns an' here are some suggestions.

Ayrshire, which has a coast lined with sandy beaches and fringed with noted golf links, has played its part in Scottish history. The Battle of Largs in 1263 saw the Scots defeat the Vikings and win back the Hebrides and the Isle of Man. William Wallace started on his road to fame as an outlaw in Ayrshire. Robert the Bruce was born at Turnberry Castle, south of Ayr, and Turnberry was the starting point of Bruce's final triumph - lured from his retreat in Arran by a signal fire, he landed here in 1307 to begin the fight for freedom that ended at Bannockburn in 1314.

Bruce wasn't the only king to touch Ayrshire - Elvis Presley touched down at Prestwick Airport on 3 March 1960, the only place in the UK ever to be visited by 'The King'.

32 The Sunday Post

Days Out: *Around Ayrshire*

SCOTTISH MARITIME MUSEUM, IRVINE

If you are more interested in boats than castles, then don't miss the Scottish Maritime Museum at the Harbourside in Irvine. Here are some of the things you can do and see:

- **Explore the Linthouse engine shop, Scotland's 'Cathedral of Engineering', a Victorian glass-roofed building from 1872.**
- **See the collection of floating vessels, including Spartan, Scotland's last Scottish-built puffer, the harbour tug Garnock and Carola, a steam yacht built in 1898.**
- **Learn about Scotland's importance to maritime history, and about the people that built and sailed Scottish ships around the world.**
- **Visit the shipyard worker's tenement flat, a 'room and kitchen' restored to its pre-1920s appearance.**
- **Discover ship models, photographs and historic objects in the museum's Boatshop**
- **Build and test your own model boat, or learn to manoeuvre a remote-controlled boat in the museum's indoor boating ponds.**

Scottish Maritime Museum,
KA12 8QE
Tel: 01294 278283
www.scottishmaritimemuseum.org

THE AILSA COURSE AT TURNBERRY

Blairquhan, near Maybole, is a fine example of a Regency castle in Scotland, designed by the Scottish architect, William Burn, for Sir David Hunter Blair, 3rd Baronet in 1821-4. It was constructed on the site of a previous castle which dated back to 1346, and has stayed in the possession of the family.

Dunure Castle, located about 5 miles north-west of Maybole, has been a ruin for more than three hundred years. The castle as you see it now is from the 15th and 16th centuries. Here in 1570, Gilbert Kennedy, 4th Earl of Cassillis brought the kidnapped Commendator of Crossraguel Abbey, Alan Stewart, and roasted him over a fire to make him agree to sign away the abbey lands. Stewart was, however, rescued by the Laird of Bargany.

Crossraguel Abbey, near Maybole, is one of a few Cluniac settlements in Scotland, founded in the early 13th century by the Earl of Carrick. The extensive remains of the Abbey are fascinating, and the church, the chapter house and much of the domestic premises can still be viewed.

Culzean – see the next page.

Dean Castle and Country Park is situated on the edge of Kilmarnock,. The Castle is a well-preserved 14th-century keep, and the palace block with a tower and curtain wall enclosing a courtyard dates from the 15th century. The castle was restored early in the 20th century. There is a museum with a fine collection of armour and interesting musical instruments. In 1975, the castle and grounds were gifted to the town of Kilmarnock and there is now a country park with a children's area and a farm.

Kelburn Castle, the home of the Earls of Glasgow, is famous for its Castle and historic gardens. It is a place of natural beauty with waterfalls, gorges, attractive woodland, dramatic views over the Firth of Clyde and surprises, like the "Secret Forest" adventure area. A great place for a family visit.

Dunure Castle

Blairquhan KA19 7LZ
Tel: 01655 770239
www.blairquhan.co.uk

Crossraguel Abbey, KA19 5HQ
Tel: 01655 883113
www.historic-scotland.gov.uk/places

14 The Scots Magazine

The Electric Brae

THE ELECTRIC BRAE, known locally as Croy Brae, is on the A719, south of Dunure, not far from Ayr, and heading towards Maybole. Starting from the bend overlooking Croy railway viaduct, it runs a quarter of a mile to the wooded Craigencroy Glen. Whilst there is a slope of 1 in 86 upwards from the bend at the Glen, the configuration of the land on either side of the road provides an optical illusion making it look as if the slope is going the other way. Therefore, a stationary car on the road with the brakes off will appear to move slowly uphill.

The term "Electric Brae" dates from a time when it was incorrectly thought to be a phenomenon caused by electric or magnetic attraction within the Brae.

Dean Castle, KA3 1XB
Tel: 01563 522702
FREE
www.deancastle.com

Kelburn Castle, KA29 0BE
Tel: 01475 568685
www.kelburnestate.com

Ayrshire – Culzean Castle

Culzean Castle and Country Park, KA19 8LE
Tel: 0844 493 2149
www.nts.org.uk
www.culzeanexperience.org

A GREAT SPOT FOR A PICNIC

CULZEAN

CULZEAN IS one of Scotland's best-loved castles and country parks. It has a magnificent cliff-top setting on the South Ayrshire coast off the A719, near Maybole.

Records show there was a tower on the site from the 1400s. By 1759 the Kennedy family transformed the tower into a stately castle and estate – one of the grandest country houses in Scotland.

Robert Adam, the leading Scottish architect of his day, redesigned the house. The elegant circular saloon sits right on top of the cliff with amazing views out to Arran while the oval staircase makes dramatic use of space. The contr between the ordered house and garden and the wild cliff-edge site make this house very special.

In November 1945 the 5th Marquess and the Kennedy family invited General Dwight D Eisenhower, Supreme Commander of the Allied Forces in Europe, to accept the tenancy of a specially created guest flat on the top floor o the Castle for his lifetime, as a gesture of Scottish thanks f American support during the Second World War. He and members of his family stayed at Culzean on several occasi and he also lent it to friends. An exhibition on the first floor of the Castle highlights the achievements of General Eisenhower.

The extensive grounds have a lake, with lilies and ducks and a café that sells ice cream. In clear weather there are stunning views from the battlements to Arran and Ayr an to Ailsa Craig, that enormous lump of rock a few miles ou to sea. There is a vine, rose garden and rhododendrons an lots of countryside to explore, as well as a wonderful beac surrounded by rocks, where you can swim. Down by the s is the old Gas House, where gas was made for use in the house, and in the rocky cliffs are caves once used by pirate There's a visitor centre in the old Stables, to tell you all abc what is going on at Culzean. As one of Scotland's most visi places, there's always something happening!

IT'S A BRAW DAY, MAW! LET'S GO TO THE SEASIDE!
DINNA BE DAFT! IT'S STILL FAR TOO CHILLY FOR THE SEASIDE!
RUBBISH! COME ON! LET'S GET OUR THINGS!
BUS STOP
YE'D THINK YE WERE GOING TO THE NORTH POLE!
THESE SEA BREEZES ARE CAULD!
COME ON, PAW! AT LEAST TAKE OFF YER SCARF!
AWA' YE GO! MY SCARF'S BIDING ON—SO THERE!
I'M AWA' TO SEE IF THERE ARE ANY CRABS IN THE ROCK POOLS!
ARE YE NO' EVEN GOIN' TO TAKE OFF YER BOOTS?
YE'D BETTER WATCH THAT SLIPPY SEAWEED THEN!
HUH! THEY'LL NO' GET ME RUNNIN' ABOOT STRIPPED IN THIS WEATHER! IT'S NO' THAT WARM YET!
HELP! I'VE SLIPPED ON SEAWEED!
SLIP!
YE DAFT GOWK! WE WARNED YE ABOUT THE SLIPPERY SEAWEED! NOW YE'RE SOAKED THROUGH!
BUS STOP
YE'RE NO' WEARING DAMP CLOTHES—AND THAT'S THAT!
REALLY, PAW! IT'S NO' THAT WARM! HA-HA!
WHAT'S THIS?

Ayrshire – Robert Burns Birthplace Museum

ROBERT BURNS BIRTHPLACE MUSEUM
by Horace Broon

The beautiful village of ALLOWAY in Ayrshire is the birthplace of Scotland's favourite son. I have "the muse" within me and have fantasies that Robert Burns, whose father's name was BURNES, was actually born Robert BRUNES, which is the old spelling of BROONS, and that I am Rabbie's great-great-great-(very good)-grandson poet.

A brand new museum in Alloway is my new favourite place in Scotland. THE ROBERT BURNS BIRTHPLACE MUSEUM. It contains some brilliant exhibits about Burns' life and some fascinating artefacts. The Robert Burns Birthplace Museum holds the world's largest collection of artefacts relating to the bard. I especially liked Tam o' Shanter written in Burns' own handwriting. And it comprises several different locations in Alloway. In one day, you can visit on foot BURNS COTTAGE where Burns was born, stroll down THE POET'S PATH and see the ginornmous and not very timorous looking moosie, visit the MUSEUM, then visit the graveyard of the AULD KIRK OF ALLOWAY, where Tam o' Shanter on his mare, Meg, first glimpsed Cutty Sark and the witches and warlocks dancing in a bleeze, then the BRIG O' DOON. Why not also climb up the BURNS MONUMENT and get a rare view of the village where Rabbie grew up.

In BURNS COTTAGE I got goosebumps being in the very room where Rabbie came into the world as the January winds blasted outside the family's new cottage. Epic! Rabbie was born there on 25th January 1759 and it was built by Rabbie's father William Burnes.

If you are brave, after the day out is done, visit the graveyard at night and shut your eyes and IMAGINE. WOOO . . .! Scary. Rather you than me. Stand at the keystone of the Brig o' Doon where the ghouls and ghosts couldn't cross the water and feel Tam's relief and Meg's sore bottom as the pair escaped.

Now, as days oot go, this one is just sheer poetry!

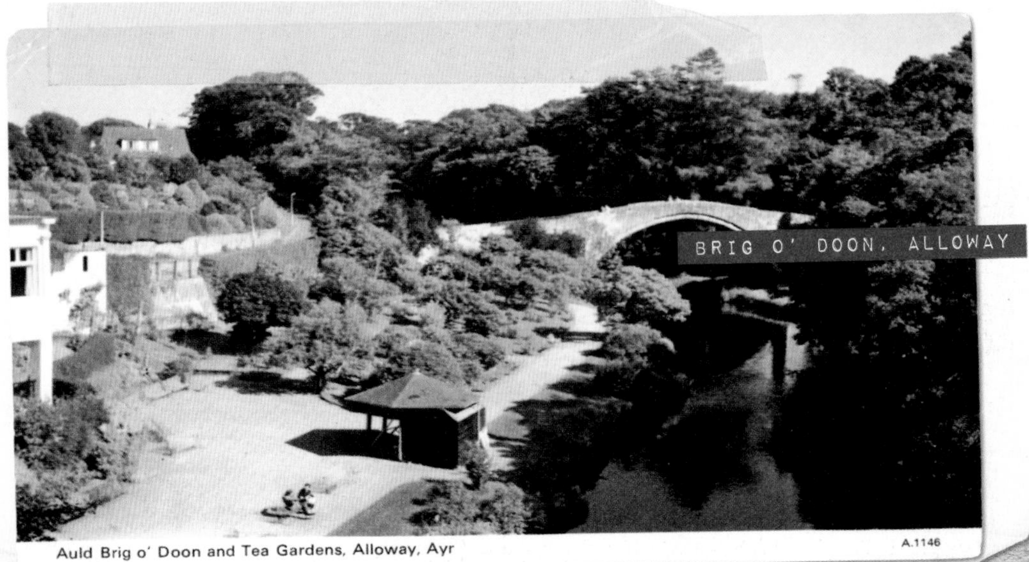

Auld Brig o' Doon and Tea Gardens, Alloway, Ayr

BURNS COTTAGE
6 Kitchen Robert was born in the boxbed. He enjoyed sitting by the fire, listening to spooky stories that kindled his imagination. This was the main living and sleeping space for the family.
EDUCATION PAVILION SHOP & WC
BURNS COTTAGE
MAP
This map will help to guide you around the site. There is no set route; you can visit as many of the destinations as you wish and in whichever order you like.
Burns Cottage
(visit takes approximately 45 minutes)
Poet's Path
(visit takes approximately 15 minutes)
Museum
(visit takes approximately 1 hour)
Alloway Auld Kirk
(visit takes approximately 20 minutes)
Brig o' Doon
(visit takes approximately 15 minutes)
Burns Monument
(visit takes approximately 20 minutes)
POET'S PATH
SHANTER WAY
AULD KIRK
FOOTBRIDGE
MURDOCH'S LONE
AULD NICK'S VIEW
RICHWOODIE PLACE
DID YOU KNOW?
THE MUSEUM COLLECTION WAS STARTED IN ALLOWAY SHORTLY AFTER BURNS'S DEATH IN 1796. OVER 200 YEARS LATER THE COLLECTION NOW STANDS AT 5,500 OBJECTS.
CYCLE PATH
DID YOU KNOW?
SOME OF THESE GRAVESTONES HAVE HOURGLASSES CARVED ONTO THEM. IT HAS BEEN CLAIMED THAT AN UPRIGHT HOURGLASS REPRESENTS DEATH BY NATURAL CAUSES BUT AN HOURGLASS ON ITS SIDE SYMBOLISES A MORE SINISTER CAUSE OF DEATH.
MUSEUM
ROUTE TO A77
B7024
BURNS MONUMENT
WC
SHOP & WC
CAFE
P
BRIG O' DOON
ROBERT BURNS
Robert Burns Birthplace Museum
Murdoch's Lone, Alloway,
KA7 4PQ
NTS member: admission FREE
www.burnsmuseum.org.uk
Tel: 0844 4932601
Email: burns@nts.org.uk

The Waverley

JOE

DOON THE WATTER
by Joe Broon

"Doon the Watter". It's an expression near a'body in Glasgow knows only too well. For a'body else, it's takin' a boat doon the Clyde to the Firth o' Clyde and the islands beyond.

And now it's "Doon the Watter" on the loveliest ship in the world. Nane o' yer ocean-goin' cruise liners can haud a candle tae the WAVERLEY. It's the last sea-going paddle steamer in the world. But dinna run awa' wi' the idea that this is some battered auld relic o' a bygone age. Launched on the Clyde in 1947, the Waverley was bought by a bunch of enthusiasts from CalMac in 1974 for ONE POUND. Bargain or what!! Restored in the year 2000, The Waverley is majestic. Some folk jist turn up at the pier tae see her. Red and white towering funnels, polished timber and gleaming brass, this ship is the pride o' the Clyde. Folk come fae all over tae sail doon the watter tae here, there and everywhere. And ye canna sing "I Belong tae Glasgow" if ye havenae been doon the Clyde on the boat.

I like tae turn up at the pier at GLASGOW SCIENCE CENTRE wi' my accordion under ma arm and play us a' oot doon the watter. A few foot-tappin' tunes soon gets a'body in the mood. But if accordion music's no' yer taste and ye canna shak' a leg at "Strip the Willow", ye can jist stand on deck and hear the music o' the mighty twin paddles swooshing the waters o' the Clyde ahent us, and breathe in the air. Or, if ye like mighty orchestra music, head doon intae the bowels o' the ship and visit the engine room. It's deafening doon there, wi' the enormous pistons o' the steam engine hammering oot the chorus of the ship's ain Clyde music. And the smell o' the hot grease will soon clear ony sair heids fae the night before.

And it's no' jist the near-at-hand ports ye can visit like Greenock and Dunoon and Largs and Rothesay and so on. The Waverley will tak' you an' yer sea legs tae amongst other spots, Armadale on Skye, Tobermory, Fort William, Brodick, Campbeltown and Ayr. And my favourite destination is Inverie on Knoydart. Ye'll get a rare welcome fae the accordion lovers at the Old Forge pub there!!

OVERLOOKING GOUROCK AND THE CLYDE FROM THE FREE FRENCH MEMORIAL AT GREENOCK

Waverley Excursions
Tel 0845 130 4647
www.waverleyexcursions.co.uk

Waverley enthusiasts
www.pswaverley.org

30 The Sunday Post

A Day Out On The Waverley

THE WAVERLEY only sails at certain times between Easter and October. It travels off to other parts of the country during its season. You will need to check on its sailing times. This is best done online at the Waverley Excursions website (www.waverleyexcursions.co.uk) or by telephone (0845 130 4647) or in person at most Tourist Information Centres or Travel Agents. Weekend sailings can be very busy, so it's wise to book. Get online or phone. This is one time you really don't want to MISS THE BOAT. Come on doon!! . . . Doon the Watter!

PIER CLOCK, DUNOON

THE WAVERLEY APPROACHES DUNOON

GREETINGS FROM DUNOON

HOLY LOCH

JB210961

THE WAVERLEY

NEW LANARK – THE MILLS ARE ALIVE WITH THE SOUND OF MUSIC
by Maggie Broon

I'd aye read stories in "The Bunty" and the like when I was young aboot orphans and cruel mill owners, stories that kept me aff my sleep. In Scotland, there's a village less than an hour fae Glasgow and Edinburgh that was once a monument to the "good" mill owners. It's now a World Heritage Site and it's called NEW LANARK, a beautifully restored living village in a bonnie setting on a bend in the River Clyde. It's richt below the Falls of Clyde. The Clyde's waters powered the cotton mills that David Dale built over 200 years ago. Dale's son-in-law Robert Owen provided decent hooses for the workers, fair wages, FREE health care and a new education system for his employees, includin' the first nursery school in the world. He telt his workers in 1816 that society could exist withoot crime, withoot poverty, with good health service, little misery and wi' intelligence and happiness increased. Some guy he must hae been.

It was jist me an' Daphne that visited New Lanark, but we'll tak' a' the family wi' us next time we go. Ye can easily spend a happy day here.

At the Visitor Centre there's a ride ca'd THE ANNIE MCLEOD EXPERIENCE. It takes ye intae the spirit world of New Lanark and ye travel back in time. It's awfy excitin'. We were taken on a fascinatin' journey by the ghost of mill girl Annie McLeod who magically appears and tells her ain story of life in New Lanark in 1820. You can explore all the attractions in the village with just one passport ticket.

Ye can also see in the restored houses how the village workers lived and ye can pop in tae ROBERT OWEN'S AIN HOOSE. No' many mill owners wid let ye dae that nowadays. We took hame some wool yarn spun on the restored 19th century mill machinery. I canna tell a lie, though. We took hame some NEW stuff fae the shops in the Mill No. 2, braw knitwear and cashmere.

We finished aff oor day wi' a lovely walk fae the FALLS OF CLYDE VISITOR CENTRE (run by the Scottish Wildlife Trust) along the walkway and through the woods tae the big waterfall at Corra Linn. Fascinatin' tae think this is the same watter that runs doon under the Kingston Bridge and floated a' thae big ships that Glasgow once made.

Ye can get tae New Lanark by bus or train tae Lanark itself and there's a link bus every hour fae the Lanark Tourist Info Centre. Only aboot a mile. It's a lovely day oot and it really is a wee gem.

Preston Mill,
EH40 3DS
Tel: 0844 493 2128
www.nts.org.uk

Stanley Mills, PH1 4QE
Tel 01738 828268
www.historic-scotland.gov.uk/places

New Lanark
WORLD HERITAGE SITE

Expect the unexpected!

Explore one of Scotland's top visitor attractions, less than an hour from Edinburgh & Glasgow

UNESCO WORLD HERITAGE SITE

European Heritage Medal Winner

British Tourism Trophy

Scottish Tourism Oscar

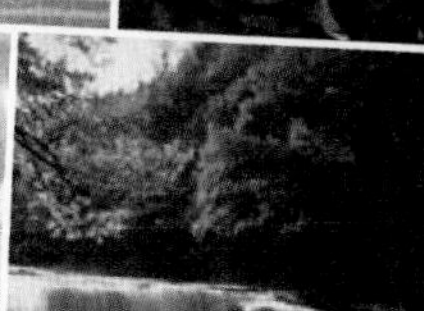

Heritage

New Lanark, ML11 9DB
Tel: 01555 661345
www.newlanark.org

Falls of Clyde Visitor Centre,
ML11 9DB. Tel: 01555 665262
www.swt.org.uk

A day out to the mills

Preston Mill

IN EAST Lothian, near East Linton, visit PRESTON MILL. Powered by water this mill grinds oats to get as much as possible from the grains, including flour and oatmeal (it is often referred to as a meal mill). Stunningly picturesque, the present buildings date from the 18th century, though there has been a mill on this site since the 16th century. The mill was used commercially until 1959 and visitors can still experience the working machinery on a tour today. There is an exhibition room to tell you about the mill, those that lived there, and the life of a miller. Close by is the Phantassie Doocot. It is about 500 years old. When it was built, the birds that were kept in the doocot were used for food.

NORTH of Perth is another cotton mill, STANLEY MILLS, on the banks of the Tay. Stanley Mills is one the best-preserved relics of the 18th-century Industrial Revolution. It was established as a cotton mill by local merchants, with support from the English cotton baron Richard Arkwright. Textiles were produced here for 200 years. The mills, and Stanley village built for the workers, were built from the 1780s onwards at a bend in the river, where tremendous water-power was available.
It is now possible to explore the mill buildings and discover the many changes that took place over two centuries. The Visitor Centre tells the stories of those who worked there and the products they made. The interactive displays let you discover if your fingers are as nimble as a child labourer's or compete to see if you are tough enough in business to make the mills profitable. Hear the clamour of the factory floor and see how engineers harnessed the energy of the Tay as well as the machinery that turned raw cotton into products sold around the world.

A Day of Rural Life

Nae a trip tae the But an' Ben, but a visit tae the National Museum o' Rural Life on the edge o' East Kilbride. While there aboots, visit Blantyre tae see the birthplace o' David Livingstone, oor great African explorer an' missionary, but check for information afore visitin'.

NATIONAL MUSEUM OF RURAL LIFE

THE EDGE of the new town of East Kilbride might seem an unlikely place to find a museum of rural life – but it does mean it is easy for lots of people to get to it. It's a fairly new museum (the main building was only finished in 2001) and consists of two parts, a museum building which contains lots of exhibits about farming, which has been created from the collection of the National Museum of Scotland and, close by, a 170-acre working 1950s farm, Wester Kittochside, that belongs to the National Trust for Scotland. Linking the two, you can enjoy the tractor ride provided between the two sites.

The Museum

The Museum building has three main galleries covering the land, the people who worked the land and the tools they used. Together they tell the story of Scottish country life from around 1750 onwards. You can learn about how we changed the landscape to meet our needs, how people were affected by poor harvests and how tools helped to increase food production and change the landscape.

You can follow the progress of farm machinery from horse-pulled equipment through to the combine harvester and see the Clayton Combine, the first European-built combine harvester. There are also lots of tractors to see, including a cut-away tractor that you can see working when you press the button! Find out about how Scotland led the way with many farming innovations across two centuries of rapid change.

The Farm

The Wester Kittochside farm has never been intensively cultivated so that the Reid family, who farmed the land for generations, gifted the museum an environmentally rich and diverse farm, with many traditional rural features that have vanished elsewhere. The farm illustrates the period of intense change around 1950, which allows visitors to look back to man- and horse-power and forward to the tractor and combine harvester.

Following the pattern of seasonal work, you can see ploughing, seed time, haymaking and harvest. You can also see cows being milked and sheep, pigs and chickens being reared using traditional methods. The farm house and the steadings around the house, including the stables and the milking parlour, are also open. Depending on the time of year, there will be different things to see on the farm and there is a big programme of activities and events throughout the year.

i

National Museum of Rural Life, G76 9HR. Tel: 0131 247 4369
www.nms.ac.uk/rural

David Livingstone Centre, G72 9BY. Tel: 0844 493 2207
www.nts.org.uk
Check before visiting.

FRIDAY
THERE'S WIR NEIGHBOURS THE SMITHS! THEY'RE A' TOGGED UP AWFY POSH!
DAE YE SEE MRS SMITH'S FUR COAT? WHIT A BEAUTY!
THERE'S THAE BROONS A' DRESSED UP AGAIN!
JESSIE SMITH'S NO' LOOKIN' AT YE, MAGGIE!
AN' I KEN WHY! SHE'S JEALOUS O' MA FUR!
AYE! I WONDER WHIT SHE THINKS O' YER FEATHER BOA!

AT HAME
I'M JUIST BACK FRAE THE TATTIE PICKIN' – AN' FAIRMER WILSON SAYS HE COULD DAE WI' MAIR HELPERS THE MORN, AN' I TELT HIM I'D GET YOU ANES – HE'S DEPENDIN' ON YE! YE'LL GET A BUS AT THE CORNER AT EIGHT IN THE MORNIN'!
AYE, WE COULD A' GO! YE GET WEEL PAID!
BUT WE CANNA LIFT TATTIES IN WIR ORDINARY CLAES. WE'LL NEED TAE LOOK OOT WIR AULD ANES THE NICHT!
A' RICHT THEN – IT'S A' FIXED FOR THE MORN!

THAT'S THE THING, RAKE OOT A' WIR AULD TACKETTY BOOTS, AN' AULD SKIRTS AN' COATS!
WELL! I HOPE THAE SMITHS OWER THE ROAD DINNA SEE WIS THE MORN DRESSED IN THAE AULD RAGS – OR I'LL TAK' A RED FACE!

NEXT MORNING
WE'LL NO' GANG OOT THE FRONT WAY BY THE CLOSE, IN CASE THAE WEEL DRESSED SMITHS SEE WIS – WE'LL CLIMB OWER THE BACK WALL!

LOOK! THAE ITHER TATTIE PICKERS ARE WAITIN' FOR THE BUS TAE, WE'LL STAND IN AMONG THEM, THEN NAEBODY WILL SEE WIS THAT KEN'S WIS – ESPECIALLY THAE SMITHS!
NICKIE TAMS!

IT'S THE SMITHS!!
HULLO! YOU GAUN TAE THE TATTIES TAE AN' DRESSED LIKE TINKS! WE WIS FEARED SOME O' YE WID SEE WIS IN WIR AULD CLAES!
HA! HA! HA! THAT'S FUNNY – ME AN' WULL WIS JUIST SAYIN' – I HOPE THE BROONS DINNA SEE US IN OOR AULD CLAES!

OOH! MA BACK!
HEY, YOU TWA! STOP GASSIN' GET ON WI' YER JOB!
GOSSIP!
CHATTER
THE BEST O' PALS
CHATTER
BEND
GET DOON ON YER HAUNDS AN' KNEES TULT!

Glasgow: Kelvingrove Museum

"LET US HASTE TO KELVINGROVE, BONNIE LASSIE O . . ."
by Paw Broon

As a day oot in Glasgow, a visit tae KELVINGROVE MUSEUM has tae be number one on anybody's list. BUT, ye'd be surprised tae learn how many folk fae Glasgow have never been through its doors . . . and that's a shame, so get aff yer backside, get there and see what ye've been missing. Kelvingrove was Scotland's leading attraction in 2009.

Get aff the wee orange underground train (some folk ca' it the Subway) at Kelvinhall and it's a ten minute stroll tae the venue or get aff at Hillhead and hae a family stroll doon lively BYRES ROAD or even doon fae Kelvinbridge and through KELVINGROVE PARK. That's really bonnie.

My lot get aff at Kelvinhall and tak' a wee diversion up Byres Road to the legendary UNIVERSITY CAFE. Hasnae changed in years. This wee gem was founded by an Italian fae Barga in Tuscany. Seems half Barga's population emigrated years ago tae Scotland tae open chip shops, ice cream parlours and the like. And I'm glad they did!

Early coffees and munchies snaffled, head for Kelvingrove Museum. It really is a fantastic sight. World famous and rightly so. Glasgow is and should be rightly proud o' this . . . and it's FREE tae get in. Handy when yer family numbers eleven. The building originally cost £250,000 tae build and as ye'll probably know that might buy ye a guid tenement flat in Partick now if ye're lucky. Recently completely renovated at the cost o' nearly £30 million, it's been worth every penny.

Kelvingrove is probably Glasgow's favourite building and ye can easily see why. Its big towers I'm telt were inspired by the great pilgrimage kirk of Santiago de Compostela in Spain. And it's nae exaggeration tae say that the building itself is as worthy o' interest as the stuff inside. And what stuff. There's something here for everybody and that's everybody of a' ages. It wid be impossible for the likes o' me tae describe what's here.

Get ane' o' the leaflets or guide books at the shops inside and just wander aboot gawpin'. It's that good. As I read in ane o' the guides, "one of the finest collections in Europe". Oor family jist loved it, and we've been back dozens o' times. Granpaw and me even managed tae sneak oot for a "hauf an' a hauf" an' naebody missed us. If ye're five or ninety-five, haste ye tae Kelvingrove!

KELVINGROVE PARK

CHARLES RENNIE MACKINTOSH DESIGNED FURNITURE

Kelvingrove Art Gallery and Museum, G3 8AG
FREE
Tel: 0141 276 9599
www.glasgowlife.org.uk/museums

Nae Park-in'... get it? Tee hee!

STATUE OF LORD KELVIN

PART OF THE MACKINTOSH TEAROOM DISPLAY

Just the richt location for an auld relic like Granpaw!

Glasgow: The Tenement House

The Tenement House
G3 6QN.
Tel: 0844 493 2197
www.nts.org.uk

THE TENEMENT HOUSE
by Maw Broon

Now, wha would hae believed it? Me visitin' a museum that's really jist anither tenement hoose like oors and lovin' every minute o' it. An' me that's been naggin' awa' at Paw for fifty years an' mair tae move us tae a nice bungalow wi' a wee gairden.

This particular tenement flat is in Glasgow at NO. 145 BUCCLEUCH STREET in GARNETHILL. It's only a five-minute walk fae Sauchiehall Street near where the M8 roars by.

The TENEMENT HOUSE was built in 1892 and it still looks today exactly like it did when it was built. A lot o' that's due tae the fact it was owned by the same woman for 50 years. Inside the hoosie, it's like steppin' back in time tae when Glasgow was the industrial power hoose o' the British Empire. There's the auld-fashioned bed recesses and lots o' period furniture. It looks like a film set fae a Victorian television series. There was even a lovely auld grandfather clock. The kitchen range was great tae see. It's original and once upon a time we a' had them. It brought back sae many happy memories. Mind you, I still prefer ma new gas cooker.

The building itself is spotless tae. A puckle o' Glasgow tenements I ken could well dae wi' haein' a look at how things SHOULD look. But although the hoose itsel' hasna changed in near ower a hunner an' twenty years, the outlook fae the flat certainly has. I shudder tae think how many cars and trucks race past on the M8 that ye can see jist ootside the front window.

This is a wee gem and well worth visitin'. I've been back a few times and had a rare time. Now I'm off doon the road for a wee Chicken Rogan Josh. Nane o' that in 1892 I'll bet!

I Think Horace has spilled curry on his Typin. Hee Hee

THE TENEMENT HOUSE

145 Buccleuch Street, Garnethill (third left off Rose St or Cambridge St. NW of Sauchiehall Street pedestrian shopping area), Glasgow city centre. G3 6QN

A typical Victorian tenement flat of 1892, this was the home of a shorthand typist for over 50 years, and little has changed since the early 20th century. It retains many original fittings, including the splendid kitchen range, and fascinating family items. Exhibition on tenement life.

• Shop

1 Mar to 31 Oct, daily 1–5.

WEAV S COTTAGE

More tae do in Glasgow

Glasgow Cathedral

The Cathedral is the largest surviving medieval building in Scotland and is dedicated to Glasgow's patron saint, St Mungo. It was mainly built in the 13th century and provides a remarkable reminder of what Glasgow might have been like before the Industrial Revolution. It's well worth a visit and it is free to go in. While there, you could visit the Necropolis, a grand cemetery for the good and the great of the city, which is next to the Cathedral, and also the St Mungo Museum of Religious Life and Art and Glasgow's one medieval house, Provand's Lordship.

Glasgow Cathedral, G4 0QZ. FREE
Tel: 0141 552 6891 www.glasgowcathedral.org.uk
For the St Mungo Museum and Provand's Lordship, visit: www.glasgowlife.org.uk/museums

Riverside Museum

Riverside Museum on the River Clyde, open from summer 2011, is Glasgow's brand new museum of transport and travel. It showcases the City's outstanding transport collection including trams, trains, cars and model ships, and includes three recreated Glasgow streets spanning 1890 to 1980.

The Riverside Museum, G3 8RF. FREE
Tel: 0141 287 2660
www.glasgowlife.org.uk/museums

The People's Palace

The People's Palace is Glasgow's social history museum and tells the story of the people and city of Glasgow from 1750 to the present. After seeing the museum, you can relax in the Winter Gardens, a vast Victorian conservatory attached to the museum.

People's Palace G40 1AT. FREE
Tel: 0141 276 0788 www.glasgowlife.org.uk/museums

The Burrell Collection

The Burrell Collection, in the beautiful Pollok Country Park, houses an enormous collection of over 9000 artefacts, bequeathed to Glasgow by Sir William Burrell. The astonishing range of beautiful objects from around the world includes medieval art, Oriental art, ancient civilizations and works by Rodin, Degas and Cézanne. Close by is Pollok House (admission charge), an 18th century country house.

The Burrell Collection, G43 1AT. FREE
Tel: 0141 287 2550 www.glasgowlife.org.uk/museums

The Glasgow Science Centre

For all who want a hands-on experience of science this is the place to go. As well as the interactive exhibits, there is a planetarium and an IMAX cinema. There is also a 300-ft tower (with a lift) – from the top you will see great views of the city, but check first to see if it's open as it sometimes has to shut for maintenance and because it's too windy.

Glasgow Science Centre, G51 1EA.
Tel: 0871 540 1000 www. glasgowsciencecentre.org
Admission charge.

GLASGOW SCIENCE CENTRE

Botanic Gardens

Botanic Gardens

Glasgow's Botanic Gardens are located at Kelvinside in Glasgow's West End between the River Kelvin, Great Western Road and Queen Margaret Drive.

The Kibble Palace Glasshouse, situated within the Botanic Gardens, is one of the most amazing iron and glass buildings remaining from the Victorian era. The main part of the building formed a conservatory at John Kibble's home at Coulport on Loch Long. He dismantled it in 1872 and it was taken up the Clyde by barge and by cart to the Botanic Gardens, where it was re-assembled and enlarged. Restored in a multi-million pound project completed in November 2006, it has a national collection of tree ferns in and amongst which are a selection of Victorian marble sculptures, including "Eve" by Scipione Tadolini.

In the main range of glasshouses there are several important collections including tropical orchids and begonias, and in the park, as well as sweeping expanses of grass, there are many special trees and shrubs. There is a 200-year-old weeping ash tree, and large black oaks and beech trees. Other key features of Glasgow's Botanics are the world rose garden, a herb garden, an uncommon vegetable garden and a flower garden.

Dawyck Botanic Garden

Dawyck, at Stobo near Peebles in the Borders, is one of the world's finest arboreta – that's a collection of trees – and has an award-winning visitor centre. Open daily Feb–Nov from 10am.

Dawyck Botanic Garden EH45 9JU. Admission charge.
Tel: 01721 760 254, email: dawyck@rbge.org.uk
www.rbge.org.uk

Logan Botanic Garden

Logan Botanic Garden at Port Logan in Stranraer in Dumfries & Galloway is a very exotic garden, benefitting from a climate warmed by the Gulf Stream. Try out the Potting Shed Bistro for lunches, light snacks and home baking.

Logan Botanic Garden, DG9 9ND
Tel: 01776 860 231 email: logan@rbge.org.uk
www.rbge.org.uk

DUTHIE PARK

BIG LILY PADS AT GLASGOW BOTANICS

Glasgow's Botanic Gardens,
G12 0UE. FREE
Tel: 0141 276 1614
www.glasgow.gov.uk and search for "Botanic Gardens"

Edinburgh's Royal Botanic Garden at Inverleith comprises 70 acres of stunning scenery, just a stone's throw from the city centre. Home to the largest collection of wild-origin Chinese plants outside China, including many rhododendrons, the Botanics are also worth visiting for their collection of heathers, the world-famous rock garden, and the 400 ft-long herbaceous border, which is backed by a 100-year-old beech hedge as well as its conifers and Sierra redwoods from North America. There is a also a special tour of climatic zones. There is a charge to enter the glasshouses.

The garden was first established in 1670 near Holyrood Abbey, for the "culture and importation of foreign plants", and was one of Britain's first botanic gardens. It moved to the head of Nor' Loch, now the site of Waverley Station and then in 1763 to a site on the road to Leith. In 1820 it moved again to Inverleith, but this move took three years, and used transplanting machines invented by the curator, William McNab, for the mature trees.

During the last century Edinburgh's Botanics acquired three regional gardens – Benmore in Argyll, Dawyck in the wooded hills of the Scottish Borders and Logan in Dumfries and Galloway.

Dundee Botanic Garden is open throughout the year, and is situated near Dundee's airport. Dundee prides itself on running a low-cost garden that was established on a shoestring in 1966. The founding principles of the garden are science, education and conservation. A Visitor's Centre was opened in 1984. A feature of the garden is the "native plant communities unit" that contains a representative range of plants that grow within the British Isles. Trees are now also a major part of the display, and include birch, ash, oak, beech and pine. Exotic plants include a Brazilian fern and plants that have adapted to different environments.

Duthie Park, Aberdeen, by the banks of the River Dee, is a park of 44 acres which was donated to the city by Lady Elizabeth Duthie in 1880 and opened to the public in 1883. Within the park is the spectacular David Welch Winter Gardens, which were rebuilt in 1970 after the original glasshouses of 1899 were badly damaged in a storm. These house many exotic plants including tree ferns, Spanish moss, banana trees and one of the largest collections of cacti in Britain. The park has many other features including a Japanese Garden, a bandstand, fountains, ponds and statues. This is a park for all the family, with activities from boating in the ponds to cricket on the lawns.

THE BOTANICS AT DUNDEE

THE PALM HOUSE AT THE ROYAL BOTANIC GARDEN

Glasgow: Charles Rennie Mackintosh

Glasgow has a world-famous architect and he was called Charles Rennie Mackintosh. Here's what I've found oot aboot him.

CHARLES RENNIE MACKINTOSH

Charles Rennie Mackintosh is recognised internationally as "the father of the Glasgow style" and as a major influence in the development of modern architecture – and all his most famous buildings are in Glasgow or close by.

He was born in 1868 and lived in Dennistoun. Aged fifteen, he began evening classes at Glasgow School of Art. Towards the end of the 19th century, the art school was one of the leading art academies of Europe. A year later Mackintosh joined John Hutchison's architectural practice as an apprentice draughtsman. In 1889 he joined the larger architectural practice of Honeyman and Keppie, where he later became a partner in 1901. In 1900 Mackintosh married Margaret Macdonald, whom he met at Glasgow School of Art. She was a key influence on his interior designs. Over the next few years he designed the buildings he is famous for. They left Glasgow in 1913, and Mackintosh spent most of the rest of his life in the south of France, where he painted. Both he and his wife died in London. Today Mackintosh is celebrated for his skill and talent as an architect, designer and watercolourist.

The most significant buildings that he designed in Glasgow include the Glasgow School of Art, the old Glasgow Herald offices in Mitchell Lane (The Lighthouse), the Willow Tearooms, Scotland Street School, Queen's Cross Church, The Hill House in Helensburgh and Windyhill in Kilmacolm.

THE GLASGOW SCHOOL OF ART TOUR
Charles Rennie Mackintosh's greatest architectural achievement.

THE BEST MACKINTOSH BUILDINGS:

The Hill House, Helensburgh

The Hill House is rated as Mackintosh's finest house. With views over the Clyde at Helensburgh, and designed for the publisher Walter Blackie in 1902, the house's design, furniture and formal gardens are classic Mackintosh style. It is now run by the National Trust for Scotland and is open from April to October.

The Hill House G84 9AJ. Tel: 0844 493 2208
www.nts.org.uk Admission charge

Scotland Street School, Glasgow

Designed in 1903-6, Scotland Street School has been restored to Mackintosh's original designs. It was the last major building by Mackintosh in Glasgow. The building is now a museum of education and contains three classroom reconstructions to show the changing nature of the schoolroom from the Victorian era, through the Second World War to the classroom of the 1950s. There are interactive displays and exhibitions.

Scotland Street School G5 8QB. Tel: 0141 287 0500
www.glasgowmuseums.com FREE

The Glasgow School of Art

Mackintosh's design for the new Glasgow School of Art in 1896 was the birth of a new style in 20th-century European architecture. Since the extension that he designed in 1906, which includes his spectacular library, the building has remained the heart of the art school. Regular tours are run for visitors to the building.

Glasgow School of Art G3 6RQ. Tel: 0141 353 4500
www.gsa.ac.uk Admission free. Charge for tours.

The Willow Tearooms, Glasgow

Working for Kate Cranston, Charles Rennie Mackintosh designed The Willow Tearoom in Sauchiehall Street, including the jewel in the crown, the Room De Luxe. Visitors today will enjoy taking their lunch in this majestic setting admiring many of the original features on view. At Buchanan Street, the tearoom has been recreated in the style of the White Dining Room and the Chinese – or Blue Room – which Mackintosh also worked on.

Willow Tea Rooms,
217 Sauchiehall Street G2 3EX
Tel: 0141 332 0521,
and 97 Buchanan Street G1 3HF
Tel: 0141 204 5242
www.willowtearooms.co.uk

Queens Cross Church, Glasgow

This is the only church designed by Mackintosh to be actually built, and is now the Charles Rennie Mackintosh Society's International Headquarters. Magnificent stained glass and exceptional relief carving on wood and stonework are highlights of the interior where light and space are used to dramatic effect.

Queens Cross Church G20 7EL.
Tel: 0141 946 6600 www.crmsociety.com
Admission charge, free entry on Wednesdays after 1 pm. Closeon Saturday and Sunday.

Hunterian Art Gallery, Glasgow

Mackintosh's own house has been reconstructed here and furnished with many examples of Mackintosh furniture from the University of Glasgow's collection.

Hunterian Art Gallery G12 8QQ.
Tel: 0141 330 5431 www.glasgow.ac.uk/hunterian
Admission charge to Mackintosh House.

Oor Favourite Art Galleries

ABOOT ART GALLERIES

I dinnae think we had ever all been in a gallery together till we were caught in the rain an' took shelter - but what a magical world we found inside. There's paintings from hunners of years ago that look as if the paint's no dry yet. There are portraits of how folk used to look and how they dressed (or didn't sometimes!) - Maw tries tae rush the boys past some o' the pictures wi people wi'oot their claes on.

There's special galleries - just portraits - or just modern, but everyone likes something different. Paw's not sae keen on the modern art. He looks at ane and says "Weel, it'll be nice when it's feenished, maybe!" Daphne says she likes "The Glasgow Boys".

Now we go again and again, and I keep going back to the same paintings for another look. I've got some real favourites and every time ye look at a painting ye can see somethin' you didnae see before, that stops ye and makes ye think.

There's plenty space usually, so even if ye're tall or short or cannae see, ye can go close or stand back and take a good look. Ye can go richt close and see the strokes o' the painter's brush.

Granpaw's never talked about art, but he really likes a wander in a gallery, but what he really likes best is an exhibition of photographs - he likes the auld ones. "Those were the days" he says - aboot everything. The auld days cannae all have been good can they? The galleries have special exhibitions as well as pictures that are there all the time. Exhibitions are usually on for a wee while so there's plenty time tae go, and go back again!

I went to see sculptures the last time. It's amazing what some artists can do with their hands. I'm not so sure about that Turner Prize though. Sometimes I think folk are just havin' a laugh. Maybe if I hung all of Daphne's shoes on a washin' line oot the windae at Glebe Street it would be art.

ⓘ Galleries not to be missed. These are some of the most popular galleries in Scotland.

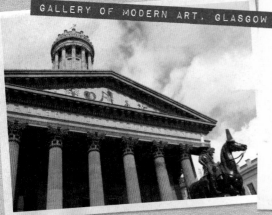

GALLERY OF MODERN ART, GLASGOW

Art Galleries

Gallery of Modern Art, Glasgow G1 3AH.
Tel: 0141 287 3050 www.glasgowmuseums.com

The Burrell Collection, Glasgow G43 1AT.
Tel: 0141 287 2550 www.glasgowmuseums.com

Scottish National Gallery of Modern Art, Edinburgh EH4 3DR. Tel: 0131 624 6200
www.nationalgalleries.org

Aberdeen Art Gallery,
AB10 1FQ. Tel: 01224 523 700 www.aagm.co.uk

National Gallery of Scotland, Edinburgh EH2 2EL.
Tel: 0131 624 6200 www.nationalgalleries.org

Perth Museum and Art Gallery, PH1 5LB.
Tel: 01738 632488 www.pkc.gov.uk

Hunterian Art Gallery, Glasgow G12 8QQ.
Tel: 0141 330 5431 www.glasgow.ac.uk/hunterian

Kirkcaldy Museum and Art Gallery, KY1 1YG.
Tel: 01592 583213 www.fife.gov.uk

Dundee Contemporary Arts, DD1 4DY.
Tel: 01382 909900 www.dca.org.uk

Pier Arts Centre, Stromness, Orkney KW16 3AA.
Tel: 01856 850209 www.pierartscentre.com

HOLD STILL, DAPHNE! MA TUTOR AT THE NEW ARTS COURSE'LL NO' BE IMPRESSED IF I CANNAE GET THIS FINISHED.
AH'M A' STIFF. COULD YE NO' HAE TOOK A PHOTOGRAPHY COURSE INSTEAD? YE'D GET YER PICTURE MUCH QUICKER.

OOT O' HERE! OOT YE GO! THERE'S IMPORTANT WORK GOIN' ON IN HERE!
AWA'! YE'RE JIST DAEIN' PICTURES! I DAE THEM A' THE TIME.

NEXT DAY . . .
MAW, HAE YE SEEN MA ART COURSE STUFF?
AYE. JIST WHAUR YE LEFT IT WITHOOT TIDYIN' IT AWA'. I'VE PACKED IT A' IN YER CASE FOR YE. HERE.

AND . . .
AH, HORATIO, MY BOY . . . AND WHAT ARTISTIC TREASURE HAVE YOU BROUGHT TO INSPIRE AND DELIGHT OUR WEARY SPIRITS?
WEEL . . . ER, WELL, I'VE BEEN EXPERIMENTING WITH PORTRAITURE, MAINLY.

MY WORD! THESE ARE . . . WHY THEY'RE EXCELLENT! SO BOLD! SO DARING! SO MOVING!
REALLY? OH . . . I MEAN, THAT'S JUST WHAT I WAS AIMING FOR.

WOULD YOU MIND IF I ADDED SOME OF THESE TO A SMALL EXHIBITION I'M PLANNING?
MIND? MY WORK ON SHOW? MY, MY . . .

IT'S A BIG HONOUR TAE . . . OH, MY!

THE OPENING NIGHT . . .
SUCH A SOPHISTICATED USE OF PRIMITIVE STYLISTIC TECHNIQUES . . .
ABSOLUTELY, YET THE POWER IS IN THE RAW EMOTIONS THEY EVOKE . . .
YA. SUPERB.
HEY!

THEM'S MA PICTURES. I PIT THEM WI' HORACE'S TAE SHOW HIM HOO EASY IT IS.
DINNAE SAY A WORD AN' I'LL BUY YE AN ICE LOLLY. I COULDNAE TELL ONYBODY. EFTER A' THAT PRAISE, I'D HAE LOOKED A RICHT EEJIT!
IT'S A GUID JOB NANE O' THEM'S A PICTURE O' ME!

Country Parks

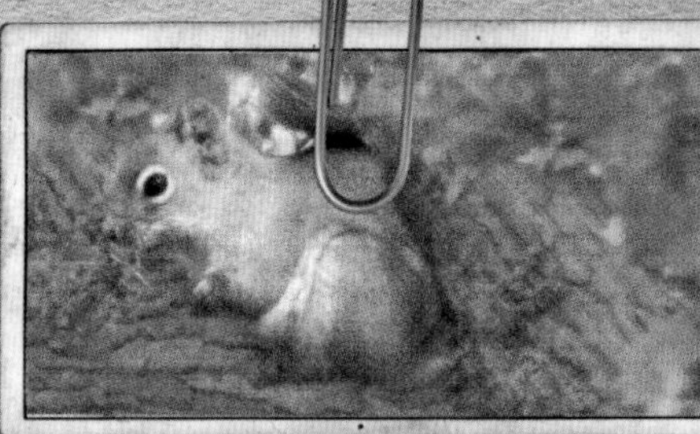

Scotland abounds with country parks, woods, forests and areas of outstanding natural beauty. Many are within easy reach of Scotland's towns and cities, and are free.

Country parks tend to have good paths and are specially managed to make them easier to explore and appreciate. Most have well-marked paths of different lengths and difficulty, and substantial areas where you are free to roam. Natural beauty, wildlife and our cultural heritage are easy to appreciate in them, and the country parks are designed so that we can enjoy and understand our country more. Most country parks are used for walking, dog walking, or cycling and mountain biking.

(i) Strathclyde Country Park, ML1 3ED
Tel: 01698 402060
www.scotlandsthemepark.com
www.northlanarkshire.gov.uk

Country Parks: Information

Volunteering to help

Many of the agencies and trusts that manage woodlands and parks run volunteer events to get you involved, and they encourage volunteers to help make paths and assist with conservation projects, or activities such as being involved in a wildlife watch. The Forestry Commission in Scotland, for example, actively promotes woodlands for healthy exercise, and their website will also direct you to the best places to catch a glimpse of a red squirrel and or a rare bird, such as the peregrine falcon.

More information on country parks, woodlands, forests, areas of outstanding natural beauty and internationally recognised heritage sites can be found on the following websites:

Forestry Commission: www.forestry.gov.uk/scotland
Their properties include Glen Affric, Bennachie, Galloway Forest Park, Queen Elizabeth Forest Park, Glenmore Forest Park Visitor Centre.

John Muir Trust: www.jmt.org
Their properties include Ben Nevis, Schiehallion, part of the Skye Cuillins, properties in Knoydart.

RSPB (Royal Society for the Protection of Birds): www.rspb.org.uk/ourwork/around_the_uk/scotland.asp
Their properties include Lochwinnoch, Inversnaid, Vane Farm (Perth and Kinross), Coll.

National Trust for Scotland: www.nts.org.uk
Their properties include Brodick, Culzean and Crathes Castle.

Scottish Natural Heritage: www.snh.org.uk
Their properties include Clyde Valley Woodlands, Loch Lomond, Beinn Eighe (Torridon).

Woodland Trust: www.woodland-trust.org.uk

Wildlife Trust: www.wildlifetrusts.org

Local authorities: check your local council's website for country parks near you.

UNESCO: (international designations, e.g. New Lanark) http://whc.unesco.org

(i) Calderglen Country Park, G75 0QZ
Tel: 01355 236644
www.southlanarkshire.gov.uk

JUST A FEW OF SCOTLAND'S COUNTRY PARKS

Strathclyde Country Park, Motherwell

Its 400 hectares of countryside in between junctions five and six of the M74 motorway make it a bit of an oasis. There are a huge range of activities available. Footpaths, nature trails and a Roman Fort and bathhouse sit alongside nature reserves and sports facilities.

Sailing, walking, birdwatching, cycling, water ski-ing – the park is a licensed outdoor activity centre with a great range of water activities available. You can also camp on the site in a specified area. Look out for major events throughout the year, from 10k races to a spectacular fireworks night.

Also on the site is M&D's, Scotland's Theme Park, with rides suitable for children and adults. It boasts Scotland's only inverted rollercoaster called the "Tsunami", the "Tornado" rollercoaster with a 360° loop and many more attractions including a 35-metre-high Big Wheel. There's also a soft-play area, amusements, bowling and minature golf.

THE BIG WHEEL AT M&D'S

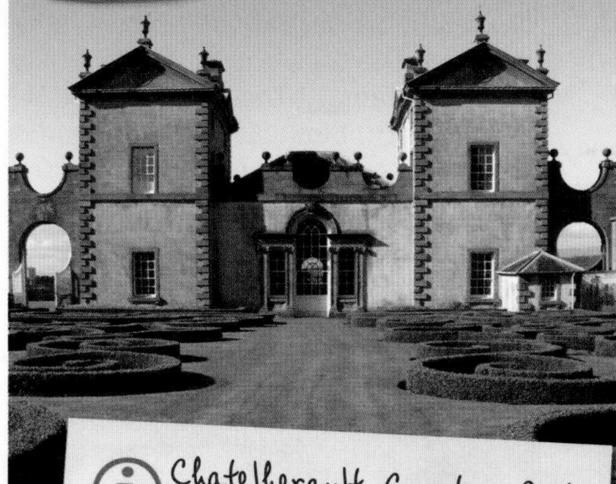

ⓘ Chatelherault Country Park and Visitor Centre, Hamilton, ML3 7UE
Phone: 01698 426213
www.southlanarkshire.gov.uk

Chatelherault, Hamilton

Chatelherault was the Duke of Hamilton's hunting lodge. The Country Park has a playpark, contains the ruins of Cadzow Castle and great woodland walks. Exhibitions and a full programme of ranger-led activities (call for further details). Apr–Oct, Mon–Sat, 10am–5pm; Sun noon–5.30pm.

Calderglen Country Park, East Kilbride

Calderglen country park has an ornamental garden, a children's zoo and a host of walks and nature trails. South Lanarkshire Ranger Service provides a full programme of countryside activities. Reduced opening hours operate from Oct–Mar.

ⓘ Balloch Castle Country Park, Loch Lomond and the Trossachs National Park, G83 8EG
Tel: 0845 345 4978
www.lochlomond-trossachs.org

Polkemmet Country Park, Near Whitburn

The former private estate of the Baillie family, who lived here for over 300 years. Enjoy beautiful woodland and riverside walks, picnic and barbecue areas and a pleasant visitor centre. Look out for roe deer, foxes, herons, water voles, bats, badgers and a white squirrel which all make their home in the park. From the M8 motorway you'll see Polkemmet's giant aluminium "horn" art sculpture. A coloured trail in the park leads to it.

Polkemmet has a 9-hole golf course and children can learn to play through a structured programme.

www.clubgolfscotland-youth.co.uk/news71.html

Balloch Castle Country Park, Balloch

Enjoy a pleasant woodland walk around several interesting sites of restoration. Worth the visit just for the beautiful Fairy Glen. Within Loch Lomond and the Trossachs National Park. Balloch is on the A81, just off the A82 from Glasgow to Crianlarich.

Loch Lomond

Loch Lomond is our biggest loch and it's really close tae Glasgow, so lots of us enjoy it. Here's some more aboot it, and some suggestions of things ye can do.

THE BONNIE, BONNIE BANKS...

Loch Lomond is 24 miles long. It is narrow at the top (about three-quarters of a mile wide) and widest at the bottom, where it is 5 miles wide. It is also much deeper towards the top – the deepest part is around 600 ft deep. It is the largest loch in Great Britain. At the northern end it is surrounded by ranges of high mountains – Ben Vorlich, Ben a Chroin and Ben Lomond, while, as it widens towards the south, it embraces a charming group of 30 wooded islands. At Balloch at the southern end of the loch, the River Leven flows south out of the loch and joins the Clyde at Dumbarton, a few miles away.

The loch holds a great number of fish. Salmon and sea trout come back up the River Leven into the southern parts of the loch, and brown and rainbow trout, pike, roach, chub, perch and dace add to the variety.

(i)

You can find out lots more about Loch Lomond at:
www.loch-lomond.net
www.lochlomondangling.com
www.visit-lochlomond.com
www.maidoftheloch.com

LOCH LOMOND

Boating on the Loch

Loch Lomond has always had a boating tradition and the loch has been well used by folk wanting to enjoy the area from the loch. The first commercial pleasure steamer started service in 1827. Since that time there has been a steady increase in the numbers and type of craft using the loch.

The Maid of the Loch

At Balloch Pier is "The Maid of the Loch", a paddle steamer that used to work on the Loch and which you can now visit. It was the last paddle steamer built in Britain and is now being restored. Leaving Balloch Pier, on the right bank you can see Balloch Park and Boturich Castle, once an ancient seat of the Lennox family and now a country park.

Loch Lomond Shores

On the left you can see Loch Lomond Shores, where there is a Visitor Centre for the Loch Lomond and the Trossachs National Park, which has lots of information about the loch (and a fascinating woodland path, complete with modern sculpture). There's a modern building that looks a bit like an old castle, now the rather surprising home to a sea-life centre. Then Glen Fruin opens up on your left, while, in the middle of the loch lies Inchmurrin ('grassy isle'), the largest and most southerly of the islands, at the south end of which are the ruins of old Lennox Castle. Both this island and Inchlonaig used to be places of "internment for drunken and insane persons".

Balmaha

To the east of Inchmurrin is the village of Balmaha and, immediately opposite it, Inchcailloch, the "island of old women" – so called from a former nunnery there. This island was the burial place of the MacGregors and the yew trees of this sacred island provided the wood for the fiery cross of "The Lady of The Lake". Rising above Balmaha is Conic Hill – a relatively easy climb to the top and great views of the loch and the line of islands that show the position of the Highland Fault Line.

Ben Lomond

North of the islands you approach Luss picturesquely situated on the west bank, and then, on the east side, is Rowardennan, a common starting point for the ascent of Ben Lomond, the most southerly Munro peak, which dominates the scene. Onwards to Tarbet on the west side and ahead a view up Glen Falloch at the head of the loch.

Rob Roy

At Inversnaid, on the east, the route from the Trossachs comes in. On the rocks to the right, high up, is Rob Roy's cave where Bruce is said to have sheltered in 1306 and a little farther on is Eilean Vow, an islet with a ruined castle of the Macfarlanes. Yews are said to have been planted on the islet by Bruce to provide bows for his successors.

At Ardlui, at the top of the loch, there is a station on the West Highland Railway, another picture postcard opportunity.

When it's Wet

WET WET WET DAYS
by Paw Broon

Wet days, days when it's jist rainin' big cats an' Rottweilers. What is there tae dae? Well, oor lot sometimes dae the usual things like goin' tae "the picters" (cinema, folk ca' it now) an' as ye ken, there's nae end o' fine museums and the like for damp days.

But here's OOR favourite wet day oot, well MY favourite actually. It took a bit o' persuadin' wi' the rest o' the gang, but now they a' like it tae. Get oot the wellies an' the waterproofs and jist head oot an' enjoy the weather. That's right, ENJOY the rain. When the Scottish rain has been bucketin' doon for days, head for some o' the maist spectacular WATERFALLS ye'll ever see. Ye mebbe winna want tae walk ower far in the downpour, so jist mak' for the beauty spots a stone's throw fae the road an' yer car. Ye'll never beat the Falls o' Watterytogle aboot a mile doon fae the Linty Loch near the But an' Ben, but that's OOR secret.

Just aff the A9 aboot a mile north o' Dunkeld, look oot for THE HERMITAGE. Park yer car in the National Trust for Scotland car park and follow the wellies in front, under the railway bridge and through the trees. It's no' far, mebbe aboot twenty minutes or so. Soon ye'll come tae what's known as a "folly". It's like a wee hoosie, perched on the edge of a cliff, wi' one side open so ye can look richt doon intae the thunderous waters o' the River Braan. This is ca'd OSSIAN'S HALL and it's spectacular and if ye dinna like this, ye'll no' like onything. Better than a Harry Potter movie and a big bag o' popcorn onyday. And right beside Ossian's Hall there's an amazin' stone bridge spanning the torrent below.

Mair waterfalls? Well, there's the FALLS O' CLYDE at New Lanark and there's the GREY MARE'S TAIL on the road fae Edinburgh doon tae Moffat. When this Mare is in full spate, Cutty Sark hersel' wouldna go near her. ROGIE FALLS between Dingwall and Garve is another belter well worth the effort ony day and richt by the road. And there's the ane I like just ower fae the Inverarnan Inn (The Drover's) at the top o' Loch Lomond, a big white scar on the side o' the hill when its waters are bilin'. The list jist goes on and on. GO AND SEE THEM A'. It could be like baggin' Munros, only it's watter. Mebbe someone should mak' up a list.

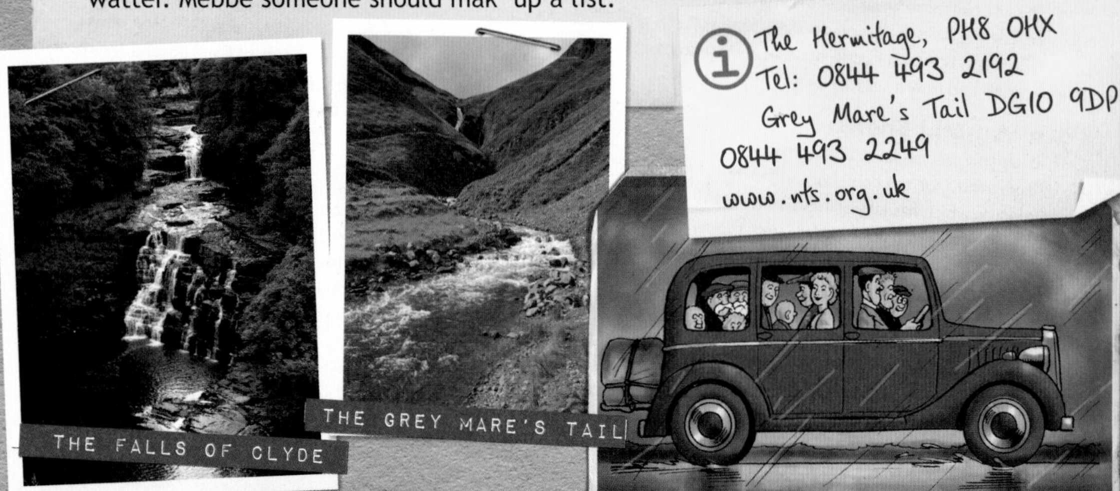

i
The Hermitage, PH8 OHX
Tel: 0844 493 2192
Grey Mare's Tail DG10 9DP
0844 493 2249
www.nts.org.uk

THE FALLS OF CLYDE

THE GREY MARE'S TAIL

LOOK! THERE'S THE STOURIE FALLS NOW, MAW. LET'S HAE OOR PICNIC AT THE TOP.
WHIT'S THE IDEA BRINGIN' THIS MUCKLE THICK TRAVELLIN' RUG ON A HOT DAY LIKE THIS?
IT'S JOE'S TURN TAE CARRY IT NEXT.
WHAT A HOPE. IT'S YOUR TURN.
ACH! STOP MOANIN' ABOOT THE RUG.
LISTEN! WE CAN GO AFF THE ROAD AN' TAK' A SHORT CUT TO THE FALLS.

AYE! WE'LL CUT ACROSS THE MUIR!
IT DOESNA LOOK SAFE ~ IT LOOKS LIKE IT'S A BOG!
WATCH YERSELS, NOW!

WHIT A PITY! WE'LL NEED TAE GO BY THE ROAD.
AYE, THEY'VE FA'EN IN. I THOCHT THEY WID!
HOI! WATCH THAT GOOD TRAVELLIN' RUG.
HELP!
W-OW!

YOU THREE LOOK AWFY SICHTS WI' THE MUD RICHT UP YER BREEKS.
WE'LL GET IT AFF WI' WATER WHEN WE GET UP TAE THE FALLS.
HUH! THEM AN' THEIR TRAVELLIN' RUGS, AN TAKIN' SHORT CUTS.

WE'LL SCRAPE THE WORST O' THE MUD AFF WHILE THE REST O' THEM ARE LOOKIN' AT THE FALLS.
ROAR

WE'LL NEED TAE HANG THEM UP TAE DRY.
THEY'LL NO' TAK' LANG. THERE'S A STRONG WIND.

HAND US OOR TEA OWER THIS STANE, MAW. WE CANNA SIT THERE WITHOOT OOR TROOSERS.
ON HIS DIGNITY
HA! HA! HA!

OH, CRIVVENS! OOR BREEKS HAVE BLAWN AWA'!
HA! HA! WHIT A LAUGH!

THAT'S THEM GONE FOR EVER! WHIT ARE WE GOIN' TAE DAE NOW?

GOING HOME
NOW THEY'RE GLAD TAE HAE THE TRAVELLIN' RUG.
THERE'S A RICHT NEW LOOK ~ A THREE-MAN KILT!
DUDLEY D. WATKINS

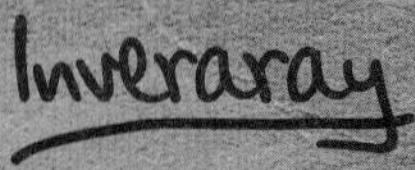

A FYNE DAY OOT at INVERARAY
by Daphne Broon

Inveraray, on the shores o' Loch Fyne, is that special ye'd actually think it was built jist for the tourists.

Naebody should come tae the toon withoot visitin' INVERARAY CASTLE, the ancient seat o' Clan Campbell. What a stately pile that is. And what a setting! Hen an' Joe were fascinated wi' the collection o' arms in the great Armoury Room. What is it aboot men that mak's them sae fascinated wi' swords an' guns an' the like? There's a display in the basement o' auld cookin' bits an' pieces they once used in the Old Kitchen. I swear I could still smell a big roast o' venison, but maybe it was jist wishful thinkin'. And dinna miss the Clan Room on the 1st floor, wi' its history of Clan Campbell. No' recommended for MacDonalds!!

A quick big bag o' fresh prawns tae eat by the pier and we a' found oorsels in jail. No, we hadna run aff withoot payin' for the prawns! It was INVERARAY JAIL, ane o' the maist unusual tourist attractions ye'll ever visit. It's ca'd "The Living Prison". If that was livin', I'll gie it a miss. There's fowk actin' oot the parts o' guards an' warders, judge an' the like. Ye actually get tae feel what it was like tae be a prisoner. I pretended I'd been locked up for haein ower many boyfriends and pies. Chance wid be a "fyne" thing.

Aboot six miles south o' Inveraray, there's AUCHINDRAIN MUSEUM, a restored farming village, takin' ye back in time in the wee cottages tae a life that the Dukes o' Argyll never knew much aboot in Inveraray Castle. Ane o' the cottages was jist like oor But an' Ben, richt doon tae the pots an' pans an' mangle for the clathes. Maybe we should open the But an' Ben as the Auchentogle Museum, complete wi' Granpaw Broon, the living museum piece.

We had the usual delay settin' aff for hame when Granpaw and Paw discovered the Loch Fyne Whiskies shop in the main street in Inveraray. They do hae a fine selection and oor bold lads were in a "fyne" state when they had their whisky tastin'. I'd happily hae locked the two auld rogues up in Inveraray Jail.

Inveraray Maritime Heritage Museum, PA32 8UY
Tel: 01499 302213
www.inveraraypier.com
Inveraray Castle, PA32 8XE
Tel: 01499 302203
www.inveraray-castle.com

The Scots Magazine 43

The boats at Inveraray

Alongside the pier in the centre of the town you can see two fascinating old boats. *The Arctic Penguin*, built in 1910 in Dublin, was one of the last iron sailing ships ever built. For 56 years she worked as a lightship. She is now a museum and you can explore all round the boat and find out about the maritime heritage of the west of Scotland.

You can also see the *Vital Spark*. This was not its original name, but it was re-named in 2006 to commemorate the boat of that name in Neil Munro's books about skipper Para Handy and his motley crew, Dan McPhail, Dougie and Sunny Jim, as they sailed around the coast of Argyll. The stories were made even more popular in the TV series. The *Vital Spark* is the last working example of a Puffer, boats that went chugging about the west coast for years and years delivering all kinds of supplies. Puffers were a maximum of 67 ft so that they could travel through the Crinan Canal.

INVERARAY JAIL & COUNTY COURT

WITNESS HISTORY

OPEN ALL YEAR

Inveraray Jail, PA32 8TX
Tel: 01499 302381
www.inverarayjail.co.uk

Auchindrain Museum,
PA32 8XN
Tel: 01499 500235
www.auchindrain-museum.org.uk

Loch Fyne Whiskies, PA32 8UD
Tel: 01499 302219
www.lfw.co.uk

LOCH FYNE

Loch Awe and Oban

LOCH AWE AND OBAN

Loch Awe – 23 miles long with an average width of 1 mile, is one of the largest and most beautiful of Scottish lochs, the third largest freshwater loch in Scotland. The head or southern end is comparatively tame, while the foot is magnificently grand. Unusually the loch flows out of the northern end by the Awe into Loch Etive (although a long, long time ago it more naturally emptied out of the southern end towards Loch Crinan).

Cruachan, the hollow mountain – Ben Cruachan, at 3,672 ft, is one of the high mountains at the north end of Loch Awe – but it contains a surprise. Over half a mile below the peak, a huge cavern has been blasted out of the mountain to hold a hydro-electric power station, and what is more, you can actually visit it! A bus takes you from a visitor centre on the banks of Loch Awe, just by the A85 to Oban, into the mountain, and it's so warm there that sub-tropical plants grow.

Kilchurn Castle – This castle stands at the head of the Loch – an oblong structure with a square keep. It was built around 1440 by Margaret, the wife of Sir Colin Campbell, the first Laird of Glenurquhay. This castle, a 5-storey keep, faced a siege by Royalists during the Civil War. Later, it was used to garrison Hanoverian troops in the days of the Jacobite Risings. You can get to it from the carpark off the A85 and by following the marked footpath that takes you under the railway line or, in season, by boat from Loch Awe Pier.

In Loch Awe village is the extraordinary **St Conan's Church**. It was designed by Walter Campbell who was not a professional architect but knew what he liked and was able to afford to turn his ideas into reality. It was built between 1881 and 1930, and the result is a magical and moving building. St Conan is said to have been a contemporary of St Columba and is connected with this area.

Bonawe Ironworks – In and amongst all this beauty at Taynuilt, on the banks of Loch Etive, are the substantial remains of a charcoal-fuelled ironworks, established in 1753. You can see how iron used to be produced, using charcoal made from the local trees as the fuel.

ST CONAN'S CHURCH

KILCHURN CASTLE

MCCAIG'S FOLLY, OBAN

Cruachan Visitor Centre,
PA33 1AN. Tel: 01866 822618
www.visitcruachan.co.uk
Bonawe Iron Furnace,
PA35 1JQ. Tel 01866 822432
www.historic-scotland.gov.uk

Oban Distillery, PA34 5NH
Tel: 01631 572004
www.discovering-distilleries.com
Scottish Sealife Sanctuary,
PA37 1SE. Tel: 01631 720386
www.sealsanctuary.co.uk
For details of cruises, adventure specialists and watersports:
www.oban.org.uk

OBAN

Oban ("little bay" in Gaelic) is the "Gateway to the Isles" – the unofficial capital of the West Highlands. The town's continuing popularity owes a great deal to the Victorians, as the town was a base for visitors touring Staffa and also pilgrims and visitors to Iona. It is now the ferry terminus for Mull, Colonsay, Coll, Tiree and Lismore; and there are also sailings from Oban to Barra and South Uist in the Western Isles. It is also home to excellent seafood.

Dunollie Castle – This ancient stronghold (12th or 13th Century) stood guard over the narrow entrance to the sheltered bay. It is now reduced to a keep, but is wonderfully situated on a bluff overlooking Loch Linnhe and was originally protected on the landward side by a moat.

The Oban Distillery (1794) is unusual as it is right in the centre of the busy town, but it makes it easy to visit. On the hill behind the town is **McCaig's Folly**, an uncompleted circular structure from 1897 which a local banker, John McCaig intended to be a viewing tower, museum and art gallery, but only the outside walls were ever built. Still, it is a good spot for a picnic and you get a great view of Oban.

The island of **Kerrera** is a natural breakwater protecting the harbour of Oban. Here Alexander II died in 1249 during an attempt to subdue the Norsemen of the Hebrides. At the south end of the island is Gylen Castle an old Norse fortress – long a MacDougall stronghold.

The Scottish Sealife Sanctuary at Loch Creran is set in picturesque surroundings and hosts a wonderful collection of marine creatures. You can visit the SOS seal rescue facility, and the seal pup nursery, learn about octopus and sharks, rays, starfish, salmon and crabs. There are talks and feeding demonstrations from marine experts.

Glencoe

It's no' really dark unless ye happen tae arrive at night, which isnae very helpful on a day oot.

Dark Glencoe by Joe Broon

GLENCOE is ane o' the most popular places in Scotland for climbers and walkers. I've been comin' here for years an' years. There's something for a'body fae the wee Bairns tae the auldest rambler like Granpaw, he himsel' once known as the Rannoch Fox. Folk tell me it was because he kent the Glencoe hills an' Rannoch Moor like the back o' his hand. Masel', I think he got his nickname for scroungin' other folk's cheese sandwiches an' beers in the twa famous hotels, the KINGS HOUSE and the CLACHAIG.

The Clachaig Inn has a notice ootside saying 'Nae Campbells', a reference tae the Campbell militia that massacred the MacDonalds in Glencoe in 1692. Ye can find oot a' aboot that at the NTS VISITOR CENTRE just aff the main road a mile or so ootside Glencoe Village. The Kingshouse Hotel sits nestled at the foot o' Glencoe's most popular mountain, BUACHAILLE ETIVE MOR ('The Great Shepherd of Etive' tae English speakers). The GLENCOE MOUNTAIN SKI CENTRE is also just a stone's throw fae the Kingshouse (well, a big stone's throw . . . an Olympic record throw mair like). Even if ye're no' a keen skier like me, ye can still have a trip on the ski lift up intae the hills on Meall a'Bhuiridh. What a view, but mind an' pack yer thermal undies. It's nae place for a real Scotsman in a kilt.

Of course, if ye're a strappin' hill man like masel' there are a' manner o' exciting climbs, including the traverse of the Aonach Eagach ridge that forms the north "wall" of the glen. It featured in a Harry Potter film and Dumbledore's Castle was also thereaboots, but ye either hae tae be a magician or a serious rock climber tae tackle this, so just best enjoy the view fae the road.

"Roond the corner" fae Glencoe, there's the wee village o' KINLOCHLEVEN. It straddles the popular WEST HIGHLAND WAY (the long distance path fae Glasgow tae Fort William) so there's plenty o' places for food an' drink. There's also THE ICE FACTOR, an indoor ice climbing wall that's worth a look-see. It's housed in the auld KINLOCHLEVEN ALUMINIUM WORKS.

After a day oot in Glencoe the best thing tae demolish (massacre even!) is a fish supper fae the chippie in Kinlochleven.

HIGHLAND
COACH TOURS
8D
FARE
STAGE 3
SINGLE
Show ticket on demand
from inspector
PRINTED IN INVERNESS X2734

12 The Scots Magazine

A favourite Glencoe walk

A WALK that almost anyone can manage starts right in the heart of the glen. Park your car in one of the high car parks, just before the road going east heads into the obvious gorge with a waterfall.

Head down and across the river by a scary bridge (children and dogs on a lead!) and then it's uphill through thriving young native trees and into the LOST VALLEY.

It's a big flat area you would never guess was there and you get no idea of what it's like from the road. It's where the MacDonald Clan reputedly kept their stolen cattle. The cattle must have been very fit, like mountain goats, for it's a steep walk all the way into the Lost Valley. The walk is well worth all the panting and sore legs.

There are many forest walks down in the heart of the glen near the village. The visitor centre has all the information you need for these walks.

Ahh! The skirl o' the pipes. Music tae ma ears!

The Kings House Hotel, PH49 4HY
Tel: 01855 851259
www.kingy.com
The Clachaig Inn, PH49 4HX
Tel: 01855 811252
www.clachaig.com

(i)

Glencoe Visitor Centre, NTS PH49 4LA
Tel: 0844 493 2222
www.nts.org.uk
Glencoe Mountain (ski lift), PH49 4HZ
Tel: 01855 851226
www.glencoemountain.com
The Ice Factor, PH50 4SF
Tel: 01855 831100
www.ice-factor.co.uk

26 The Sunday Post

Days Out: Slates of Scotland

RIGHT AT the back of the village of Ballachulish is an enormous slate quarry, that once upon a time supplied nearly all the houses in Scotland. It's not working now but it's a spectacular sight and Ballachulish slates are still sought after for re-use when old buildings are demolished.

Ben Nevis

THE BIG MUNRO, BEN NEVIS,
by The Broons' Mountaineering Club

4,408 ft - awfy high!

Hen Broon, team leader

It was my idea tae get the family oot on the highest mountain in Britain. Easy for me of course wi' my long legs. I'm like a mountain goat. But no' sae easy for the likes o' the Twins or the Bairn. Here's a tip . . . there's nae need tae go a' the way tae the summit tae enjoy the day oot. More o' that later.

The Ben sits looking doon on FORT WILLIAM in the West Highlands. There's a good footpath a' the way tae the very top. Easiest start point is from the car park at ACHINTEE. Ye'll find it well marked, but the Tourist Info Office in Fort William will help if ye need it. They'll no' help ye get UP, that's YOUR problem. Best tae get an early nicht and an early start.

We set off at six in the mornin', wi' a'thing we needed in the rucksacks . . . spare waterproof clothes, plenty o' drinks an' enough sandwiches tae feed the Black Watch. Ye need it all!! Even the Bairn an' Granpaw were there. The bigger folk took turn aboot tae gie the Bairn a piggyback fae time tae time. The path is actually easy to begin with, as it angles gently up above bonnie GLEN NEVIS on yer right-hand side. Ye look doon on the camp and caravan sites and the Youth Hostel, rare places tae spend a few days. Ye'll be amazed at the number o' hills ye see soaring up around aboot.

Now, even at oor "family" pace and a few stops tae drink from the burns, we arrived in good order at the halfway lochan (Lochan Meall an t-Suidhe) at around nine o' clock. This is the secret o' a good DAY OOT on the Ben. Early birds!! Now, it was about here that Granpaw, Maw and the Bairn decided tae picnic an' then mak' their way back doon tae enjoy Fort William, and the Bairn skipped a' the way doon!

Good advice tae remember is that it can snow on this biggest of Munros (hills over 3,000 ft) even in the summer. Check the weather forecast.

Fort William Tourist Information, PH33 6AJ. Tel: 08452 255121
www.visithighlands.com
Lochaber Leisure Centre, PH33 6BU. Tel: 01397 704359
Crannog Seafood Restaurant, PH33 6DB. Tel: 01397 705589
www.crannog.net
Glen Nevis Youth Hostel, PH33 6SY
Tel: 01397 702336
www.syha.org.uk
Ben Nevis information: www.mountainwalk.co.uk/benneviswalk.html
FORT WILLIAM AND BEN NEVIS

Maggie Broon

Me an' Daphne were near on oor knees at this point, but as the laddies said we'd never mak it tae the tap, we had nae choice but tae carry on. Never make it indeed! Cheek! We just had a wee breather, checked the make-up and the lipstick and set off in the lead. We'd show thae men. (Famous last words).

Joe Broon

At the halfway point, ye can turn left doon past the lochan and head without more climbing roond the shoulder o' the Ben tae the SCOTTISH MOUNTAINEERING CLUB HUT below the vast and REALLY impressive cliffs of the Ben. In some ways, this is a better day than goin' a' the way tae the top. It's the most impressive view in Scotland.

Paw Broon

I couldna let the lassies go on withoot their faither tae look efter them, so I took a deep breath and sauntered on wi' the Twins an' Horace. Horace offered tae carry ma pack, so I let him (just so he wid look the part, ye understand!).

Ben Nevis – continued

Daphne Broon

The path fae the "halfway" lochan to the very top took me anither three hoors. It winds backwards and forwards and backwards and forwards and upward and upward. They tell me the view was braw on the way up, but I had that much sweat pooring doon ma face, the first I saw was at the summit when I wiped ma red moosh wi' Joe's bandanna. I had tae look ma best for this walker fae Paisley wha helped me up the last hunner feet. Erchie Munro, by name, and the best-looking Munro I saw a' day I can tell ye.

THE PATH UP BEN NE

CAMPING BELOW BEN NEVIS

A RARE VIEW FAE BEN NEVIS

An we Thought it was BED nevis

26 The Sunday Post

Out & About: *Ben Nevis facts*

- Ben Nevis is the highest mountain in Britain. It is 4,408 ft (1,344 metres) high.
- In a year, twice as much rain falls on the top of Ben Nevis as in Fort William.
- On average, the top is in clouds nine days out of ten.
- The first recorded climb was made in 1771 by James Robertson.
- A bed, a wheelbarrow and an organ have also been pushed to the top.
- Around 100,000 people climb Ben Nevis every year.
- Clement Wragge climbed Ben Nevis every day from 1 June to 14 October 1881 to take weather readings.
- There was an observatory on the summit that was manned all year round from 1883 to 1904.
- There was a Temperance Hotel with four bedrooms at the summit which functioned in the summer until 1916.
- In 1911 a Ford Model T car was driven to the top of Ben Nevis – but it did take five days.

Hen Broon

So there we were, on the summit looking like folk that had run twa marathons, but it was worth it. Ye can literally see for miles in a' directions and richt oot tae the Outer Hebrides on a good day like we got. Ye'll never forget being here if ye can mak' the effort.

Some hill runners can run tae the summit an' back tae Fort William in less than twa hours and it had taken us six just tae get up . . . six hours, 25 stops and four picnics, but what's the hurry? Easy does it. And it was only mid-day. The only anes o' oor team no' oot o' breath were the Twins and Horace. Piece o' cake tae them . . . them that normally canna go tae school withoot gettin' a lift!

And then it was a' doonhill tae Fort William . . a few blisters an' a few aches and pains (well, a lot for some in truth), but WHAT a day oot. We met up wi' Maw, Granpaw and the Bairn who spent the afternoon in the LOCHABER LEISURE CENTRE. Efter we'd soaked in hot baths for what seemed like hours, we treated oorsel's tae real seafood in the CRANNOG SEAFOOD RESTAURANT. And Jings! you can fair eat efter a day like that. Paw was that knackered he didna even check the bill!

So, get yer boots looked oot and get oot there. What are ye waitin' for? The Big Ben beckons!!

The West Highland Railway

HEN

THE WEST HIGHLAND RAILWAY
by Hen Broon

Surely the maist famous stretch o' rail track in Scotland. An unbroken ribbon of metal rail a' the way fae GLASGOW QUEEN STREET tae the fishing port of MALLAIG looking across the sea to Skye. It touches the Clyde, Loch Long, Loch Lomond, the vast deer-filled and bog-filled expanses o' Rannoch Moor, Fort William, Glenfinnan and oot tae the sea past bonnie Morar Sands. What an incredible journey!

Of course, the trip fae Glasgow tae Mallaig and back is a day oot in itsel'. Yer nose will be pressed tae the train windae the whole way. It's like lookin' at the best ootdoor TV programme ye've ever seen. But there's so much to see along the way, ye'd be daft no' tae hae as many days oot on this line as yer wallet will allow. I've been up an' doon it for years and still no' seen everything there is tae see. Oh, and there was this bonnie lassie Mary fae Arisaig . . . but that's anither story. I'll just gie ye a quick train ride a' the way fae Glasgow and then come back and fill in a' ma favourite gaps later.

All aboard at Queen Street Station and doon the watter, doon the Clyde, under the ERSKINE BRIDGE and intae HELENSBURGH at the foot o' the GARE LOCH. Alight here tae see Charles Rennie Mackintosh's THE HILL HOOSE, sorry HOUSE.

see page 53 for
the Hill Hoose

MALLAIG HARBOUR

he world's most memorable rail journeys

ut in autumn, when the
urs flare into purple, gold,
w and brown.
oard the train in winter,
h the glinting snow adds
w dimension, and the
s of deer come to forage
he moors.
e for all seasons...
hanks to the vision and
rage of the entrepreneurs,
gineers and labourers who
ve this track through some
Britain's most dramatic,
autiful and sometimes
rciless terrain.

Connel Ferry
Oban
Taynuilt
Falls of Cruachan
Loch Awe
Pass of Brander
Ben Cruachan
Loch Etive
Kilchurn Castle
Dalmally
Glen Lochy
Upper Tyndrum
Tyndrum Lower
Fillan Water
Crianlarich
Falls of Falloch
Ardlui
Arrochar & Tarbet
Ben Lomond
Loch Long
Loch Lomond
Garelochhead
Gare Loch
Helensburgh Upper
Dumbarton
Greenock
Port Glasgow
Clyde
Dalmuir
GLASGOW

Glasgow
Crianlaric

Your journey s
Glasgow Quee
station, from whe
climbs in tunnel up
Bank, turning left thr
Maryhill and Westerto
to Kilpatrick, with the
lines of the Erskine Bri
You're running parallel
Clyde, cradle of so ma
ocean liners.

Then it's on to Bowli
the Clyde estuar
before yo

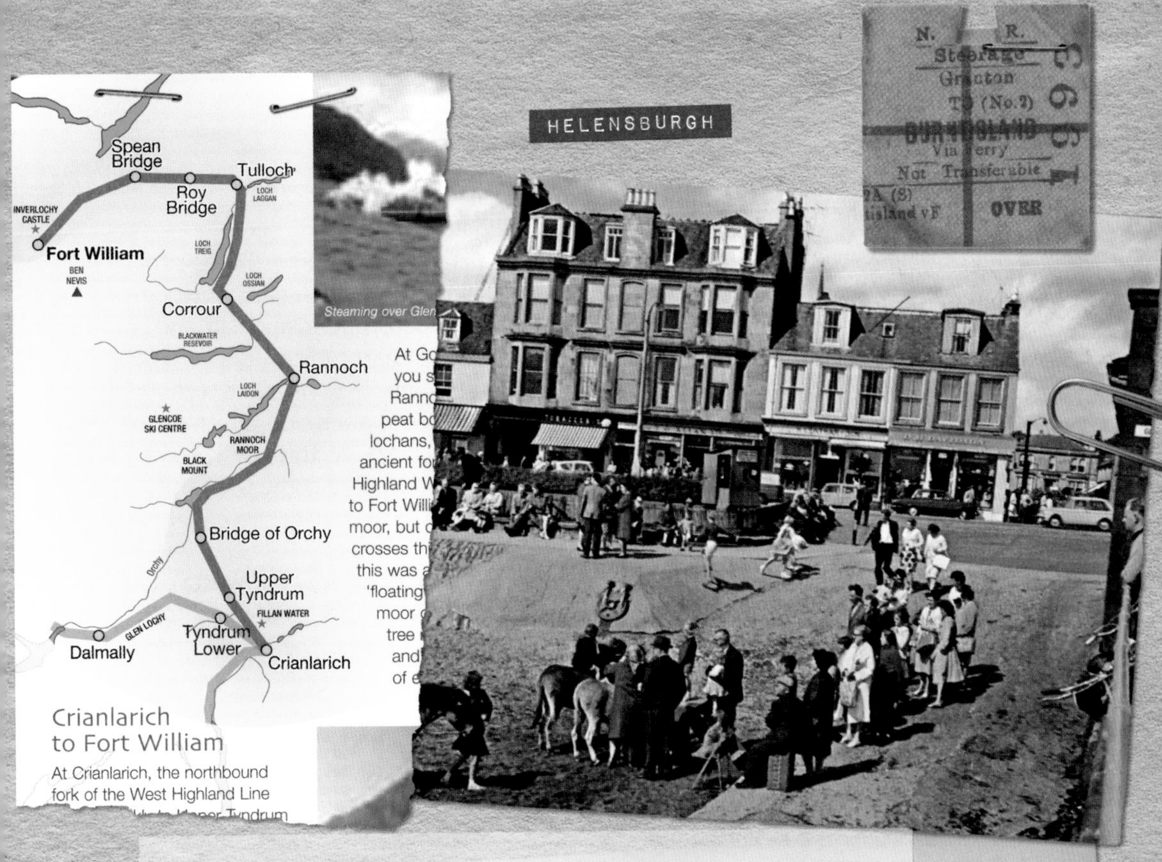

Gare Loch to Rannoch

Now on up the Gare Loch past a' the military bases and oot intae the sunshine on Loch Long and afore long ye'll see the outline of one of Scotland's most famous hills appearing on yer left, the COBBLER. Only 2,891 ft high but a gem . . . and a rock climber's paradise. LOCH LOMOND comes suddenly into view at TARBET and if ye're quick, ye'll see BEN LOMOND across the waters of the loch on yer right (ye'll need tae be sittin' on the right-hand side o' the train of course, or move folk aside tae get a wee keek).

Scotrail steams on (it disnae really, it's diesel) passing ARDLUI and then running alongside the WEST HIGHLAND WAY footpath that came up the other side of Loch Lomond. Up GLEN FALLOCH now, past old Caledonian pine trees and into CRIANLARICH under mighty BEN MORE. Ye can change trains here and head out west tae OBAN, but it's over late for that now, for ye've got yer ticket tae MALLAIG already paid for.

Clicketty-click, clicketty-click (I love sayin' that on trains) to TYNDRUM where the rail track heaves the train uphill and north towards GLENCOE. But there's only tantalising glimpses o' Glencoe for me (a bit like Mary fae Arisaig really) and the train swings away north-east from Glencoe and parts company with the West Highland Way as we rattle across Rannoch Moor to RANNOCH STATION.

The West Highland Railway – continued

<u>Rannoch to Glenfinnan</u>

Rannoch Station is in the middle o' nae place, but stunningly bonnie. There's that much wet bog aboot here, parts o' the railway line are floating on piles of wood, so it's a bit like the Rannoch Ferry at this point. From here to Corrour Halt and Tulloch Station, the train really does show you the wild heart of Scotland ye'd never otherwise see withoot walking for miles. Not a car in sight. Just hills and lochs and red deer. And then we're back with the cars and buses alongside the track as we shoot doon past SPEAN BRIDGE and intae FORT WILLIAM. At this point, spare a thought for the walkers on the WEST HIGHLAND WAY who've come the same distance as yersel' on foot!!

There's usually a wee halt in Fort William before we continue way oot west, past the CALEDONIAN CANAL at BANAVIE (Neptune's Staircase, a series of canal locks on your right-hand side is impressive. Boats on a ladder really). The train inches by slowly here so ye'll no' miss it.

Then it's the Wild West past GLENFINNAN and the visitor centre that commemorates the raising of the standard at Glenfinnan by Bonnie Prince Charlie in 1745. Right across from the National Trust for Scotland centre is a tall tower with a Highlander on top framed by the beautiful view doon LOCH SHIEL. It's no' Charlie, but lots o' folk think it is. Afore ye reach the station at Glenfinnan, ye cross the world's first viaduct made just from concrete. This is the magnificent viaduct featured in the Harry Potter films with the Hogwarts Express whisking Harry off to school. There is a steam train that runs on the Fort William to Mallaig line in summer, affectionately known, to locals at least, as the Harry Potter Express.

Glenfinnan Monument,
PH37 4LT
Tel: 0844 493 2221
www.nts.org.uk

'Harry Potter Express' going over the Glenfinnan viaduct

West Highland Line: the World's Top Journey

In 2009 the West Highland Line was voted the Top Rail Journey in the World by the readers of ***Wanderlust***, the magazine for independent travellers. It was the first time the award has been made and over 400 journeys were nominated. The journey was recognised for its breathtaking and varied scenery. The Editor-in-Chief of ***Wanderlust***, Lyn Hughes, said, 'Having a Scottish winner for this award is particularly exciting, and shows you don't have to travel far for truly world-beating scenery'. Here are the results:

1 The West Highland Line
2 Cuzco to Puno, Peru
3 Cuzco to Macchu Picchu, Peru
4 Trans-Siberian Railway
=5 Eurostar
=5 Rocky Mountaineer, Western Canada
7 Darjeeling Himalayan Railway, India
8 TranzAlpine, Christchurch–Greymouth, New Zealand
9 Orient Express
=10 Devil's Nose, Ecuador
=10 The Ghan, Darwin–Adelaide, Australia

West Highland Line, Scotrail
www.scotrail.co.uk
Luxury cruise trains on the West Highland Line
www.royalscotsman.com

The Jacobite steam train, Fort William to Mallaig
www.westcoastrailways.co.uk

And so to Mallaig

The line from here is my favourite bit of railway in Scotland. It just weaves about slowly amongst hills and lochs before bursting out ontae the west coast at ARISAIG and the stunning views of the islands floating on the sea . . . Rum, Eigg, Skye . . . wonderland. Then it's MORAR SANDS, the quaint level crossing in MORAR village itself and the scenic railway stint to MALLAIG and the end of the line right on the sea.

I have to get off here and find some fresh prawns tae eat and then I'm ready for the train back. The fresh fish shop is just roond the corner. Now, I'll tell you aboot a' my favourite walks from the train on the journey back . . . wait a minute, the train's awa'. I'm stranded in Mallaig for the night. But it's no' a' that bad. It's only a wee walk back doon the coast tae Arisaig and bonnie Mary. What was her address again . . .?

MORAR SANDS

Loch Ness

Nessieland Castle Monster Centre,
IV63 6TU
Tel: 01456 450342
www.loch-ness-monster-nessieland.com

Loch Ness Monster
www.nessie.co.uk

26 The Sunday Post

Did you know?

Before the railway was built to Inverness, the quickest way from Glasgow to Inverness was by steamer through the Crinan Canal, stopping off in Oban and then up to Fort William and through the 60 miles of The Caledonian Canal to Inverness. What a great way to travel!

LOCH NESS
by Maw Broon

Nae book aboot days oot in Scotland would be complete withoot mention o' the world famous Loch Ness and its monster.

I've been comin' here since I was a lassie, and in a' thae years, I've never had as much as a glimpse o' the monster in Loch Ness. Mind you, we were ha'en a picnic on the bonnie beach at DORES aye day when a tourist got fair excited aboot seein' the beast. "Look, there it's there . . . ower yonder!" he was yelllin' as he clicked awa' wi' his camera. "Can ye see its lang neck and its black body thrashing aboot in the watter?" I could see what he was lookin' at richt enough, but it was jist oor Hen takin' a photo of Daphne swimmin' in the loch to cool doon.

Dores is a bonnie spot, on the wee road on the "ither" side o' Loch Ness. Ye can drive doon here on the east side o' the loch fae Inverness. Aboot 12 miles doon the same road ye come tae FOYERS. Even at my age I never miss the chance tae walk tae the big waterfall. It's aboot 100 ft high and it's set in the bonniest woodland ye can imagine. In fact, a' roond the loch there are miles o' paths and cycleways through the trees.

Now, as maist folk ken, Loch Ness is part o' the CALEDONIAN CANAL, the famous waterway that splits Scotland fae Inverness on the east tae Fort William on the west coast. And for me, the bonniest part o' the canal is at the south end o' Loch Ness at Fort Augustus. I do like tae sit by the locks and watch a' the boats goin' up an' doon the ladder o' locks. The whole place is buzzin' wi' boats an' chatterin' fowk on holiday. And here's what's braw, naebody is in any hurry. Locks fillin' up, locks emptying, wi' boats goin' up and boats goin' doon. An' there's cafes an' shops dotted aboot the place. I jist love it.

The main road runs up the north shore o' the loch fae Fort Augustus, passin' through Drumnadrochit, whaur ye can visit the Monster Visitor Centre. It's jist past Urquhart Castle. The views are stunning and if ye're no' drivin', keep yer eyes on the loch an' see if ye can spot "Nessie" herself.

THE REAL NESSIE GOT A RICHT FRICHT WHEN DAPHNE GOT IN THE WATTER

LOCH NESS AT FORT AUGUSTUS

4 The Sunday Post / April 8

MONSTER HOAX!

The Sunday Post

No. 4506 April 1, 1992 Price 40p

NESSIE SIGHTED!

By A Sunday Post Reporter

EXCLUSIVE!

See page 10 for more

AMAZING NEW evidence of Nessie, the Loch Ness Monster, was made available exclusively to the Sunday Post this week.

The Sunday Post can reveal the stunning new photo which adds substantialy to the growing evidence that the Loch Ness monster does, in fact, exist.

The crucial picture was taken by Loch Ness fishermen last weeknd and rushed to our offices for publication .

INSIDE: Waether 2, The Doc 23, TV and Radio 26-27, Horoscope 34, Sport 29-48

■ Last week's Sunday Post cover.

■ Hen Broon's picture of his sister Daphne.

IT SEEMED as though The Sunday Post news team was duped by a holidaymaker whose photograph sparked "Nessie Mania" in the Highlands around the Loch Ness area last week.

Hen Broon aided the Sunday Post in our April fools day hoax which unfortunately led to hundreds of excited calls to our busy telephone switchboard.

The picture in question was simply a silhouette of his sister, Daphne, who was having a dip in the Loch to cool down on what was the hottest day of the year so far this summer in Scotland .

We do hope that all our readers can see the funny side of our practical joke. Watch this space next year!

Urquhart Castle

URQUHART CASTLE
by Horace Broon

Heading down the busy A82 from Inverness along the west shore of mighty Loch Ness, I could hardly wait for my first wee glimpse of Urquhart Castle, and then, aboot fourteen miles doon the loch, there it was. And what a sight. A jagged set of fantastic ruins on an outcrop sticking out intae Loch Ness. Through the bay past wonderfully named DRUMNADROCHIT village and we were there. I near fell oot o' the car wi' excitement.

History tells me this was once one of Scotland's largest castles and I believe it. The Visitor Centre was opened in 2002 and it's built intae the hillside below the main road. Great views of the loch fae here. There's a shop and a cafe of course (isn't there always?) and great audio visuals . . . but what caught my attention was the model of the castle afore folk started knocking lumps aff it. It looks like something frae "Lord o' The Rings" and ye can easily imagine armies stormin' the gates and gettin' their fingers burned fae the defending sojers.

Don't whatever ye do, miss the view from the top of the GRANT TOWER . . . or what's left of it, that is. I just loved wandering up and down the steps and paths connecting the various parts of the castle that still remain. Ye'll see that the castle was once narrow in the middle as it was built on two separate rocky tops. Ye can also see that well in the model in the Visitor Centre.

So there ye have it, a day oot in bloody Castle Urquhart. I only get tae say bloody now and again, but it's true here. This is a castle tae gladden every schoolboy sojer's warring heart, and mind an' keep an eye on the 600-ft deep still waters of Loch Ness. Who knows WHAT lurks doon there. A monster mebbe? And if IT has a day oot, RUN!!

URQUHART CASTLE

ⓘ

Urquhart Castle,
IV63 6XJ
Tel 01456 450551
www.historic-scotland.gov.uk

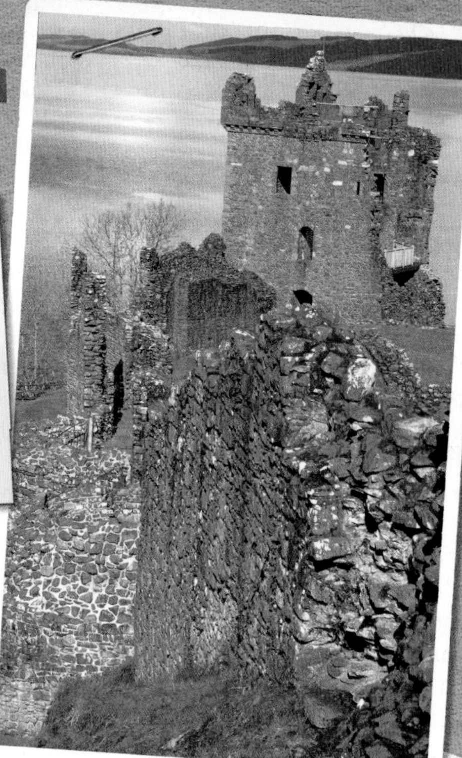

My history of Urquhart Castle

Jist how lang there's been a castle here, naebody is really sure, but my history teacher tells me St Columba passed through here on his way fae Iona tae visit the King o' The Picts in Inverness aboot AD 580. Columba was called to see an auld Pictish nobleman ca'd Emchath at his big hoose at Airdchartdan. Whether this Airdchartdan WAS the original fort on this rocky outcrop we canna say. Mind you, Airdchartdan is aboot as hard tae pronounce as Urquhart, so I'd say the story's true.

I love tae read in my history books aboot "bloody conflicts" and "turbulent times" and this place has seen mair than its share. The castle sits astride the major route through the Highlands and it seems a'body and his brother was keen tae own it by fair means or foul. As a medieval fortress from the 13th to the 17th century it was a case o' "never a dull moment". Edward I of England, known to his chums as the "Hammer of the Scots", stole the keys o' the door aboot 1296 and saw off an assault by us Scots later, and then we took it back and Edward's lot came crashin' back in again. Robert the Bruce broke in and took ower again afore he became King of Scots efter Bannockburn, and in 1332 efter The Bruce died, Urquhart was the only Highland Castle holdin' oot against the Auld Enemy. And then, nae sooner had the English lost interest than the MacDonalds fae the Western Isles came battering at the door fighting again and again against the castle folk.

When the last sojers marched oot in 1692, they blew it up so NAEBODY could have it. What aboot that for extreme measures? Part of the big GRANT TOWER (the main bit ye still see) crashed tae the ground in 1715 during what was described as a violent storm. A thousand years of history disappeared under the rubble.

A Day Oot Aroond Inverness

INVERNESS and Roond Aboot
Granpaw Broon

INVERNESS is the fastest growin' toon in Scotland and it's hardly recognisable now as the sleepy wee place I first visited as a laddie. Comin' doon the hill on the main A9 road intae Inverness, ye can see the KESSOCK BRIDGE above a' the new commercial buildings, takin' the main road across the firth and on intae the Black Isle. It's a rare panorama. As a laddie on a youth hostel tour, I had tae cycle a' the way tae Beauly roond the Beauly Firth and roond first ae firth an' then anither. Now ye can speed past Inverness in yer car and be on yer way north tae Wick and Thurso afore ye ken whaur ye're goin'. That's progress or so they tell me.

Now, comin' doon the hill intae Inverness from the south, ye'll pass the turn off for CULLODEN BATTLEFIELD. Even the maist dunder-heided laddies in my primary school history class a' thae years ago knew a' aboot Culloden, if little aboot onythin' else. I've been tae Culloden many times and now with the new Battlefield Visitor Centre, it's proving to be ane o' Scotland's big tourist attractions.

Lying no' that far north o' Culloden on the shores of the Moray Firth at Ardersier is FORT GEORGE, built followin' Charlie's demise at Culloden. This is the mightiest artillery fort in Britain. It took near 21 years tae build and it never saw a single shot fired in anger. Fort George is almost in its original 18th century new-build condition. It has hunners o' arms and bits o' military equipment and fair bristles wi' cannons. And on a cheerier note, ye can often spot dolphins fae whaur the cannon peek oot tae the Moray Firth.

Tired o' blood and glory and stirrin' tales o' battle? Head along the coast tae Fochabers and visit BAXTERS visitor centre. Baxters is as famous as Bonnie Prince Charlie, its soups and home bakes mooth-wateringly wunnerful. As guid as Maw Broon makes. Mair I canna say. And there's a kids' adventure playground. Goin' tae or comin' fae Fochabers, pop intae ma favourite grocers at ELGIN. "Gordon and MacPhail" have enough different kinds o' single malt whisky tae wet the throats of whisky lovers richt across the world. Their Elgin shop's my favourite "retail therapy" day oot.

i

Culloden Battlefield, IV2 5EU
Tel: 0844 493 2159
www.nts.org.uk/Culloden

i

Baxter's Highland Village, Fochabers, IV32 7LD
Tel: 01343 820666
www.baxters.com
Gordon & MacPhail, IV30 1JY
Tel: 01343 545110
www.gordonandmacphail.com

The Sunday Post 32

Days Out: *CULLODEN*

ULLODEN is where Bonnie
rince Charlie's Jacobite Rising
nally ended, his Highland men
ıtchered under the withering
re of the muskets and cannon of
e Redcoats led by "Butcher"
umberland, a son of George II,
nt up from London. Less than an
our after it started on 16 April
'46, the battle was over and
er 1,000 men lay dead or dying.
nnie Prince Charlie escaped from
e battlefield and headed off into
ling, song and legend, faithfully
eltered by the Highlanders whose
es he had helped shatter forever.
the words of the famous song
'ill ye no' come back again?"
Charlie didn't. He escaped to France and died a sad old man in Rome, leaving behind a broken way of life.

You can find all this out at the visitor centre and experience what it was like in the centre of the bloody battle in a four-minute film in the new "immersion theatre". It's like you were there in the thick of the battle. Take time to walk through the battlefield itself, visit old Leanach Cottage and stand quietly amongst the Highlanders' graves, the men lying asleep on the field of the last pitched battle on British soil.

Fort George, IV2 7TD
Tel 01667 460232
www.historic-scotland.gov.uk/places

Black Watch sojers at the Fort

THE BATTLE
OF CULLODEN
WAS FOUGHT ON THIS MOOR
16TH APRIL 1746.
THE GRAVES OF THE
GALLANT HIGHLANDERS
WHO FOUGHT FOR
SCOTLAND & PRINCE CHARLIE
ARE MARKED BY THE NAMES
OF THEIR CLANS.

Memorial cairn at Culloden moor

Birds of Scotland

RSPB www.rspb.org.uk

FEATHERED FRIENDS
by Horace Broon

Scotland is one of the best places in the world to be a "twitcher". That's the funny name for folk that are mad about birds. Now, jist so ye dinna get the wrong idea, we're talking aboot days oot tae see feathered birds . . . no' nights oot like Hen and Joe have tae see "the birds" at The Dancin'!

There are so many great places to go bird watching, ye'd need a hale book or twa tae list a' the guid places and the many different birds ye can spot. Visit the RSPB website to get the latest news aboot arctic geese or oor wee summer visitors fae the South. I've been to lots of RSPB reserves and my favourite is at LOCH GRUINART on Islay where ye can see THOUSANDS of geese from all over the world in the autumn and crane yer neck for the rasping sound o' the corncrake (no, it's no' a breakfast cereal) in the spring. Throw in the odd golden eagle if ye're lucky and that's a day oot in itself tae remember.

Near Aviemore, LOCH GARTEN is the home of the OSPREY. It's no' that long ago that there were nae ospreys left in Scotland, but that's a' changed now. Ye can watch the magnificent birdies through CCTV at the visitor centre. We were luckier than that when we went tae visit. On the A9 near Pitlochry, Joe spotted ane flying richt alongside oor car on the River Tay. It jist dipped doon intae the watter richt ootside the car windae (in a' that traffic!!) and came up quick as ye like wi' an enormous salmon in its talons. That's what I call fishin'. Nae bother at all. I could hardly believe it.

POST CARD

CORRESPONDENCE

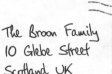

Printed in Gt. Britain

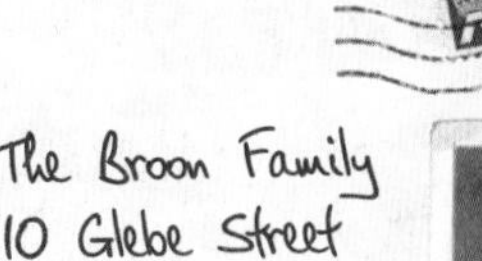

Great twitching here! My best sighting was on LOCH NEVIS near Mallaig, when twa sea eagles flew richt ower the boat tae Inverie. Michty. Whit a size. They tell me the wing span can be aboot eight or nine feet wide. That's even bigger than Hen . . . OOR Hen, that is, no' a chicken.

Horace x

The Broon Family
10 Glebe Street
Scotland UK

A YOUNG GOLDEN EAGLE

THE OSPREY NEST

AN OSPREY CATCHING ITS TEA

THE OSPREY CENTRE AT LOCH GARTEN

My other favourite reserves are at:
VANE FARM near Kinross, where there's lots of bird hides and walking trails on the shores of Loch Leven. If ye're awfy unlucky no' tae spot onything rare, ye'll at least spot the castle in the middle o' the loch whaur Mary, Queen of Scots was imprisoned for a year before escapin'. LOCHWINNOCH just off the A737 near Beith, the favourite watering hole of the Bonnie Glasgow Birds (Joe made me say that). FAIRY GLEN near Fortrose (The Bairn loved that, but I think it was jist the name), CULBIN SANDS north of Nairn and INVERSNAID on the east shore of the Bonnie Banks of Loch Lomond.

However, even though ye can visit dozens o' bird reserves, a great day oot can be had wi' jist a packed lunch and a guid pair o' binoculars. There's naebody locks the doors on oor Scottish birds in the reserves. Ye'll see them a' ower the countryside and in yer ain gairden. Buy some bird feeders, fill them wi' bird nuts and sit back and watch the feathers fly!

SCOTTISH Wildlife

No.12
FROM A SERIES OF 35
INFORMATIVE CARDS

THE GOLDEN EAGLE

The golden eagle is one of the most magnificent birds of prey in the Scotland. The females are much larger than the males. Golden eagles range across Europe, Asia, N. Africa and N. America. In the UK, they are predominantly found in the Scottish Highlands. These large birds prefer mountainous habitats, although they require large trees or rock faces for nesting. Golden eagles hunt mammals, such as rodents, rabbits, and young deer. They also hunt birds. They can remain in the air for hours at a time. Golden eagles can attain speeds of 80 mph. They are resident birds and do not migrate. They have exceptionally good eyesight, and when prey has been spotted, they dive down to seize and kill the victim with their curved talons. Golden eagles mate for life. Pairs normally have territories of up to 35 square miles.

SNOWY OWL

PEREGRINE FALCON

PUFFIN

The Vikings

GLEBE STREET SCHOOL PRIZE ESSAY
THE VIKINGS

By Horace Brown

Well done Horace! Very good.

The raids of the Vikings (Norsemen) on the west coast of Scotland began around 792. Between 795 and 806, Iona was attacked at least three times. By the latter date it was clear that the Vikings were a very serious threat to all the established kingdoms of the British Isles. Their paganism added a sinister aspect to what, even by the standards of the time, was appalling brutality.

With little space in their ships to take slaves, they killed men indiscriminately but carried off girls and women. Their language and their customs were equally strange. There is ample evidence that they were found to be utterly terrifying. The monasteries and religious hermitages of the Western Isles had been generally safe since around 617, when St Donnan, abbot of Eigg, and his community were killed by pagan Picts (according to legend, ruled by a queen). They had no protection and the surprise nature of the raids made organised defence very difficult. No one could tell where the longships would strike next.

By the early ninth century, the Vikings were settling in Orkney and Shetland, causing the existing population to take emergency measures, like the burying of treasures in the church on St Ninian's Isle (to be discovered in 1958). There is no record of any Pictish expedition to drive out the invaders. The Picts had a long tradition as seafarers, though their boats were inferior to the Viking longships. Such lethargy is not what might have been expected from a strong kingdom with a long tradition of rule in the northern isles. The lack of response suggests that there was no well-established authority in the north at this time.

Some evidence has been found of local resistance on the islands, with hastily thrown-up earthworks on promontory sites. But, by 820, hundreds of little farming-fishing settlements, with Norse names, were established in the islands. Their new proprietors might have gone off on "summer raids" but they were essentially farmers with boats. Many of the Pictish islanders moved to the northern mainland and there can be no doubt that many Pictish communities were displaced. The record of Viking behaviour elsewhere suggests that for those who could not leave, the future held the bleak alternatives of slavery or death.

horace is swotty and spotty

The Scots Magazine 53

Jarlshof

AT THE end of the 19th century, storms ripped open the low cliffs at Jarlshof, near the southern tip of Shetland. They revealed an extraordinary settlement site embracing 4,000 years of human history. Upon excavation, the site was found to contain a remarkable sequence of stone structures – late Neolithic houses, Bronze-Age village, Iron-Age broch and wheelhouses, Viking longhouse, medieval farmstead, and 16th-century laird's house.

Visible remains from this first settlement include a Bronze-Age smithy, built around 800 BC, and houses with distinctive cells formed by buttresses extending into the living space. The broch (a circular broad tower of uncertain use) now stands to a height of 2.4 metres but was probably much higher; Mousa Broch, 10 miles to the north, still stands 13 metres high. The broch was soon joined by other dwellings, including a large aisled 'roundhouse' and a byre.

During the first centuries AD, the broch collapsed to be replaced by structures called wheelhouses because their roofs were supported on radial piers, like the spokes of a wheel. Vikings from Norway settled at Jarlshof in the 9th century. The longhouse forming the heart of the farm is still clearly visible. The farmstead expanded and contracted over

time – some 12 to 16 generations. By the 13th century, it had been replaced by a farmhouse, with barn and corn kilns attached.

Shetland passed from Norway to Scotland in 1469, and came under the control of Earl Robert Stewart. His son, the tyrant Earl Patrick, built 'the Old House of Sumburgh' that dominates the site. The name 'Jarlshof' (earl's house), though it sounds old, was actually created by Sir Walter Scott, in his novel *The Pirate*.

Jarlshof, ZE3 9JN
Tel: 01950 460112
www.historic-scotland.gov.uk/places
Information about Up-Helly-Aa: www.uphellyaa.org

14 The Scots Magazine

Battle of Largs

THE battle took place between 30 September and 4 October 1263 at Largs, on the Ayrshire coast. At that time King Haakon IV of Norway controlled Shetland, Orkney and the Hebrides down into western Argyll. Haakon's fleet of longships had anchored off Largs and were badly damaged in a storm. A series of skirmishes with the Scots arose along the shore over a number of days. Eventually Haakon had to withdraw and the fleet broke up. Haakon died on Orkney in December and his son, Magnus V, agreed to hand the Hebrides and the Isle of Man to the Scots under Alexander III. And so it came about that the seaside town of Largs played a key part in making the west coast of Scotland Scottish.

Visit the Vikingar! exhibition at Largs to find out more.

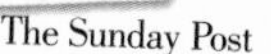

The Sunday Post 33

Shetland: Up-Helly-Aa

Reflecting Shetland's Viking aditions, an amazing festival of re called Up-Helly-Aa is held Lerwick on the last Tuesday January. The celebrations are esided over by the Guizer Jarl, 10 dresses as a figure from Norse ythology. There is a torch-lit ocession of over 900 Guizers, made of nearly 50 squads (with the Jarl Squad representing the Viking) and a Viking galley is pulled through the streets. At the end of the procession the torches are thrown into the galley which then burns. After the burning of the galley there are parties at a dozen halls in the town until the morning and each squad of Guizers have to perform at each hall. It's a long night of celebration!

for more on Shetland see page 184

The Cairngorms

AVIEMORE and ROTHIEMURCHUS

by Horace Broon

I first discovered this bit o' the country wi' the Boy Scouts, but it's really popular wi' folk o' all ages. It's fabulous. Ye'll see walkers and bikers o' Granpaw's age and as young as oor Bairn at every turn in the track here. And now, of course, it's all part of the CAIRNGORMS NATIONAL PARK, so ye have to respect the countryside and no' drop litter or cut doon trees and the like.

I like tae arrive on the train as it drops you right in the middle of AVIEMORE at its bonnie wooden station. After you get yer supplies, hire a bike (or bring yer ain, of course). There are miles of safe places tae cycle wi' the family here and good camp sites, the one at GLENMORE/LOCH MORLICH (four or five miles along the B970 from Aviemore) being aboot the biggest I've seen. There's wind-surfing and boating and kayaking at Loch Morlich and the maist fantastic sandy beach this side of Torremolinos.

If yer legs are up tae it, ye can bike from here a' the way tae the end of the road at COIRE CAS car park, where the funicular railway will whisk you right tae the highest restaurant in Britain, the Ptarmigan, nearly at the top of CAIRNGORM itself (4,084 ft high). Needless to say, the views are immense. Don't forget your camera.

If cycling's no' yer cup o' tea, there's a regular bus from Aviemore to the ski car park. But for me, the treat is to freewheel on my bike doon, doon, doon from the mountain for miles and miles and the canny ride past Loch Morlich and ROTHIEMURCHUS FOREST (what a great name !!) back to Aviemore and the train, or if ye're lucky, a night in one o' the braw hotels or guesthouses. Or camping wi' the Scouts like me.

At Coire Cas, you are in the middle of a winter playground. On snowy winter days, the place is thronged with skiers and snowboarders. If you're not up to skiing, just be like The Broons and take a ride up the mountain on the train and hire a sledge at the top. There's lots of safe areas to pretend you're still young at heart. Granpaw and the Bairn are the Glebe Street sledging champs.

e Ptarmigan Restaurant and
irngorm funicular railway,
22 1RB. Tel: 01479 861261
ww.cairngormmountain.co.uk
thiemurchus Estate, PH22 1QH
l: 01479 812345
ww.rothiemurchus.net

The Sunday Post 32

Days Out: *Our Favourite Cycle Ride*

■ Head out on the cycle track beside the road to Coylumbridge, the B970.

■ Turn off after Inverdruie and follow the signs for Loch an Eilein. It's an easy cycle run.

■ At the loch, there's an information kiosk and you can cycle round the loch on the track.

The old Caledonian pine trees here are wonderful and the sweet smell of the pine needles in the summer sun is amazing. Keep your eyes peeled for big ant hills, too. The ants just love making these big stacks with the millions of pine needles.

There's an island in the middle of the loch with a ruined castle that was once the home to a man called the Wolf of Badenoch, the bad grandson of Robert the Bruce (the Wolf burnt down the towns of Forres and Elgin).

You'll love this spot, with its backdrop of the big Cairngorm Mountains and trees, trees and more trees.

24 *Cairngorms / Coire Gas*

Funicular facts

- The building of the funicular started in 1999.
- It opened on 23 December 2001, 40 years after the first chair lift opened.
- It cost around £14.8 million.
- It is about a mile and a quarter long and goes up nearly 1,600 ft.
- It carries 120 passengers (standing) or 60 (seated).
- It takes 4 minutes (winter) and 8 minutes (summer – slower to see the view).
- Steepest gradient is 40 per cent.
- Powered by electric motors at the top and bottom.

Information about Aviemore
www.visitaviemore.com
Cairngorms National Park Authority, PH26 3HG
Tel: 01479 873535
www.cairngorms.co.uk
Glenmore Campsite, PH22 1QU
Tel: 01479 861271
www.forestholidays.co.uk

THE FUNICULAR IS PIPED IN
COTTISH
Wildlife
No.12
GOLDEN EAGLE

Camping

A NICHT OOT CAMPING   by Paw Broon

Now here's a real treat. No' a DAY oot but a NICHT oot "under canvas". It's a nicht oot ye'll never forget. Ye micht never want tae go on anither ane, but there's mair guid than bad.

If ye're lucky and can find a big open space in the countryside, like we do, near the Lintie Loch at Auchentogle, ye can mak' a big campfire. There's nuthin' as tasty as tatties roasted on a stick on an open fire. Organised camp sites are no' keen on campfires. They have a point I hae tae admit. But ye can jist as happily barbecue sassidges and burgers an' spare ribs an' chops on wee disposable barbecues. Ye'll find lots o' things tae tempt the al fresco (that means no' in yer hoose) chef in MAW BROON'S BUT AN' BEN COOKBOOK.

Now here's guid advice fae someone who knows aboot thae things . . . dinna leave onything behind at the hoose in terms o' food and drink (bein' ootside ye'll need mountains o' things tae shovel doon yer throat!) and dinna leave onything behind like litter when ye leave. Jist bring awa' yer memories.

When ye get tae yer camp site, pit the tents up. Ye'll need lights on yer picnic tables of course so ye can see what ye're daein'. Big candles are fine unless it's windy and they keep blawin' oot. Citronella candles keep awa' (whisper it) the dreaded midges. Midges dinna need lights, beds OR candles tae hae a guid nicht oot. They jist need you. And there's nae "bein' ower fu' tae eat ony mair" at a midges' picnic. So that's anither essential, midge repellent. I find a wee dab o' single malt ahent the ears works wonders.

So there ye are, oot there in the wilds, yer bellies fu', yer beds ready ony time ye feel like it and ye can sit back an' hae a campfire sing song and hopefully watch the embers fae yer campfire float aff up intae the night sky. Ye canna buy that.

And that's aboot it....and ye'll find there's a guid camp site no' that far fae ony place in Scotland.

List o' things tae tak camping

- a tent ... or fower tents for us
- Sleeping bags and mats
- warm clothes and waterproofs
- plates, mugs, cutlery, pots and pans fae the hoose
- camping stove and gas / barbecue
- midge repellent
- plenty o' food and drink
- toilet paper and a wee shovel
- candles and torches
- picnic table and chairs

THIS IS A GOOD PLACE TO PITCH OOR TENTS!
AYE! IT'LL DAE FINE!
NA! NA! THAE COOS WOULD KEEP YE AWAKE A' NICHT!
MOOO!

HOW ABOUT HERE?
NO! YE WIDNA GET A WINK O' SLEEP FOR THE ROARIN' O' THAT WATERFALL.

IT'S GETTIN' AWFY MISTY!
HOW ABOOT CAMPIN' HERE?
NO! IT'S OWER ROCKY!

HERE'S A RARE, SOFT, GRASSY SPOT. WE'LL CAMP HERE.
OKAY, PAW.

THIS IS A RARE SPOT, HEN.
AYE! WE'RE LUCKY GETTIN' THIS, PAW.
I BET WE'LL GET A BRAW VIEW IN THE MORNIN'!
OH, DAPHNE! I'VE COME AWA' WITHOOT MY CURLERS!
AN' I'VE FORGOTTEN MY HOT-WATER BOTTLE.
BE QUIET, YOU ANES. WE WANT TO SLEEP.

6 A.M.
BRRRRRRR
?
BUR-BUR-BURRR
PEE-EEEP
HONK-HONK
BRRRR

PEEP!
OH, CRIVVENS!
RATTLE
KEEP LEFT
WINK
CHUG! CHUG!
BRRR-BRRR
PHUT
DUDLEY D. WATKINS

MARK COTTAGE, LOCH LONG, ARGYLL. THERE'S A BRAW VIEW FAE THIS BOTHY WINDAE!

WHAT IS A BOTHY?
By Joe Broon

I've done a fair bit o' hiking in ma time and ane of my favourite things tae do tae get away fae it a' is tae take masel' off up into the mountains and stay in a bothy. Now a bothy is NOT a holiday cottage. It's really no'. You need a' the same equipment you need for camping. It is basic ... very basic ... really basic.

There's nae running water, nae sink, nae beds, nae lights, nae electricity, nae hair straighteners, and probably nae toilet. If there's a fireplace there might no' be any fuel for it. It will probably be in quite a remote place, up a hill, and awfy cold at night, even in summer. There might no' be a nearby fresh water supply.

There might be a sleeping platform, but you might hae to sleep on the floor, and that floor is no' going to be covered in a nice carpet – it's going to be stone or earth. You might have to share. You need to be prepared to get alang wi' strangers. If that worries you this is NOT for you.

It is a BIG no-no, if you get to a bothy first, to say to a newcomer "sorry – we got here first". Not the done thing at a'. Follow the bothy code and be respectful to others and of the building – the bothy owners and the MOUNTAIN BOTHY ASSOCIATION put a lot of effort, money and love into the upkeep o' bothies.

So why do I love bothy life? Real quietness. No roads or traffic. You really see the stars. If you meet anyone they'll probably be like-minded. You'll hae a roof ower your heid that's sturdier than a tent on a windy night and you'll wake up to a braw view – guaranteed.

THE BOTHY CODE

The Bothies maintained by the Mountain Bothy Association are available by courtesy of the owners. Please respect this privilege. Please record your visit in the Bothy log-book.

Note that bothies are used entirely at your own risk.

Respect Other Users

Please leave the bothy clean and tidy with dry kindling for the next visitors. Make other visitors welcome. If they are not MBA members set a good example.

Respect the Bothy

Tell us about any accidental damage. Don't leave graffiti or vandalise the bothy. Please take out all rubbish which you can't burn. Avoid burying rubbish; this pollutes the environment. Please don't leave perishable food as this attracts vermin. Guard against fire risk and ensure the fire is out before you leave. Make sure the doors and windows are properly closed when you leave.

Respect the Surroundings

If there is no toilet at the bothy please bury human waste out of sight. Use the spade provided, keep well away from the water supply and never use the vicinity of the bothy as a toilet. Never cut live wood or damage estate property. Use fuel sparingly.

Respect our Agreement with the Estate

Please observe any restrictions on use of the bothy, for example during stag stalking or at lambing time. Please remember that bothies are for short stays only. The owner's permission must be obtained if you intend an extended stay.

Respect the Restriction On Numbers

Because of overcrowding and lack of facilities, large groups (6 or more) should not use a bothy or camp near a bothy without first seeking permission from the owner.

Bothies are not available for commercial groups.

http://www.mountainbothies.org.uk/

COME ON! THIS IS THE QUICKEST WAY TAE THE BONNY BANKS O' THE SNECHTY! OWER THE BRIG!
DINNA BE DAFT! THIS IS THE SHORTEST WAY— AN' IT'S BONNIER — THROUGH THE WOOD!

A' RICHT! GO THAT WAY IF YE LIKE! I'LL BET YE WE'RE THERE FIRST!
WE'LL SEE YE IN ABOUT AN HOUR AT THE FAR END O' THE WOOD — WE'LL BE WAITIN' FOR YE!
CHEERIO!
WE'RE STICKIN' TAE MAW AN' PAW! THEY'VE GOT THE GRUB!
AYE! THE OTHERS HAVE ONLY THE POTS AN' PANS!

MY! IT'S A BONNY BRIG, THIS!
IT'S AN AULD, AULD BRIG!
YE SEE THE ROAD GOES UP OWER THE BRAE— BUT WE'LL FOLLOW THE PATH BESIDE THE RIVER!

THERE'S NAE SIGN O' THE OTHERS YET! MAYBE THEY'RE IN FRONT— OR FAR AHENT!

AN HOUR LATER
LOOK! THERE THEY ARE! ON THE OPPOSITE SIDE O' THE RIVER!
HEY! YOU'RE ON THE WRANG SIDE O' THE BURN!
IT'S YOU THAT'S ON THE WRANG SIDE, YE DAFT IDIOTS!

THIS IS A FINE MESS WE'RE IN! WE'VE GOT THE FOOD, BUT WE CANNA COOK IT BECAUSE YOU'VE GOT THE POTS AN' PANS!
WE CANNA GET ACROSS! THE RIVER'S OWER DEEP, AN' WE'RE OWER TIRED TAE GO A' THE WAY BACK AGAIN! WHIT ARE WE GOIN' TAE DAE?
WE'LL NEED TAE FIX UP SOME WAY O' PASSIN' THINGS TAE EACH OTHER! DAE YE HAE YER ROPE?

IF YE WANT SOME MAIR TEA, JUIST PASS YER CUP!
HERE'S SOME MAIR FORKS AN' KNIVES!
HEY, MAW! THERE'S TEETH-MARKS IN THIS CREAM-COOKIE!
I'M SENDIN' MA CUP O' TEA BACK, MAW, YE FORGOT TAE PUT SUGAR IN IT!
JINGS! I HOPE IT DISNA SINK!
HERE'S YER SAUSAGE AN' TATTIES, HORACE!

Highland Wildlife

No, not Joe and Hen up some Ben, but some advice aboot the wild animals that live in the hills – and where ye can see them avoidin' the climb.

The Wildlife of Scotland (with ma thanks tae Visit Scotland)
By Horace Broon

In an unspoilt area with a low population, there is plenty of room for wildlife, which means the Scottish Highlands provide ideal habitats for a wide range of birds and beasts. In fact, unless you travel with your eyes shut, you are sure to encounter some special creature. Best of all, you don't have to tramp for miles to enjoy exciting wildlife views. Red kites, for example, are easily seen from the car as you travel through the Black Isle north of Inverness while ospreys are everyday birds in the Cairngorms National Park and elsewhere.

Red deer, Scotland's largest wild creatures, also abound in the Highlands and can often be seen from the road, especially in the cooler months when they move down from the high tops.

Another creature closely associated with this area is the golden eagle. Its home is the high moors, crags and mountain corries in many parts of the area. If you are very lucky you may also encounter the spectacular sea eagle in a few places on the west coast, where they have been successfully re-introduced.

There are also lots of places where wildlife spotting uses modern technology to provide unrivalled views of various species such as red kites, ospreys and hen harriers. At Boat of Garten, for example, discreet cameras allow you to watch the activities in the ospreys' nests at close-quarters.

From dramatic sea-bird colonies to pine martens and reindeer, the Highlands offer fantastic wildlife displays.

Highland Wildlife Park, PH21 1NL
Tel: 01540 651270
www.highlandwildlifepark.org

The Cairngorm Reindeer Herd

This herd is Britain's only herd of reindeer, found free ranging in the Cairngorm mountains in Scotland. These extremely tame and friendly animals are a joy to all who come and see them. There are currently around 150 reindeer, approximately 50 of them ranging the Cairngorm Mountains and the remainder on the Glenlivet Estate; the locations being some 30 miles apart. There is a daily visit to the reindeer, weather permitting, starting from the Reindeer House at Glenmore, near Aviemore. During the winter months, the visit may be dependent on whether they can be found – they say they're free-ranging and they mean it! Under the supervision of trained guides, visitors can feed and stroke the reindeer.

Cairngorm Reindeer Herd,
PH22 1QU
Tel: 01479 861228
www.cairngormreindeer.co.uk

The Highland Wildlife Park

The Highland Wildlife Park at Kincraig, near Aviemore, is run by the same people who look after Edinburgh Zoo (see page 18), so they know how to do things well and look after all the animals.

At the Wildlife Park, you can discover the amazing variety of wildlife found in present day Scotland, such as the pine marten, wildcat, otter and capercaillie - then step back in time and meet the creatures that roamed the earth hundreds, even thousands of years ago - the animals of your ancestors, such as wolves, lynx, reindeer and wild horses.

The Highland Wildlife Park has expanded its collection further afield to include endangered animals of the world's mountain and tundra regions. Already home to snow monkeys, red pandas, yak and Amur tigers, the Park recently welcomed polar bears.

Drive around the Main Reserve in your own car and then investigate the walk-round area by foot. Throughout the day animal wardens give feeding talks on some of the many creatures in the walk-around area. Watch as some of the animals are fed and hear some more fascinating facts about them!

Distilleries – by Granpaw

THE WATER OF LIFE (a day tae remember or maybe not)
by Granpaw Broon

Uisge Beatha, the water of life, amber nectar, call it what ye will, WHISKY has been Scotland's great international symbol since lang afore Irn Bru was ever thought aboot. Ma laddie said he'd write aboot a great whisky day oot, but he's still a youngster when it comes tae bein' a whisky expert . . . no' like masel', wha's been tipplin' the "hard stuff" (in moderation, of course) since afore Paw Broon was a twinkle in ma eye. I do mind "wettin' his heid" wi' a fine wee Laphroaig way back in . . . och, I canna mind, it's that lang ago.

Let's start off oor day wi' folk that'll be able tae explain the magic o' the dram, near Forres, just east alang the road fae Inverness and Nairn. Run by Historic Scotland, DALLAS DHU distillery is a whisky museum, well signposted off the A96 fae Inverness tae Aberdeen. There's nae whisky distilled there nowadays, but ye can still buy "the cratur", the last Dallas Dhu being distilled in 1983.

Dallas Dhu was the last distillery tae be built in the 19th century in Scotland and one o' the first tae be built wi' the pagoda chimney that soon became common on nearly all the distilleries makin' Scotch. While ye're there, visit the visual presentation wi' the free audio guide . . . and the FREE DRAM! Canna ask fairer than that. (See Speyside Trail page 96.)

Dae ye ken, Scotland still produces mair whisky than any other country in the world? As well as bein' oor national drink, it's loved by folk fae Alaska tae New Zealand. So now ye ken how it's made, I'll let ye intae the secret o' how it's enjoyed. And then ye'll be able tae hae braw days oot and many nichts in, savouring the malts o' Auld Scotia. I'll be tellin' ye a' this for FREE, so pay attention. I'll no' be tellin' ye again.

The Scots Magazine 23

Scotch whisky

Scotch whisky, or 'water of life' as it is called in Gaelic ('uisge beatha'), is whisky made in Scotland. It can only be called Scotch whisky if it is made at a distillery in Scotland from water and malted barley, to which only whole grains of other cereals may be added, and it must be stored in oak casks for over three years. The main type of Scotch whisky sold around the world is blended Scotch whisky. There are two main categories of whisky: single malt and blended. Single malt Scotch whisky means the whisky comes from one distillery only, and blended Scotch whisky means that the whisky is composed of malt whiskies from a number of distilleries, and also contains some Scotch grain whiskies.

The first written records of Scotch whisky date from 1494. The ancient Celts knew how to brew, and probably got their skills in distilling from Ireland. Distilling is a craft.

Scotch whisky is made from a mash of cereal grains, which, when it ferments with the addition of yeast, produces alcohol and carbon dioxide. This is then distilled. The majority of Scottish malt whisky distilleries use double distillation. There are distinct distilling regions in Scotland, and it is their natural characteristics that help give each region its particular flavours. Speyside, for example, is home to two-thirds of Scotland's malt whisky distilleries, due to the quality of its soft water. Colour is normally imparted to whisky while it is matured in casks. The casks used are made of oak, and are usually ex-sherry or ex-bourbon casks.

Quality whiskies

There's different areas and kinds o' malt whiskies as far as I mind, Island, Highland, Speyside, Lowland, Islay and Campbeltown. But there's only really twa kinds o' whisky . . . guid and better still. But here's ma expert opinion. There's that much keech (no' a word ye'll find in the dictionary - it means somethin' like bird droppings or the stuff ye bag efter yer dog's done its business) talked aboot whisky, it wid put ye aff drinkin'. Here's ane I read no' that lang ago, "10-year-old Glentammynoorie has a long finish, lingering, with hints of old socks, seaweed, warm tarmac, dark chocolate and notes of dandelions. Superb." Superb? Wha's kiddin' wha? Onythin' tastin' like that wid pit a mannie aff his mince. So, jist ignore a' the experts an' taste them til ye find ane ye like.

- Speyside has lovely smooth drams, anes ye'll enjoy if ye're watchin' the rugby at Murrayfield.
- Highland anes wi' a bit mair bite for a day oot in yer kilt.
- Island malts like Highland Park (fae Orkney) and Talisker (fae Skye), perfect for a day oot in yer boat.
- Lowland malts jist rare for a' yer family (over eighteen!!).
- Campbeltown drams like Springbank are Maw Broon's choice. Need I say mair?
- Then there's the peaty Islay giants, Granpaw Broon recommended.

Speyside – The Malt Whisky Trail

The main malt whisky tour in Scotland is in Speyside, the hame o' rich, sweet, hearty drams that are juist richt for sipping in front of a roaring log fire as the snow falls outside. You can stay in Dufftown or Rothes and visit a' the places on the MALT WHISKY TRAIL in a couple o' days.

(i)

Malt Whisky Trail
www.maltwhiskytrail.com

Speyside Cooperage
www.speysidecooperage.co.uk

In Dufftown there is a saying, 'Rome was built on seven hills and Dufftown was built on seven stills.' In Dufftown, ane of those 'stills' is GLENFIDDICH, the world's most popular malt whisky. The distillery, built in 1886-7, is one o' the biggest malt whisky distilleries in the world, with 28 stills producing 11 million litres of spirit every year. There's the usual tour wi' drams at the end and a guid shop to get your souvenirs in. All the places tae visit on the trail offer tours, tastings, good grub and plenty o' shopping so don't go spending a' your pocket money in the first place you visit!

A wee bit further north is the ABERLOUR distillery. This whisky is double-cask matured – in old sherry and bourbon casks, then it is blended together. If you fancy buying a bottle, at the end of your tour you can hand-fill a bottle of Aberlour straight from the cask.

Next up is the SPEYSIDE COOPERAGE where ye can see how the oak casks are made that all Scotch whisky must be matured in. If the whisky disnae stay in cask for at least three years, then it cannae legally be ca'd Scotch whisky. This is an amazing place wi' a' the clattering and hammering. You can see how skilled these lads are as they build up or repair a' the wooden barrels that pass through. Look out for barrels from America that used to hold bourbon, and Spanish casks that once held sherry. Both of these are very popular for maturing oor national drink in.

Then there's the GLEN GRANT DISTILLERY (1840). Glen Grant is the maist popular malt whisky in Italy. Have a look at the stills; they have strange bulbs at the bottom of their necks. The tour guide will explain how this influences the character o' the whisky. The distillery's Victorian Garden is world-famous so you can take a dram and have a great walk as well. Look out for Major Grant's secret whisky grotto! It's a really beautiful place to be on a sunny day.

(i)

Glen Grant
www.glengrant.com

Cardhu Distillery
www.discovering-distilleries.com/cardhu

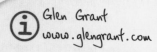

Glenlivet Distillery
www.glenlivet.com

Strathisla Distillery
www.maltwhiskydistilleries.com

Glen Moray Distillery
www.glen-moray.co.uk

Aberlour Distillery
www.aberlour.com

CARDHU DISTILLERY can also be reached after the Speyside Cooperage – it's just to the west of it. This distillery was built in 1824 after the local farmer, John Cumming, wis convicted of distilling 'privately'. His wife, Helen, wis the real culprit. A lassie makin' whisky – that's my kind o wummin! He got thegither wi' some other distillers and took oot a licence to distil legally. An awfy lot of Cardhu goes into the Johnnie Walker blends. It's also a really popular malt in Spain.

The next distillery is a bit further afield and taks ye into some mair remote countryside. The famous GLENLIVET DISTILLERY was the first to go legal when the government changed the distilling laws in 1823. George Smith, the original owner, had to cairry twa pistols wi' him everywhere he went because the local illicit distillers were not at a' happy wi' his new legal status. They soon came roond though and soon after that almost a'body went legal. The distillery is in a beautiful bowl right in Glenlivet and it maks ane o' the really braw Speyside drams.

Heading back tae Dufftown, we go east to the town o' Keith, the hame o' STRATHISLA DISTILLERY, one of the bonniest there is with its Japanese pagoda hats sitting on top o' the malting kilns. This style o' roof was adopted in the late 1880s after an Elgin architect, Bill Doig, renovated the kilns at DAILUANE DISTILLERY and soon it was a' the rage everywhere. This distillery has been on the go since 1786, which makes it ane of the oldest in Scotland and it is the spiritual home of the famous blend, CHIVAS REGAL.

From Strathisla it's time tae head alang the A96 to Elgin and visit GLEN MORAY DISTILLERY. It started in 1897 but was originally a brewery. It seems to enjoy a much milder climate than a lot o' other Speyside distilleries. Also its warehouses are quite low-lying and they flood from time to time and a' that helps the whisky to mature a bit differently. If you like your pudding – and who in their richt mind disnae – this is the dram for you … a' fruity and sweet. The French must really like it because a French company owns it now!

The next twa distilleries are further tae the west near Forres. The first, BENROMACH, means "shaggy mountain" in Gaelic. It was built in 1898 but had a topsy-turvy history until 1992 when the famous independent whisky bottlers and blenders, GORDON & MACPHAIL, bought it. It reopened in 1998 and since then it has never looked back. They are a pretty innovative bunch at Benromach and were the first to produce 100% organic malt whisky! You can even fill your own bottle if you want to.

Finally, we head south of Forres to visit DALLAS DHU. This is a really pretty place but it's actually a museum as it hasn't produced whisky since 1983 when it was closed. Luckily, the owners decided not to knock it down or sell it but instead handed it over to Historic Scotland who have taken care of it since then. The distillery started up in 1899 to supply whisky for a famous, long-forgotten blend called Roderick Dhu but it changed hands quite a few times before closing for good. You can still buy the whisky they used to produce here though, but it's getting pricey the less there is of it!

Dallas Dhu Distillery,
IV36 2RR
Tel: 01309 676548
www.historic-scotland.gov.uk/places

Benromach
www.gordonandmacphail.com

Granpaw's guide on how tae enjoy a dram . . . get yer pals and find a wee hoose like the But an' Ben or a wee cottage or bothy wi' an open fire, wi' wood or peat. Get candles. Pour everybody a guid dram. Cup the glass in yer hand tae warm it a bitty and pit yer nose in it. Lovely. Nae hints o' tarmac or auld socks here. Jist whisky. No, no, hae patience, dinna drink it yet. Look at yer bleezin' fire through the whisky in yer glass and watch it dance, smell it again and then tell tales wi' yer auld cronies aboot yer first girlfriend or yer days when ye were near picked tae play for Scotland. We're nearly there now . . . in a wee bit o' quiet, raise yer glass, toast yer auld cronies and doon she goes . . . oh, man, is that guid or what!! Slainte!

"Should auld acquaintance be forgot an' never brought tae mind . . ."

www.drinkaware.co.uk

Distilleries – The Whisky Coast

There's another way to visit some of Scotland's distilleries, but it'll take a bit longer than the Speyside trail! This trail is alang Scotland's glorious west coast and is called THE WHISKY COAST. It covers 16 distilleries from CAMPBELTOWN to the ISLE OF SKYE and you can start wherever you want and end up wherever you want. You can even take a yacht if you feel adventurous! Whatever you dae ye'll need a guid few days tae dae it so plan ahead.

We started at the bottom in CAMPBELTOWN which used to hae dozens o' distilleries in Victorian times with names like Ardlussa, Dalaruan and Dalintober. The town fell on hard times in the 1920s and a whole lot of them closed down forever, but there are three survivors and you can visit two of them: SPRINGBANK and GLENGYLE. These are sister distilleries owned by the same company but Springbank is the more famous as it has always stayed open whereas Glengyle had a period when it was closed so it's really only just getting a head of steam up again after all those years.

They do everything at SPRINGBANK so you can see the old floor maltings covered in barley before it is dried in the kiln and you can see them bottling the whisky as well! They even make more than one malt whisky here. Longrow is their peated variety and if you shut your eyes when you taste it, you could be on Islay!

A short walk away is the rejuvenated GLENGYLE DISTILLERY which reopened in March 2004. It was originally built in 1872 before it closed in 1925 so it's had a long rest and is now raring to go! Its 10-year-old will be ready in 2012 and goes by the name of Kilkerran, so look out for it.

ⓘ Caledonian MacBrayne:
Kennacraig, PA29 6YF
Tel: 01880 730253;

Port Ellen, PA42 7DW
Tel: 01496 302209
www.calmac.co.uk

ⓘ

The Whisky Coast

www.whiskycoast.com

Springbank, PA28 6EX

www.springbankwhisky.com

Glengyle Distillery, PA 28 6EX

www.kilkerran.com

Laphroaig, PA42 7DU
www.laphroaig.com

Lagavulin, PA42 7DZ
www.malts.com

Ardbeg, PA42 7EA
www.ardbeg.com

Old Kiln Café, PA42 7EA
Tel: 01496 302244

After Campbeltown ye could head for Claonaig in Kintyre to catch the ferry for Arran and the ISLE OF ARRAN distillery at Lochranza. It's quite a young distillery and there's a page aboot it in this book. page 154

Or tak' the ferry to ISLAY AND JURA frae Kennacraig near West Loch Tarbert up on the west side of Kintyre, just south of the picturesque fishing port of Tarbert.

Ye'll arrive at PORT ELLEN on ISLAY. As ye approach the island, watch oot for the white distilleries peekin' oot fae their sheltered spots alang the Islay coast . . . names tae mak' yer mooth watter – Ardbeg, Lagavulin, Laphroaig – and then the boat's intae Port Ellen.

Islay has eight distilleries – ARDBEG, LAGAVULIN, LAPHROAIG, BOWMORE, BRUICHLADDICH, BUNNAHABHAIN, CAOL ILA and a new ane at KILCHOMAN – so you need to keep your wits aboot ye wi' the tasting samples!

'PAGODAS' AT LAGAVULIN

Head west first to visit LAPHROAIG, LAGAVULIN and ARDBEG. Ardbeg is the maist peaty o' the Islay malts – and a braw dram – and last time I was there, I also had awfy fine clootie dumplin' at the OLD KILN CAFÉ (as nice as Maw's). Only a few of the distilleries on Islay have a café.

Look oot for the unusual pear-shaped stills that make rich, peaty LAGAVULIN. At LAPHROAIG ye'll be able tae see the floor maltings like at Springbank (and Bowmore too) and if you want tae join the Friends of Laphroaig, ye'll be given a square foot o' land near the distillery for life! An' the best bit is, when you visit after that, the distillery have to give ye a free dram for the rent!

Returning to Port Ellen you pass by the PORT ELLEN MALTINGS at the end o' the village (which supplies all the Islay distilleries with their malted barley) and head north to BOWMORE across the massive Laggan Moss. This is where the peat is cut that gives most of the Islay whiskies their big, peaty flavour. Bring yer bathing suit because the waste heat frae the distillery heats the local swimming pool! Bowmore is right at the heart o' the community. They use the hall at the distillery for a' sorts o' events an' the ISLAY WAVE BUS, which runs on electricity from the island's wave-power station, is kept here to recharge overnight. They're canny people these Islay folk! If you feel like staying at the distillery there's some bonnie cottages you can rent as well.

Head to Bridgend next and turn left ower the bridge on to the A847 to PORT CHARLOTTE. After a few miles take the B8018 on the right and head along this road until you see the signs for KILCHOMAN DISTILLERY. This is Islay's newest distillery, built in the yard at Rockside Farm in 2005. Everything is wee here and the whisky is still quite young but it's really good for its age. There are some floor maltings here as well, where barley they grow on the farm is malted. If you fancy a bracing beach walk, this is a good place to do it by continuing down the road to Islay's Atlantic shore at MACHIR BAY.

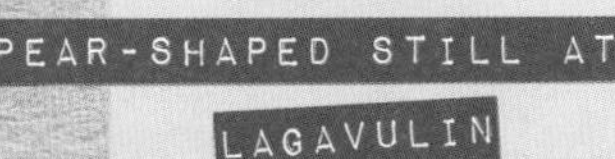
PEAR-SHAPED STILL AT LAGAVULIN

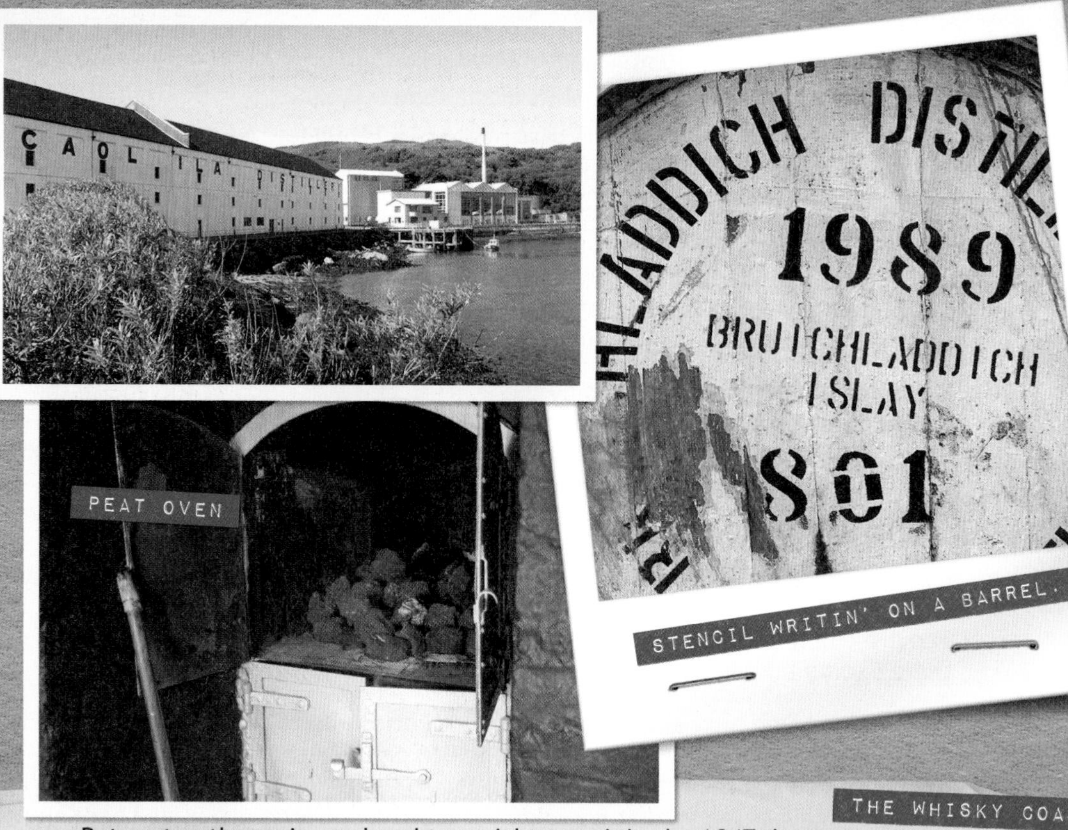

STENCIL WRITIN' ON A BARREL.

Return tae the main road and turn right to rejoin the A847 down to BRUICHLADDICH (pronounced *Brew-ick-LAAD-ie*) which was built in 1881 at the same time as Bunnahabhain. This distillery has also had its fair share of misfortune and, like Glengyle, it was rescued after closure by some canny folk who didn't listen to the doom and gloom merchants! The result is magic and the distillery is doing really well. They even produce gin here in an old still ca'ed Ugly Betty (because she is!).

The next stops are up on the north o' the island at CAOL ILA and BUNNAHABHAIN (pronounced *Cull EE-lah* and *Bunna-HAAV-inn*) so head back to Bridgend and on towards Port Askaig. They're both signposted off the road just south of Port Askaig down a single-track road, so take care. At the end o' the road ye'll find Bunnahabhain. This distillery has some o' the tallest stills in the world. It's ane o' the lighter Islay malts with no big peaty flavours. Maw likes a wee nip o' this ane.

Retracing your steps to Caol Ila you go doon a switchback road and roond the front o' the warehouse to the car park. When you enter the stillhouse the view over to the Paps of Jura across the Sound of Islay fair taks yer breath awa. By the way, Caol Ila means "Sound of Islay".

Now it's time tae tak the short ferry crossing fae Port Askaig ower tae Feolin on JURA and on tae the only village on the island, Craighouse, the home o' ISLE OF JURA malt whisky. Don't worry aboot directions, there's only ane road on Jura! Isle of Jura is another resurrected distillery which was built in 1963 on the site of the old one that closed in 1910. Jura whisky isn't peaty at all. A good time to go and do the grand tour of Islay and Jura is when the FEIS ILE (Islay Festival) is on at the end o' May each year. There's music, food, distillery events and the weather is usually braw, but book ahead.

Back to ISLAY now and then the big ferry back tae the mainland where we head up the coast tae bonny OBAN tae find that its distillery began as a brewery back in the 1790s. A couple o' enterprising brithers by the name o' Stevenson started it a'. The distillery is tucked awa' up a street just aff the harbour, so it's aye been a wee totie affair but it has a guid visitor centre. From Oban you can tak' the ferry direct to MULL and visit the distillery at TOBERMORY. Just like Springbank, Tobermory makes another peaty malt called Ledaig so you're spoilt for choice. see page 163 for a picture o' the Tobermory distillery

Now it's off to FORT WILLIAM and the BEN NEVIS DISTILLERY which sits in the shadow o' Britain's highest mountain. It was "Long John" MacDonald who began it in 1825 which explains why for years it was the main malt in the famous Long John blend. Although the distillery claims to have been the first one in Lochaber, I bet there were a few more hidden away in the glens that naebody knew aboot!

Finally, we tak the road tae the isles ower the sea to SKYE to visit TALISKER DISTILLERY. This is a very famous malt whisky that is aye winning prizes and no wonder, it's a lovely dram that's perfect to end your tour with. Each year there is a special MALTS CRUISE that you can join if ye have yer ain yacht and go sailing from distillery to distillery in some o' the maist bonnie scenery in the world.

ⓘ Bowmore Visitor Information Centre, PA43 7JP
Tel: 08707 200 617

Oban, PA34 5NH
www.malts.com

Tobermory, PA75 6NR
www.tobermorymalt.com

Talisker Distillery, IV47 8SR
www.malts.com

maltscruise
www.worldcruising.com

AT BALMORAL
by Maggie Broon

I've aye wanted tae be the Queen. And as that's no' likely tae happen (but I was once the carnival queen), the next best thing was tae be invited tae tea with Her Majesty and get a' dressed up. But that's no' likely tae happen either. So I had tae settle for a day oot in Her Majesty's hoose. Actually, I had tae pay tae get in, alang wi' the rest o' the family, no' the Royal Family, jist oor lot fae Glebe Street. We had a day oot tae Royal Deeside and oor first stop was BALMORAL CASTLE. We drove alang the course o' the River Dee fae Aberdeen. This is such bonnie countryside.

Balmoral Castle sits on the banks of the Dee with "Dark" Lochnagar, the mountain, towerin' up oot o' its back garden. Actually, Lochnagar wisnae dark at a' when we were there. It was bathed in sunshine. The castle was bought by Queen Victoria in 1848 and has been the Scottish home of the Royals ever since. Good Queen Vic's man, Prince Albert, added an extension to the castle made oot o' gleaming white marble fae a local quarry. Apparently 'Bert didna think there was enough room for them in the original castle. He wouldna have been much good in oor wee tenement flat. I jist loved wandering aboot inside the castle, knowing that I was walking through the places the Queen ca's home.

I was in my element in the Castle Ballroom. I jist imagined myself a' dressed up for the ball and the Prince makin' straight for me and sayin', "Miss Broon, will you do me the honour of having this dance?" I would have accepted tae. Granpaw said he used tae go tae dances in a place called Mar Lodge just up the road in what he called the Stag Ballroom. There were stags' heads all over the ceiling and walls. When the Highland dance got goin' the hale place shook and the teeth used tae fall oot o' the old stags' heads and fowk wid slip on them. Trust him tae remember some story aboot teeth fa'in oot.

The castle's only open from the beginning of April until 31st July (it's closed in August, September and October when the Queen and her family are bidin' there and during the winter). But if she's readin' this, I would still like an invitation for ma tea!!

Balmoral Castle,
AB35 5TB
Tel: 01339 742534
www.balmoralcastle.com

GEORGE MELVIN RENNIE
Aw, that's awfy pretty.
OLD BRIDGE OF DEE.
A.634
BALMORAL CASTLE
A2348
GEORGE MELVIN RENNIE
MY GREAT UNCLE
CRATHIE CHURCH
A2349
105

Codona's Amusement Park,
AB24 5EB
Tel: 01224 595910
www.codonas.com

THE NORTHERN LIGHTS – OOR DAY OOT IN ABERDEEN

by The Broons Twins

We got tae pick this day oot. It was great an' we canna wait tae go back again.

It's the oil capital o' Europe or so Paw telt us. Ye canna see ony oil rigs of course, cos they're a' offshore in the deep North Sea. But ye can see a' the boats in ABERDEEN HARBOUR that supply the offshore rigs. Walkin' roond the harbour is fascinatin'. There's boats o' every shape and size. Oor favourite was the ferry boat fae Shetland that lands in Aberdeen. It's a lang sailing and the passage over the Pentland Firth can "be a bitty rough" as an auld Aberdonian put it. It was just unloading when we passed and we've never seen sae many green faces in oor lives. We would have paid tae see them.

We didna get things a' oor ain way and Maw and the lassies insisted we visit the shops in UNION STREET. Thankfully, she didna mean a' the shops as this has got tae be the langest street in the world. Aberdeen looks as if it was just built last month. A' the buildings are built wi' granite. It's a local stone that disnae wear at a' it seems. Everything looks new. We liked the big Marischal College. It's an old university building and it's the second biggest granite building in the world.

And now we were aff tae what WE really wanted tae see, CODONA'S AMUSEMENT PARK, right doon on the beach. What could be better? When the weather's good, ye can lie on the sands, hae a swim and head off intae the amusement park. When ye're oor age, nuthin' could be better. There's too many things tae list, but we loved the Pirate Island Adventure Golf. It's 18 holes and it looks like ye're in Florida. Pirates galore and even a big pirate ship . . . and there's a second 18-hole Congo INDOORS jungle golf course wi' jungle trees, tree huts, a big waterfall and an eruptin' volcano. Then there's the Disco Waltzers (haud on tae yer stomach!) and the Super Dodgems. The Bairn loved the Safari Kiddies Train. If ye're willing tae "shoot the rapids" and ye dinna mind gettin' soaked, try the White Water Log Flume. Couldna get enough o' that, and there's Ten Pin Bowling, a huge super slide . . . and . . . and then we ran oot o' time. It was tea time.

The Twins were too busy on the beach tae visit the great hands-on science centre: The Satrosphere on Constitution Street, AB24 5TU
Tel: 01224 640340
www.satrosphere.net

Greetings from
THE BEACH
UNION TERRACE GARDENS
BALMORAL CASTLE
ABERDEEN
MARISCHAL COLLEGE
87A
THE HARBOUR

A SMALL SCOTCH FROM
THE HARBOUR
BRIG O' BALGOWNIE
UNION STREET FROM EAST END
ABERDEEN

Oh no! Horace will BATTER us for makin a mess o his book!

Ashvale Fish Restaurant,
AB10 6PY
Tel: 01224 575842
www.theashvale.co.uk

Fit fine!

Tea time

As the day oot was oor choice, we got tae pick . . . and we aye go tae the same place. The Ashvale fish an' chip shop at 42 Great Western Road. No' just the Ashvale, it's THE Ashvale, the bestest nosh north o' the Equator. There's a' manner o' things on the menu, but we twa only ever have haddock, chips and peas. It's the nicht oot tae round aff the best day oot. They have a thing on the menu called "The Ashvale Whale". The biggest fish in the sea. It comes wi' chips and peas tae and if you can eat the hale lot, ye get anither ane free. Paw said that once Daphne ate twa and wondered if there was anythin' for efters. But then again, she would.

Ah kent you twins were up tae somethin' fishy!

Highland Games

BRAEMAR GATHERING
by Maggie Broon

And while ye're on Deeside, ye jist must visit Braemar, home of the Braemar Highland Games, the Braemar Gathering as it's known. There are Highland Games all over Scotland, but this is the one Her Majesty attends, so it's the ane a'body remembers. The games are held in The Memorial Park in Braemar. It's been a richt Royal occasion since their new neighbour Queen Victoria attended in 1848 when she'd moved in doon the road. Tickets for The Games sell oot quick . . . and I mean quick. But ye can aye visit at any time and just imagine what it's like . . .the packed crowds, the Queen and her party, the Highland dancing, the pipe bands, Tossing the Caber, Throwing the Hammer and the like and a' thae big lovely young men in skirts . . . sorry, kilts.

But, if ye're no' lucky enough tae get tickets for the Braemar Bash, look out for the hundreds of Highland Games all over Scotland. It really does make a grand day oot.

26 The Sunday Post

Out & About: *The Braemar Gathering*

THERE HAVE been gatherings at Braemar for over 900 years. The current form of the Gathering can be traced back to 1832 when the Braemar Highland Society donated money for the prizes and took on the organisation of the Gathering.

The Gathering is held on the first Saturday in September in the Memorial Park in Braemar. It has been a Royal occasion since Queen Victoria first attended in 1848.

Among the events held at the Gathering are:

- **Tossing the Caber**
- **Throwing the Hammer**
- **Putting the Stone**
- **The Hill Race**
- **The Inter-Services Tug of War**
- **Highland Dancing competitions**
- **Pipe Bands**

. . . and even the Children's Sack Race.

Looks like he'll fy aff wi' it!

Braemar Gathering
AB35 5YU
Tel: 013397 41098
www.braemargathering.org

THE STONE TOSS
THE STONE TOSS
307

OF COURSE WE WID GET STUCK ON THE DEVIL'S ELBOW ON THE WAY TAE THE BRAEMAR GAMES!
WE'LL NEED TAE DUMP THE CAR SOMEPLACE~AN' WALK. I KEN A SHORT CUT OWER THE HILLS.
YE'RE HOLDIN' EVERYBODY UP!
DEVIL'S ELBOW
CHANGE TO LOW GEAR
COME AFF AN' SHOVE

10 MINUTES LATER
WELL, WE'VE SHOVED THE CAR AFF THE ROAD~ BUT NOW WE'LL NEED TAE HURRY OR WE'LL MISS THE BEST O' THE GAMES!
IT'S GEY ROUGH GOIN' OWER HERE~MIND THE MARSHY GROUND~YE'LL SINK IN IT!
OOH! LOOK AT THAT POOR HORSE WI' A TREE GROWIN' OOT O' ITS HEID!
THAT'S NO' A HORSE~ THAT'S A BILLY GOAT!
DINNA BE DAFT. IT'S A STAG!

HOORAY
CHEERS
PIPES
WE'RE NEARLY THERE NOW— THAT'S IT OWER THE BRAE. LISTEN TAE THE FOWK CHEERIN'!
JINGS! FANCY A'BODY CHEERIN' FOR PAW AN' GRAN'PAW!
DINNA BE DAFT. THAT'LL BE FOR THE ROYAL PARTY ARRIVING.

IT'S AWFY CROWDED. WE'LL NO' SEE ONYTHING!
HERE! LOOK AT THAE ATHLETES GOIN' IN~IT GIES ME AN IDEA~YOU LASSIES~ WE'LL SWAP YOUR TARTAN SKIRTS FOR OOR TROOSERS, AN' BORROW THAT STRETCHER OWER THERE.
SPARE STRETCHERS

THERE'S A RICHT QUEER-LOOKIN' BUNCH O' ATHLETES GOIN' IN.
MAN, IF IT'S NO' SERGEANT TOSH FRAE GLEBE STREET! YE'LL LET THE WIFE IN, EH? SHE'S COME A' THIS ROAD TAE SEE US TOSS THE CABER, AN' NOW SHE'S NO' FEELIN' TOO GRAND. BUT IT'S NO' SERIOUS. SHE'LL BRIGHTEN UP ONCE SHE GETS INSIDE!
OH, AYE! AN' I SEE YOUR YOUNG TWINS HIDIN' IN THE STRETCHER. AH, WELL, IN YE GO. I DIDNA SEE YE!
WHISPER~ I NEVER FELT BETTER IN A' MA LIFE!
OH, LOOK! HERE'S SOME MAIR HIELANDERS COMIN'!

JINGS! WHIT A BRAW VIEW! WE'LL JUIST SIT HERE AN' PRETEND TAE WAIT OOR TURN FOR YOU LADS TOSSIN' THE CABER!

Pitlochry and the Centre of Scotland

by Daphne Broon

I like PITLOCHRY. The locals tell me it's the very centre of Scotland. It's but a wee stroll fae the railway station tae the Pitlochry dam on LOCH FASKALLY, wi' an ice cream shop on yer way. The big dam is part o' the HYDRO scheme built aroond here efter the Second World war. Haudin' back the waters o' bonnie Loch Faskally, Pitlochry dam is a fair lump o' concrete and it has a FISH LADDER tae help the salmon climb up intae the waters o' the loch. There's an observation room where ye can stick yer nose up against the glass and come face tae face wi' some o' Scotland's best salmon. It's as weel salmon tastes better than it looks. Some o' thae monsters look like something oot o' a scary movie. And jist a stroll doon river fae the dam is the PITLOCHRY FESTIVAL THEATRE. There's something for a' tastes here throughout the year – comedy, folk music, serious plays and near onythin' else ye can think o', includin' salmon in the restaurant.

We dropped the menfolk aff at BLAIR CASTLE jist up the road. It looks fantastic and the lads had a rare afternoon. The castle is the home o' the Dukes o' Atholl and still has its own private army, the only ane in Scotland, apart from The Tartan Army fitba' lot, of course. Blair Castle is a magnificent white building ye can see for miles, and a walk through the grounds wi' the huge trees is awesome.

But for us weemin, it was foot doon on the accelerator and up the road tae the HOUSE OF BRUAR!! It's aboot nine miles fae Pitlochry and is ane o' the best shoppin' days oot in the world. There's a'thing in the shops here fae a coffee an' a scone tae the finest tweeds and woollens the Scottish sheep can produce. Funny how ye can get sic lovely clathes fae thae smelly stupid animals! Ye'll love the braw clathes, the best o' Scottish food and near a'thing else tae warm a lassie's heart and melt her credit card. Dae ye no' jist LOVE shoppin'?

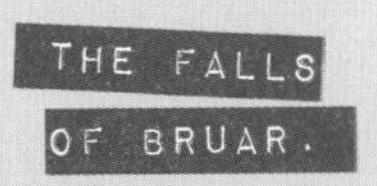

THE FALLS OF BRUAR. TRANQUILITY!

Information about Pitlochry
www.pitlochry.org
Pitlochry Festival Theatre, PH16 5DR. Tel: 01796 484626
www.pitlochry.org.uk

Blair Castle, PH18 5TL
Tel: 01796 481207
www.blair-castle.co.uk
House of Bruar, PH18 5TZ
Tel: 01796 483236
www.houseofbruar.com

Pitlochry and the Centre of Scotland

Moulin Inn & Brewery, PH16 5EH
Tel: 01796 472196
www.moulininn.co.uk
Killiecrankie Visitor Centre,
PH16 5LG. Tel: 0844 493 2194
www.nts.org.uk

The Sunday Post 32

Days Out: Good Walks

THERE ARE many well marked paths in and around Pitlochry, round the loch and through the woods at Faskally. If you are on the round-the-loch walk, stop at the boat station on the water's edge for another ice cream and feed the ducks. For climbers and hill-walkers, a favourite route is up and down Ben Vrackie (2,757 ft). Again, there are well marked paths. Stop and start at the Moulin Inn, where there's a small brewery making its own beer, just about essential after coming down off the hill.

THE PASS OF KILLIECRANKIE

This is the site of a famous battle on 27 July 1689 between the Jacobites under "Bonnie Dundee" (John Graham of Claverhouse, Viscount Dundee) and King William's troops under General Hugh MacKay. The Jacobites won a convincing victory. There's a famous spot over by the River Garry, called the Soldier's Leap, near the Killiecrankie Visitor Centre. A government soldier, Donald McBean, was being chased at the battle by a Highlander with a great sword and didn't fancy his chances, so he leapt right across the rocks over the torrent. It's an Olympic leap, as you'll see, of around 18½ ft. "Bonnie Dundee" was not so lucky, for he was killed when leading the Highlanders in a charge and lies buried in the nearby graveyard at Old Blair.

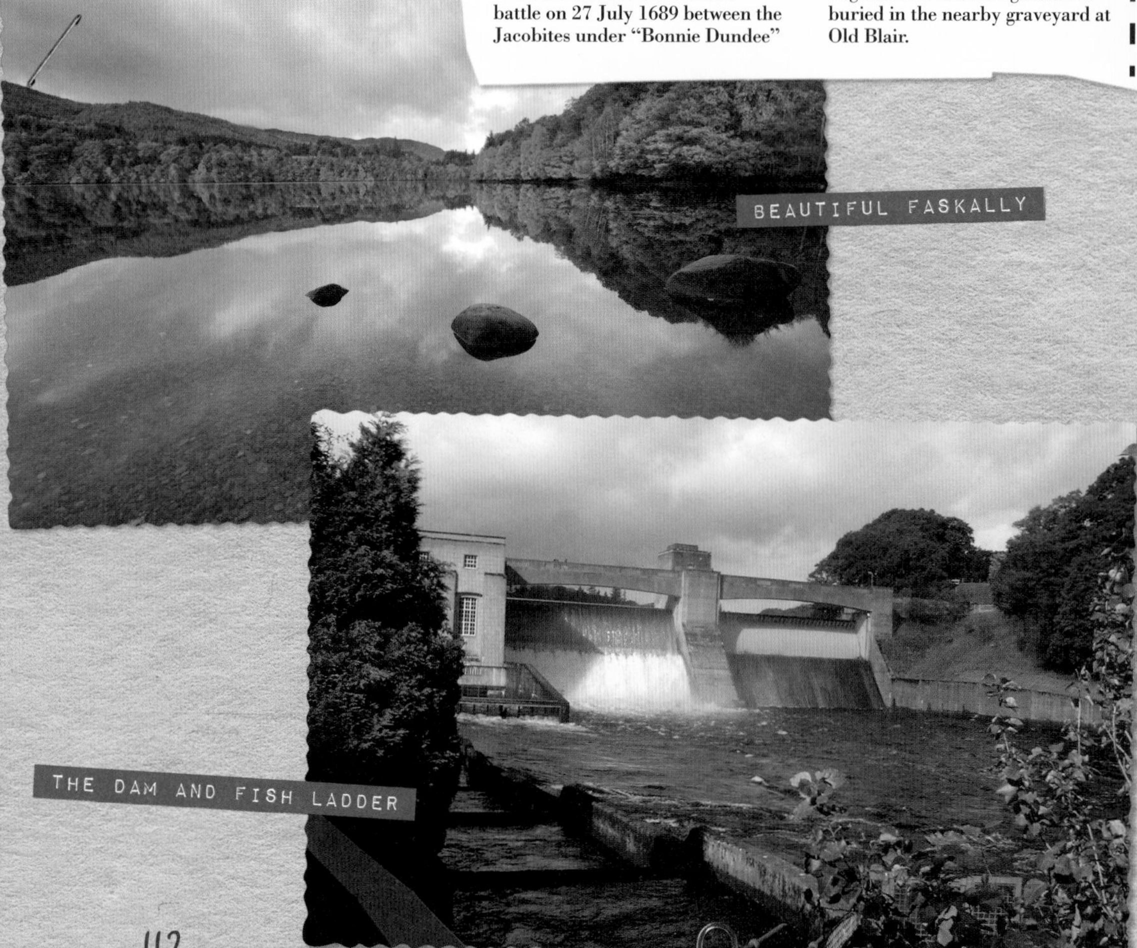

BEAUTIFUL FASKALLY

THE DAM AND FISH LADDER

CONGRATULATIONS, DAPHNE. YE'VE JUST CLIMBED YOUR FIRST MUNRO!
JINGS! THAT MEANS WE'RE THREE THOOSAND FEET UP!
AYE, THIS BEN IS THREE THOOSAND FEET AN' HALF AN INCH HIGH!
JINGS! IT'S JUST A MUNRO AN' NAE MAIR!
RICHT, YOU LOT! GET YOUR MUCKLE BOOTS AFF O' HERE BEFORE YE WEAR IT DOON AN' IT'S NO' A MUNRO ONY MAIR.
JINGS! DAPHNE'S GONE A' GREEN ON US!
AT THE GROOND LEVEL HOTEL -
FOWER SHANDIES, PLEASE.
TIME TO CHECK MA MAKE-UP'S NO' SMUDGED.
ME, TAE.
OCH, THAE CONTACT LENSES O' MINE ARE AYE POPPIN' OOT.
HAVE YE FOOND IT YET, DAPHNE?
I'LL JUST HAE A SEAT ON THIS SOFA.
NAW, IT'S NEARLY INVISIBLE.
HERE, YOU - GET AFF!
JINGS! IT SPEAKS! A TALKING SOFA!
OH-OH! 'SOFA' SO BAD!
NOO A MUNRO'S SITTIN' ON YOU, DAPHNE. MEET JOCK MUNRO, THE MOUNTAINEER.
I'M AWFY SORRY, LASS!
DOES YOUR FEMILY ACTUALLY OWN A THAE MUNROS, JOCK?
IT DOESNAE WORK THAT WAY, DAPHNE. PITY!
HAW! HAW!

Great Gardens

Maw really likes visitin' beautiful gardens, perhaps cos we dinnae have a garden at Glebe Street. The rest o' us enjoy seeing the ootside tamed. Here are some o' the best.

26 The Sunday Post

Out & About: *Gardens*

Threave Garden

THREAVE Garden, 1 mile west of Castle Douglas, is best known for its magnificent display of nearly 200 different varieties of springtime daffodils, but this is very much a garden for all seasons. Highlights of the 64-acre garden are the rose garden, the impressive walled garden and stunnin herbaceous borders. The principal rooms of the Scottish Baronial-style Threave House are now open to visitors.

The Countryside Centre features interactive displays and a live video link to one of the many nesting boxes on the wider estate, with its waymarked trails, bird hides, and wildfowl sanctuary.

12 *Sightseeing – Gardens of Scotland*

Pitmedden Garden

PITMEDDEN Garden is 1 mile west of Pitmedden village and 14 miles north of Aberdeen. It's hard to imagine a garden today being planted on such an extravagant scale. The heart of the property is the formal walled garden originally laid out in 1675 by Sir Alexander Seton. Today, Pitmedden features over 5 miles of box hedging arranged in intricate patterns to form six parterres. Each parterre is filled with some 40,000 plants bursting with colour in the summer months. The adjoining Museum of Farming Life brings the agricultural past to life.

The Scots Magazine 33

Drummond Gardens

DRUMMOND is near Muthill and south of Crieff in Perthshire. If you have seen the film "Rob Roy" you will have seen these gardens, for they are where Montrose held court. The main garden, sitting below Drummond Castle, is laid out in the formal style of the 17th century, with the overall shape of the design based on the Saltire. There is a strong north–south axis to the garden, starting with the wide flight of steps down from the castle to the 17th century sundial in the centre of the garden. This line then continues through a stone arch and the kitchen garden, and then rises through the trees to the top of the hillside opposite the castle. It is an amazing sight.

ⓘ Inverewe Garden, IV2
2LG
Tel: 0844 493 2225

Threave Garden, DG7 1RX
Tel: 0844 493 2245

Greenbank Garden, G76 8R
Tel: 0844 493 2201

Pitmedden Garden, AB41 7P
Tel: 0844 493 2177

Details for all four gardens above at www.nts.org.uk

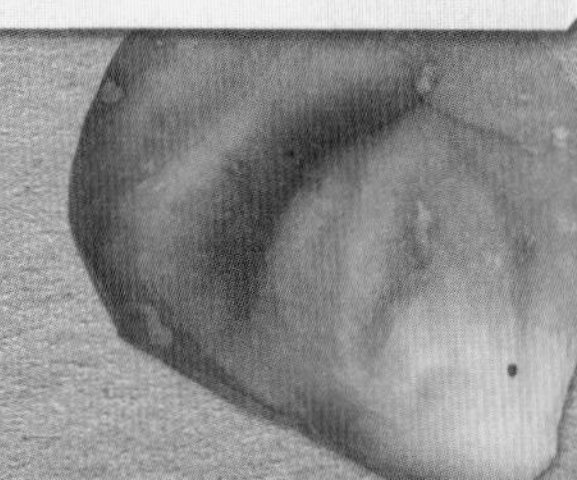

24 The Sunday Post

Out & About: *Gardens*

Logan Botanic Garden

LOGAN Garden, about 14 miles south of Stranraer, is an exotic paradise tucked away on the south-western tip of the country. Warmed by the Gulf Stream, the Walled Garden is breathtaking. From spring to late autumn, a blaze of colour greets the eye and the air is heavy with exotic scents. With a backdrop of palms and tree ferns, the atmosphere on a sunny day is truly tropical. The Woodland Garden has a host of weird and wonderful plants and trees such as the gunnera bog. It is a regional garden of the Royal Botanic Garden, Edinburgh.

The Scots Magazine 63

Great Scottish Gardens

Inverewe Garden

ONE of the world's greatest gardens, Inverewe, 6 miles north-east of Gairloch, sprang from one man's determination and his taste for the exotic. This 50-acre garden was created by Osgood Mackenzie in 1862. For many, visiting this beautiful, tranquil place is an unforgettable experience. The garden is built on a craggy hillside with a majestic setting on the edge of Loch Ewe.

It is an oasis of exotic plants, bursting with vibrant colour – thanks to the warm currents of the Gulf Stream that flow along the west Scottish coastline. Rhododendrons from the Himalayas, eucalypts from Tasmania, Olearia from New Zealand, and other species from such far-flung places as Chile and South Africa all flourish here, in a display that changes with the seasons, so repeat visits are always rewarded. The Walled Garden looks its best in spring through to late summer when flowering bulbs and plants are grown alongside vegetables which traditionally were for the "family" in the "Big Hoose".

SPOT FOR A PICNIC

Greenbank Garden

GREENBANK Garden is in Clarkston, about 6 miles south of the centre of Glasgow. It is a unique walled garden of 2.5 acres with plants and designs of special interest to gardeners. There are 447 varieties of daffodils and more than 3,700 different plants in the garden. The walled garden is surrounded by 15 acres of woodland walks. The garden is used to assess what plants are suitable for a Scottish climate. Greenbank House was built in the 1760s and is sometimes open to the public at the weekends.

Drummond Gardens, PH5 2AA
Tel: 01764 681433
www.drummondcastlegardens.co.uk
Logan Botanic Garden, DG9 9ND
Tel: 01776 860231
www.rbge.org.uk/the-gardens/logan

Dundee

THE CITY OF DISCOVERY
by Joe Broon

It's on the very banks o' the SILVERY TAY, the mightiest river in Scotland, that yer day oot in DUNDEE starts.

Get aff the train at Dundee Station and then ye canna miss the RRS DISCOVERY. It's Dundee's most famous ship, built tae transport Captain Scott tae the Antarctic over a hundred years ago in 1901. Dundee was a famous whaling city and the Discovery was built here. Ye can tour the ship and its museum at DISCOVERY POINT. Marvel at the ship's huge timbers, able tae withstand the Antarctic ice pack (and a guid job, too, as the ship was frozen in the ice for two years) and at the cramped quarters the crew shared below decks. Also berthed in Dundee is HM FRIGATE UNICORN, one of the last of the Royal Navy's wooden ships, launched in 1824.

Then there's the VERDANT WORKS, tellin' the story of ane o' Dundee's famous "Three Js" . . . Jute, Jam and Journalism. It is an old jute works and the shake, rattle an' roar o' the original machinery will transport ye back a hunner years tae when jute was King and Dundee was its capital city. The museum is just the most fascinating look back intae a time when 50,000 folk were employed in the jute trade in Dundee.

In the city centre pedestrian area is the best-known cowboy in Scotland. Cast in bronze, the statue o' Desperate Dan mingles wi' the shoppers as he strides across the foot o' Reform Street. He's Dan fae THE DANDY, one of Dundee's two famous children's comics. Sneaking up behind him is another showbiz star, Minnie the Minx from THE BEANO comic, with her catapult aimed at Dan's back. Kids love getting their photies taken beside the two giants from Dundee.

by The Twins
Oor favourite place in Dundee is the SENSATION SCIENCE CENTRE. We're no' very keen on science at school, but this is different. It's supposed tae be for kids, but Granpaw and Paw liked it as much as we did. And it's in the Greenmarket, jist twa minutes' walk from the train. We hate trailing aboot and that's what we like aboot Dundee. Lots o' the things ye want tae see are near the station.

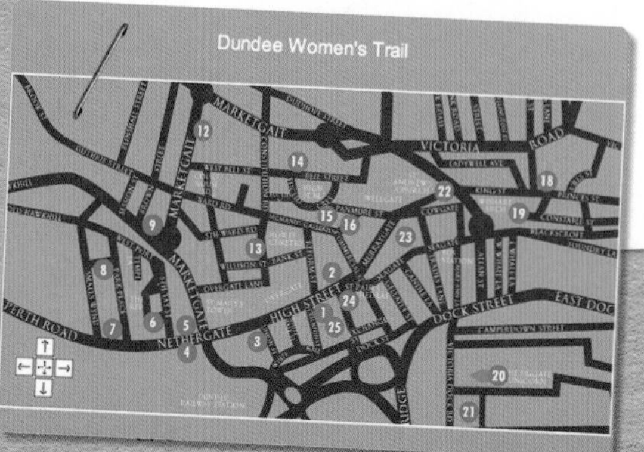

ⓘ Dundee Women's Trail celebrates twenty-five amazing women whose lives touched the city. There is a map to follow to take a walk in some great women's shoes. You can download and print a map or a copy of the Dundee Women's Trail information leaflet to take with you.
www.dundeewomenstrail.org.uk

RRS Discovery, DD1 4XA.
Tel: 01382 309060
www.rrsdiscovery.com
Verdant Works, DD1 5BT.
Tel: 01382 309060
www.verdant.works

26 The Sunday Post

Days Out: Two walks in Dundee

Walk No. 1 takes you along the river front at the railway station away from the city centre. You'll easily see what's ahead of you – the famous Tay Railway Bridge. It was once the longest in the world. The original bridge fell down in 1879 and you can see the "feet" of the old bridge sticking out of the water alongside the "new" bridge, as well as seals lying on the sand banks after eating salmon for their lunch. When you're up close to the bridge, it's a marvellous sight, with the big express trains rattling over your head.

Walk No. 2 takes you to the summit of Dundee Law, the hill that overlooks the city. There's an indicator on the top of the hill pointing out the things you can see in all directions, from the River Tay and the bridges at your feet to the high hills of Perthshire. It's worth the effort and it will give you an appetite for the world-famous Dundee peh (that's Dundonian for "pie") or an ingin (onion) bridie.

RRS Dis

Desperate Dan - Dundee City Square

HM Frigate Unicorn, DD1 3JA. Tel: 01382 200900
www.frigateunicorn.org
Sensation, DD1 4QB
Tel: 01382 228800
www.sensation.org.uk
Dundee information:
www.angusanddundee.co.uk

Abbeys tae Visit

Abbeys are places where monks used tae live, work an' pray. They were built hunners o' years ago and nearly all o' them are now ruins. I did a project on ane famous abbey – Arbroath Abbey. It's famous because o' the Declaration o' Arbroath, which is nothin' to do wi' Arbroath Smokies, but that's just one o' the reasons we like comin' here.

Arbroath Abbey

Arbroath Abbey was founded in 1178 by King William I 'the Lion' as a memorial to his friend Thomas Becket, Archbishop of Canterbury, who was murdered in 1170. William asked the monks from Kelso Abbey to start the monastery. When he died in 1214, his body was buried in front of the high altar. Traditionally, Scottish Kings were laid to rest at Dunfermline Abbey.

There are some buildings grouped to the south side of the church and another group further south. All that's left of these are foundations, but if you shut your eyes tight, you can imagine just what it was like. They say that the abbot's house is one of the most complete abbot's residences left in the whole country. Nearby are the gatehouse, the guesthouse and a long stretch of the outer wall. There's plenty of space for a picnic and room for the Bairn and the Twins to run about.

The Declaration of Arbroath is the most famous document in Scottish history. When Robert the Bruce beat Edward II of England at Bannockburn in 1314, this did not end the Wars of Independence. The English persuaded Pope John XXII to retain the sentence of excommunication passed on King Robert in 1306. In response, 40 Scottish nobles, barons and freemen despatched a note to Pope John. This letter set out Scotland's case that it was an independent kingdom. It was written down by Abbot Bernard of Arbroath, King Robert's chancellor, and was sent from here in April 1320.

The guidebook says that religious life in the abbey continued until the Scottish Reformation in 1560. In 1580 parts of the abbey were dismantled to build a new burgh church. By 1700 the buildings were in much the same condition they are now. The abbey's famous 'Round O' - the circular window in the south transept gable - became a landmark for shipping. Robert Stevenson, grandfather of the novelist Robert Louis Stevenson, rebuilt it in 1809.

In March 1951 the abbey was in the papers again, when the Stone of Destiny was found beside the high altar, three months after it was pinched back from Westminster Abbey. All quiet since then.

ⓘ Arbroath Abbey, DD11 1EG
Tel: 01241 878756

Arbroath and the other abbeys listed (apart from Paisley) are looked after by Historic Scotland
www.historic-scotland.gov.uk/places

For, as long as but a hundred of us remain alive, never will we on any conditions be brought under English rule. It is in truth not for glory, nor riches, nor honours that we are fighting, but for freedom – for that alone, which no honest man gives up but with life itself.

(from the Declaration of Arbroath)

Paisley Abbey, PA1 1JG
Tel: 0141 889 7654
www.paisleyabbey.org.uk

The Scots Magazine 33

Other famous abbeys

Cambuskenneth Abbey (near Stirling)
Cambuskenneth Abbey was the site of Robert the Bruce's parliament in 1326. James III and his queen are buried here. Today the tower is the only significant remaining section but the majority of the foundations remain.

Crossraguel Abbey (near Maybole, South Ayrshire)
The building of this abbey began in the 13th century. The following three centuries saw the abbey undergo a great deal of rebuilding. Today the remains of the abbey are largely intact, and it is possible to see the church, cloister, chapterhouse, dovecot and living quarters.

Dunfermline Abbey and Palace
(Dunfermline, Fife)
The remains of the 11th-century Benedictine abbey, founded by Queen Margaret, are substantial. Robert the Bruce is buried in the choir. Next to the abbey are the ruins of the royal palace built for James VI, which was the birthplace of Charles I, the last monarch to be born in Scotland.

Inchcolm Abbey (opposite Aberdour, Fife)
Inchcolm island in the Firth of Forth has the best-preserved group of monastic buildings in Scotland, including a 13th-century octagonal chapterhouse. The abbey was founded in 1123.

Jedburgh Abbey (Jedburgh, Scottish Borders)
This great ruin, founded in 1138 by David I, is mostly built in Romanesque and early Gothic styles. The remains include the recently uncovered cloister buildings where several finds were made, including the 12th-century 'Jedburgh comb'.

Kelso Abbey (Kelso, Scottish Borders)
This abbey, which is now in ruins, was founded in 1128 by Benedictine monks from Chartres in France who were brought to Kelso by David I.

Melrose Abbey (Melrose, Scottish Borders)
This is one of the most famous ruins in Scotland. It was founded as a Cistercian abbey in 1136 by David I but was largely destroyed by the English army of Richard III in 1385. The best surviving remains are the church, dating from the 15th century. Robert the Bruce's heart is buried here.

Paisley Abbey (Paisley, Renfrewshire)
The abbey, still used as a church today, was founded in 1163, but much of what you see today dates from the 14th and 15th centuries. There are lots of stained glass windows and its organ is one of the finest in Europe.

Festivals

FESTIVALS

Scotland loves festivals! Loves them? We invented them! Since the time of the first Christian missionaries, when the religion in Scotland was Druidism, a form of sun-worship special to the Celtic peoples, Scotland celebrated two festivals a year: Beltane (May 1) and Samhuinn (November 1), which marked the entry of summer and winter. Today the festival of Hallowe'en, on 31 October, still uses many folk customs while the original significance has been forgotten So, from Hallowe'en to art, and fire, music and Vikings. While the list below does not include all of Scotland's festivals, many provide all-round family entertainment. It's time to have a day oot, and celebrate

Hebridean Celtic Festival
www.hebceltfest.com
Up-Helly-Aa, Shetland
www.uphellyaa.org
Aberdeen International Youth Festival
www.aiyf.org
Loch Shiel Spring Festival www.lochshielfestival.com
Doune And Dunblane Fling www.dunblanefling.com
Tarbert Music Festival www.tarbertmusicfestival.com
Traquair Fair www.traquair.co.uk
The WickerMan Festival www.thewickermanfestival.co.uk
Lanark Medieval Festival www.lanarkmedievalfestival.co.uk
Pittenweem Arts Festival www.pittenweemartsfestival.co.uk
Largs Viking Festival www.largsonline.co.uk

EDINBURGH
Edinburgh International Festival www.eif.co.uk
Edinburgh Festival Fringe www.edfringe.com
Edinburgh International Book Festival
www.edbookfest.co.uk
Edinburgh International Film Festival
www.edfilmfest.org.uk
Edinburgh Science Festival www.sciencefestival.co.uk
Edinburgh Tattoo www.edintattoo.co.uk
Imaginate Festival (Children's International Theatre Festival)
www.imaginate.org.uk
Edinburgh Harp Festival www.harpfestival.co.uk
Edinburgh's Hogmanay www.edinburghshogmanay.org
Beltane Fire Festival, Edinburgh www.beltane.org

GLASGOW
Celtic Connections www.celticconnections.com
Glasgow Film Festival www.glasgowfilmfestival.org.uk
Merchant City Festival www.merchantcityfestival.com
West End Festival www.westendfestival.co.uk
Aye Write! Glasgow's Book Festival www.ayewrite.com
Southside Festival southsidefestival.org.uk
Glasgow Comedy Festival www.glasgowcomedyfestival.com
Glasgow International Jazz Festival www.jazzfest.co.uk
Glasgay www.glasgay.co.uk

BOOK FESTIVALS

January/February
PITLOCHRY WINTER WORDS FESTIVAL
Readings, children's events, writing workshops and more, organised by Festival Theatre Pitlochry.
www.pitlochry.org.uk

March
AYE WRITE! – GLASGOW
Annual March festival in Glasgow's Mitchell Library with big names and great events.
www.ayewrite.com

STANZA: SCOTLAND'S INTERNATIONAL POETRY FESTIVAL – ST ANDREWS
Poetry readings and performances.
www.stanzapoetry.org

May
DUMFRIES AND GALLOWAY ARTS FESTIVAL
10-day annual festival includes literary events, music, dance, theatre and films.
www.dgartsfestival.org.uk

PERTH FESTIVAL OF THE ARTS
Music and literary festival in various venues in Perth.
www.perthfestival.co.uk

WORD – ABERDEEN
The University of Aberdeen's Writers Festival features events in arts venues throughout Aberdeen.
www.abdn.ac.uk/word

ULLAPOOL BOOK FESTIVAL
Weekend long festival of English and Gaelic writing.
www.ullapoolbookfestival.co.uk

June
BORDERS BOOK FESTIVAL – MELROSE
Annual festival taking place over four nights and three days. Held mostly at Harmony House and Garden.
www.bordersbookfestival.org

ST MAGNUS FESTIVAL – ORKNEY
Literature and music, drama, dance and the visual arts.
www.stmagnusfestival.com

WEST PORT BOOK FESTIVAL – EDINBURGH
Diverse and quirky small book festival which has featured storytelling, readings and bookbinding.
http://westportbookfestival.org/programme

August
EDINBURGH INTERNATIONAL BOOK FESTIVAL
Largest festival of its kind in the world with over 200,000 visitors each year.
www.edbookfest.co.uk

INVERNESS BOOK FESTIVAL – AUGUST
A four-day festival with a varied programme held in the Eden Court Theatre.
www.invernessbookfestival.co.uk

September
BLACK ISLE WORDS – CROMARTY, ROSS-SHIRE
Held in the Old Brewery.
www.blackislewords.co.uk

MILNGAVIE BOOK AND ARTS FESTIVAL
Six days of readings, exhibitions and workshops.
www.milngaviefestival.org.uk

ISLAY BOOK FESTIVAL – SEPTEMBER
The beautiful setting proves enticing and brings well-known authors to this weekend festival.
www.islaybookfestival.org

NAIRN BOOK AND ARTS FESTIVAL – SEPTEMBER
Book and arts festival featuring many famous names.
www.nairnfestival.co.uk

NEW WORDS – ABERDEEN
Aberdeen and the North East's festival of new writing.
www.newwords.co.uk

OFF THE PAGE: STIRLING BOOK FESTIVAL
Library-organised events held in communities throughout the Stirling area.
www.stirling.gov.uk/offthepage

WORDPLAY – SHETLAND
Readings, signings, workshops and other book events.
www.shetlandarts.org/events/wordplay

September/October
FACLAN HEBRIDEAN BOOK FESTIVAL – STORNOWAY, HARRIS, UIST AND BARRA
Celebrating writing in both English and Gaelic, and with Hebridean themes.
www.faclan.org

WIGTOWN BOOK FESTIVAL
Biggest literary event in Scotland outside Edinburgh and Glasgow.
www.wigtownbookfestival.com

October
DUNDEE LITERARY FESTIVAL – UNIVERSITY OF DUNDEE
Includes author readings and writing workshops and an international Comic Conference.
www.literarydundee.co.uk

November
LENNOXLOVE BOOK FESTIVAL – EAST LOTHIAN
A weekend-long winter festival that complements the Borders Book Festival.
www.lennoxlovebookfestival.com

LINLITHGOW BOOK FESTIVAL
A volunteer-run weekend festival.
www.linlithgowbookfestival.org

IMPRINT BOOK FESTIVAL – EAST AYRSHIRE
Week-long library-run festival held each November, which contains a mixture of adult and children's events.
www.imprintfestival.co.uk

Oor Favourite Castles

There are lots o' castles tae visit in Scotland. I've mentioned quite a few on other pages. Here are some more great places tae explore. All these castles are looked after by Historic Scotland, and here are some o' the things they say aboot them.

(i)

Bothwell Castle, G71 8BL
Tel: 01698 816894
Huntly Castle, AB54 4SH
Tel: 01466 793191
Castle Campbell, FK14 7PP
Tel: 01259 742408
www.historic-scotland.gov.

26 The Sunday Post

Out & About: *Bothwell Castle*

Bothwell Castle is one of the outstanding monuments of medieval Scotland. It owes its origins to Walter of Moray, a northern aristocratic family who acquired Bothwell in 1242. He (or his son William, known as 'the Rich') created the mighty castle in a spectacular display of feudal pride. Not surprisingly, the Morays' great castle figured prominently in the Wars of Independence with England. Siege followed on siege. The most momentous was Edward I's great siege of 1301.

After the wars, Bothwell Castle passed to another powerful noble family, the Black Douglases. They rebuilt it in an impressive form not envisaged by their predecessors. After the Black Douglases were overthrown in 1455, the castle reverted to the Crown, and its later history was relatively uneventful.

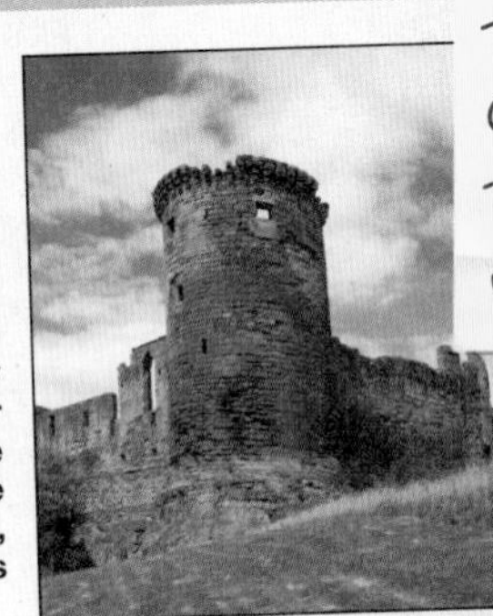

14 *Holiday Scotland: Castles*

Huntly Castle

HUNTLY CASTLE lies in the green heart of the Aberdeenshire countryside. It is a noble ruin in a beautiful setting, remarkable both for the quality of its architecture and for its eventful history. The stately palace that dominates the site is one of Scotland's most impressive medieval buildings. It was constructed around 1450 by the newly ennobled Earl of Huntly. The 4th Earl, George Gordon, 'Cock o' the North', extensively remodelled it in the 1550s.

His grandson, the 6th Earl, greatly embellished it, outside and in, to celebrate his becoming 1st Marquis of Huntly in 1599. It is the 1st Marquis's work that holds the visitor in thrall today: the great inscription high upon the south front, the heraldic fireplaces inside, and most notable of all, the splendid heraldic carving over the main door.

Amazing Scotland 22

Castle Campbell

Everyone is awestruck by Castle Campbell. The imposing ruin stands in solemn isolation upon a narrow ridge, overlooked by a crescent of the Ochil Hills. Two precipitous ravines hem it on either side, through which thunder the Burn of Care and the Burn of Sorrow. The setting couldn't be more dramatic.

The oldest part of the stone castle was built in the early 15th century. At that time it was called 'Castle Glume'. Around 1465 it passed through marriage to Colin Campbell, 1st Earl of Argyll. In 1489, the earl changed the name to Castle Campbell. And there the Campbells stayed for the next 200 years. Castle Campbell is one of Scotland's best-preserved tower-house castles. The tower house itself served as the family residence. Standing 66 ft high, it dominates the courtyard.

26 The Sunday Post

Out & About: *Castles*

Linlithgow

THE MAJESTIC royal palace of the Stewarts at Linlithgow today lies roofless and ruined. Yet the visitor still feels a sense of awe on entering its gates. It was begun by James I in 1424, rising like a phoenix from the flames following a fire that devastated its predecessor. The Stewart queens especially liked its tranquillity and fresh air. But after 1603, when James VI moved the royal court to London following his coronation as James I of England, the palace fell quickly into decline. The end came ignominiously in September 1745, when a fire swept through the ghostly rooms.

It is majestically situated in the centre of Linlithgow, beside 15th-century St Michael's Kirk, and overlooking the peel (park) and loch. The magnificent great hall – despite being roofless – still has the power to impress. In the courtyard is a beautiful three-tiered fountain. There are cellars, staircases and lots of ruined rooms – it is easy to get lost in it!

The Scots Magazine 43

Historic Scottish Castles: Hermitage

HERMITAGE, in deepest Liddesdale, is a lonely spot. The feeling of foreboding is heightened by the presence of the awesome castle ruin. It has inspired colourful local legends – of the wicked Lord Soules and of a giant Englishman with impregnable armour who drowned in the nearby Hermitage Water. In truth, though, Hermitage has no need of myths. It has a history of torture, treason – and romantic trysts – sufficient for a host of castles. It has been described as 'the guardhouse of the bloodiest valley in Britain'.

The mighty stone castle rises up from impressive earthworks. The castle was designed not so much for residence as defence, and the interior is just as dour as the outside. Even in the 16th century, Hermitage was adapted to counter the threat posed by gunpowdered artillery, with gunholes punched through its thick walls, and a massive gun defence built outside, to protect the castle's western approach.

Hermitage Castle.

Hermitage Castle, TD9 OLU
Tel: 01387 376222
Linlithgow Castle, EH49 7AL
Tel: 01506 842896
Caerlaverock Castle, DG1 4RU
Tel: 01387 770244
www.historic-scotland.gov.uk/places

Caerlaverock

Caerlaverock Castle is one of Scotland's great medieval fortresses. For 400 years it stood on the very edge of the kingdom. To the south, across the Solway Firth, lay England. For most of its history, Caerlaverock played an important role in the defence of the realm. Alexander II of Scotland, needing trusted men to secure the Scottish West March, granted the estate to his chamberlain, Sir John de Maccuswell (Maxwell). Sir John built the 'old' castle. Within 50 years, his nephew, Sir Herbert, had moved to a new castle just 650 ft away to the north. There the Maxwell lords remained for the next 400 years.

Caerlaverock's triangular shape is unique among British castles. Why it was built this way is not known. A walk around the castle gives a sense of its strength. The north tower, facing into Scotland, is a mightily impressive twin-towered gatehouse, where the Maxwells had their private suite of rooms.

We could hae a rare game o sojers in thae castles

I'd throw the pair o' ye in the dungeons!

A GREAT SPOT FOR A PICNIC

SCOTTISH CASTLES AS FILM LOCATIONS

Blackness Castle, West Lothian	*Hamlet* (1990), *Ivanhoe* (BBC TV 1997), *Macbeth* (1997), *The Bruce* (1996), *Bonnie Prince Charlie* (1948)
Ardverikie Castle, Kinlochlaggan, near Aviemore, Highland	*Monarch of the Glen* (BBC TV 1999–2005)
Castle Kennedy, Stanraer, Dumfries and Galloway,	
Culzean Castle, Ayrshire	*The Wicker Man* (1973),
Doune Castle, Doune, Stirling	*Ivanhoe* (BBC TV 1997), *Monty Python and the Holy Grail* (1975)
Duart Castle, Isle of Mull	*Entrapment* (1999)
Dumbarton Castle, West Dunbartonshire	*Gregory's Two Girls* (1999)
Dunnottar Castle, near Stonehaven, Aberdeenshire	*Hamlet* (1990)
Duns Castle, Berwickshire, Scottish Borders	*Mrs Brown* (1997)
Eilean Donan Castle, Dornie, Highland	*The World is Not Enough* (1999), *Highlander* (1986), *Highlander 3* (1994), *Highlander: Endgame* (2000), *Loch Ness* (1996), *Entrapment* (1999)
Floors Castle, Kelso, Scottish Borders	*Greystoke* (1984)
Lauriston Castle, Edinburgh	*The Prime of Miss Jean Brodie* (1969)
Manderston Castle, Duns, Borders	*The House of Mirth* (2000)
Morton Castle, Dumfries and Galloway	*The Thirty-Nine Steps* (1978)
Neidpath Castle, Dumfries and Galloway	*The Bruce* (1996)
Castle Stalker	*Monty Python and the Holy Grail* (1975).
Stirling Castle, Stirling	*Kidnapped* (1971), *Gregory's Two Girls* (1999), *Tunes of Glory* (1960), *Burke and Hare* (2010)

SCOTTISH GLENS AS FILM LOCATIONS

Glen Coe	*Braveheart* (1995), *Rob Roy* (1995), *Monty Python and the Holy Grail* (1975), *Harry Potter and the Prisoner of Azkaban* (2004), *Bonnie Prince Charlie* (1948), *Kidnapped* (1960)
Glenfinnan	*Bonnie Prince Charlie* (1948), (viaduct) *Harry Potter and the Chamber of Secrets* (2002), *Charlotte Gray* (2001)
Glen Nevis	*Kidnapped* (1960), *Harry Potter and the Philosopher's Stone* (2001), *Braveheart* (1995), *Highlander* 3 (1994)
The Sma' Glen	*Chariots of Fire* (1981)

Other Film Locations

Young Adam (2003)	Forth and Clyde Canal
The House of Mirth (2000)	Glasgow: City Chambers, Theatre Royal
Trainspotting (1996)	Edinburgh
Local Hero (1983)	Arisaig, Morar, Moidart, Pennan
Whisky Galore (1949)	Island of Barra
Gregory's Girl (1980)	Cumbernauld
Highlander (1986)	Loch Sheil, Torridon, Skye
The Wicker Man (1973)	Burrow Head, Plockton, Kirkcudbright
Breaking the Waves (1996)	Skye, Mallaig
The Thirty-nine Steps (1978)	Balquidder, Killin, Dunblane, Forth Rail Bridge
Chariots of Fire (1981)	Edinburgh, St Andrews
Mrs Brown (1997)	River Pattack, Lochan na h-Earba
Monty Python and the Holy Grail (1975)	Rannoch Moor, Loch Tay
Festival (2005)	Edinburgh city centre
Enigma (2001)	Oban, Loch Feochan

HOW LONG WILL WE BE AFORE WE GET TAE KINDREARY CASTLE?
NO' LANG, NOO! AN' IT'S GOT A REAL GHOST! THE AULD EARL O' KINDREARY HAUNTS THE PLACE! HE FELL THROUGH A TRAP DOOR AND WIS DROONDED IN THE MOAT. AN' HIS GHOST COMES BACK AN' OPENS THE TRAP DOOR WHEN ONYBOY STANDS ON IT!
THAT'S NONSENSE! THESE STORIES ARE PURELY FAIRY TALES!
GUIDE BOOK

THIS IS MA AULD CHUM, SANDY McTASKER, HE'S THE KEEPER O' THE CASTLE!
AYE, HERE WE ARE, KINDREARY CASTLE, WITH ITS FAMOUS GHOST!
NONSENSE! ALL SUPERSTITION!

JINGS! WHIT BONNY ARMOUR!
WEEL, THAT KIND O' FIREPLACE WIDNA NEED MUCH BLACK LEADIN'!
OH, THERE'S VERY LITTLE HISTORIC INTEREST ATTACHED TO THIS CASTLE! IT HAS A GOOD VIEW FROM THE TOP,— THAT'S ALL!
THIS IS ANE O' THEY THINGS THEY USED TAE STOP WOMEN GOSSIPIN' WI',— BUT YON LAD OWER THERE COULD DAE WI' IT!
RASP
TORTURE INSTRUMENTS

THIS AULD LEVER WORKS THE TRAP DOOR,— THAT'S IT ROPED OFF THERE!
WHIT ABOOT TRYIN' IT?
DANGER, KINDREARY'S DROP
LEVER THAT WORKS TRAP DOOR DOWN WHICH THE 1st EARL OF KINDREARY FELL TO HIS DEATH!

THAT'S KINDREARY'S DROP! YE'RE NO' ALLOWED ON IT, IT'S DANGEROUS!
RIDICULOUS! ANYHOW, I'M NOT AFRAID OF ANY TRAPDOOR NONSENSE STORY!
GET READY!

OW!!

WEEL, S'LONG! NOO YE KEN THE TRAPDOOR WORKS!— YE PROVED IT YERSEL'!
NOO WE CAN ENJOY OORSEL'S IN PEACE!
BUT I WONDER HOW THAT TRAPDOOR WORKED LIKE THAT!
NUDGE

Stirling and Roond About

It's a MIGHTY "Day Oot" without a doot.

STIRLING
by Granpaw Broon

STIRLING CASTLE, for my money is a much grander castle than its more popular neebor, Edinburgh Castle. Historic Scotland have done a grand job here. There wid be little point in me tellin' ye a'thing there is tae see here, as it wid fill a hale book on its own. From the newly refurbished Grand Hall tae the on-going re-creation of "The Hunt of the Unicorn", Europe's finest tapestry series, there's nae end o' things tae marvel at. See the beautiful restoration of the Renaissaince Royal Palace. Meet the characters o' the past, as costumed performers do tours every day. Mak' sure ye walk up tae the castle through the old parts o' Stirling toon and across the drawbridge intae the castle itsel' past the figure o' Robert the Bruce. Ye'll be singin' "Flower o' Scotland" afore ye've even got inside the place. And the view fae the castle ramparts!! Well, come an' see for yersel' and look doon on the plains where armies hacked themselves tae wee bits to decide the fate of Scotland.

Ye canna miss Stirling Castle of course. If ye need directions, ye need tae see yer optician. It's the gigantic stone building sitting richt across the mighty rock in the centre o' the toon. Ye can see it for miles.

Now, if ye've still enough left o' yer day oot efter seein' the castle, get yer skates on an' get roond tae the WALLACE MONUMENT. That's anither thing ye canna miss unless it's awfy misty. Ye can see it towering up intae the air no' far north o' the castle. Ye canna mistake it for the castle as it's a different shape . . . and, onyway, if ye've jist visited the castle, how would ye mistake it? This is the monument tae oor Scottish hero Sir William Wallace, better known tae some as jist "The Wallace".

And as if a' that wisnae enough history for one day, the BANNOCKBURN Heritage Centre awaits the visit o' every ane o' Jock Tamson's bairns interested in Scottish History. What a result!! What could we not dae wi' a puckle o' thae stalwart seven thoosand lads for oor fitba' and rugby teams the day? And, by the way, ye can still see Stirling Castle fae the battlefield o' Bannockburn.

Wallace Monument, FK9 5LF
Tel: 01786 472140
www.nationalwallacemonument.com

Stirling Castle, FK8 1EJ
Tel: 01786 450000
www.stirlingcastle.gov.uk

Bannockburn, FK7 0LJ
Tel: 0844 493 2139
www.nts.org.uk

THE WALLACE MONUMENT

The Sunday Post 30

Days Out: The Wallace Monument

THE WALLACE MONUMENT
Film star Mel Gibson played William Wallace in the blockbuster "Braveheart" but the monument is to the man himself. The monument was completed in 1869. It is built on the top of a rocky crag called Abbey Craig and is 220 feet tall. You will need all your puff to climb the 246 steps to the very top, but you can have a rest on floors one, two and three before you reach the top, which is in the shape of a crown.

You will see The Wallace's sword, a double-handed broadsword 5-feet 4-inches long, on the way up. There are also exhibitions about famous Scots and the building of the monument to break up the climb. From the top you can see where William defeated Edward I's English army at the Battle of Stirling Bridge in 1297. After he was defeated at the Battle of Falkirk in 1298, he was betrayed and hanged and cut into bits by his enemies at Smithfield in London. People were not very nice in his day, and some say The Wallace himself was a bit of a rascal, but he's in every true Scot's heart.

BANNOCKBURN
Although the site of the actual Battle of Bannockburn is disputed by the historians, the Heritage Centre will fill you in on the possibilities. You must stand on the historic site and look at the magnificent statue of King Robert the Bruce of Scotland on his horse.

He won the famous battle here in 1314 over Edward II's English army and "sent them homeward to think again". The battle lasted for two whole days, 23 and 24 June, and the 7,000 Scottish troops routed the 20,000 English troops around the banks of the Bannock Burn. The victory allowed Robert the Bruce to re-establish an independent Scotland.

Mackay's
Guide t
STIRLING
AND DISTRICT

Historical and Des
Notes.
By JOHN M. AMESS
with
Maps and Illustrations.
PRICE SIXPENCE.

STIRLING CASTLE

Falkirk Wheel

FALKIRK WHEEL and SCOTLAND'S CANALS
by Horace Broon

I used tae build fantastic machines wi' my Lego and Meccano sets in the hoose, but nane o' my wildest dreams would have dreamt up anything like the FALKIRK WHEEL. It's a "lift" that hoists canal boats intae the air!! It's like something ye might expect tae see in a science fiction film . . . and all it does is connect two of Scotland's canals, the Forth and Clyde and the Union. The Wheel is hard tae describe and it's best tae go and see it for yersel'. It can lift eight boats or mair fae one canal tae another. They're baith at different heights, no' something that's handy wi' waterways. I read somewhere that the Falkirk Wheel can lift the equivalent weight o' near 100 African elephants, but why onybody would want tae lift 100 elephants when they could jist as easy walk fae one canal tae anither, I have nae idea. There's an amazing view o' the wheel in operation from a sensational viewpoint at the visitor centre and ye can also go on a boat that tak's ye up the Wheel and then on for a wee canal cruise then back doon again.

THE FORTH AND CLYDE CANAL runs fae West Dunbartonshire at Bowling to the River Forth, so it connects the west and the east coasts. The Union Canal branches off at the Falkirk Wheel and runs a' the way tae Edinburgh toon. A' the canals in the central belt were once great wattery ribbons o' commerce, wi' boats an' barges carryin' a' manner o' goods an' chattels. But railways and road transport saw the canals near aboot disappear. Efter some grand restoration work costin' millions o' pounds, the waterways now have a new lease o' life. Goodness knows how many empty bottles, auld cars, iron beds and mountains o' a' manner o' junk were pulled oot o' the watter tae mak' way for the new boats. It's mainly pleasure craft nowadays, but I'd no' be surprised tae see the canals used for trade through time.

And there's lots o' walks and bike tracks running alongside the canals. It's richt popular. Check oot the braw new section and the modern lock at PORT DUNDAS in Glasgow.

i The Antonine Wall, built by the Romans between the Clyde and the Forth, goes near the Falkirk Wheel. It was made a World Heritage Site in 2008.
www.antoninewall.org

A GREAT SPOT FOR A PICNIC

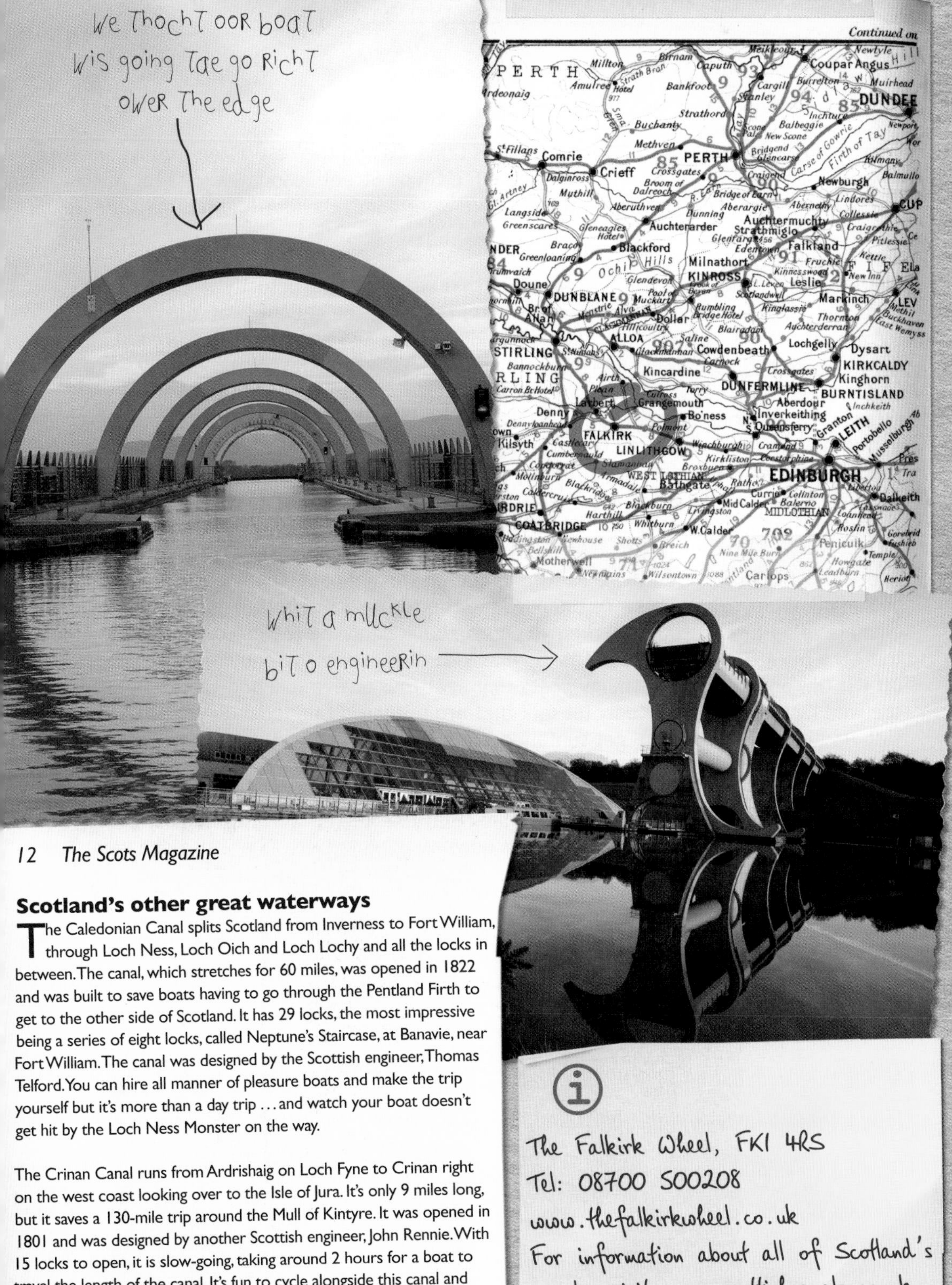
we Thocht oor boat
wis going tae go richt
ower the edge
Continued on
whit a muckle
bit o engineerin

Scotland's other great waterways

The Caledonian Canal splits Scotland from Inverness to Fort William, through Loch Ness, Loch Oich and Loch Lochy and all the locks in between. The canal, which stretches for 60 miles, was opened in 1822 and was built to save boats having to go through the Pentland Firth to get to the other side of Scotland. It has 29 locks, the most impressive being a series of eight locks, called Neptune's Staircase, at Banavie, near Fort William. The canal was designed by the Scottish engineer, Thomas Telford. You can hire all manner of pleasure boats and make the trip yourself but it's more than a day trip ... and watch your boat doesn't get hit by the Loch Ness Monster on the way.

The Crinan Canal runs from Ardrishaig on Loch Fyne to Crinan right on the west coast looking over to the Isle of Jura. It's only 9 miles long, but it saves a 130-mile trip around the Mull of Kintyre. It was opened in 1801 and was designed by another Scottish engineer, John Rennie. With 15 locks to open, it is slow-going, taking around 2 hours for a boat to travel the length of the canal. It's fun to cycle alongside this canal and watch the boats slowly making their way from one lock to the next.

ⓘ

The Falkirk Wheel, FK1 4RS
Tel: 08700 500208
www.thefalkirkwheel.co.uk
For information about all of Scotland's canals, visit www.scottishcanals.co.uk

Blair Drummond Safari Park

ON SAFARI
with the Broon Twins

We couldna believe it when Paw said he was takin' us and the rest o' the family "on safari". Just imagine it . . . us, the laddies fae Glebe Street School, headed for Africa or the Amazon or India or wherever it was we were goin'. David Attenborough here we come!

Well, it wisna Africa or any ither place like that we went tae, actually . . . but it WAS absolutely fan-dabby-tastical. In fact it didna tak' long tae get there at all. We just turned off the M9 motorway at junction 10 on tae the A84 and there we were – BLAIR DRUMMOND SAFARI PARK. I'd hardly digested ma breakfast and there we were, and the best o' it was, there were more wild animals there than ye'd EVER meet "on safari" in a month o' Sundays. Ye'll maybe no' believe this, but there's tigers and lions and rhinos and elephants (really, real ones!!) and there's wallabies, ostriches, sea lions, penguins, chimps, giraffes, bears, birds of prey, zebras and . . . and . . . och, I canna remember. There's hunners!! How often can ye say ye've seen a' that on one DAY OOT?? Oor favourites were – ye winna believe this – the meerkats. They're just SO funny.

There's just LOADS tae do there as well as see all the animals. There's a wooden castle ye can climb up. What a view o' the park fae the top . . . and ye can pick oot a' the animals ye've just visited, and then ye can zip back doon tae the ground on slides. AND there's a big ASTRAGLIDE slide. That's what kids like us like. We couldna keep Granpaw off it!! Oh, and the pedalo-thingy boats that seat four or five folk and ye can sail roond the wee loch. Mak' sure ye only let folk that are prepared tae pedal on yer boat. Daphne just wanted tae lie back an' get suntanned.

Oh . . . nearly forgot. If ye have a wee sister (and we do), make sure she visits the PETS FARM. Ye get tae stroke all the animals that like gettin' tickled – llamas, goats, piggies, sheep an' the like. The Bairn was howlin' when we left. She just didna want tae go hame. Neither did we.

RING TAIL LEMUR

GIRAFFE

list o' Things tae tak on safari

pith helmets
nets tae catch snakes an' beasties
a blunderbuss tae ward off wild animals
tents
binoculars
animal cages
food

ELEPHANT

Blair Drummond Safari Park,
FK9 4UR. Tel: 01786 841456
www.blairdrummond.com
(closed November to March)

The SCOTTISH FISHERIES MUSEUM
by Hen Broon

Situated richt on the harbour front in ANSTRUTHER, the Fisheries Museum is a gem. It's actually worthwhile tae hae a day oot aboot here just tae visit the wee toons and harbours all along the East Neuk o' Fife. But ye'd be missin' a treat no' tae spend time in this history of Scottish fisher-folk and their hard-won sea harvest.

The museum itself is a fascinatin' collection of historic hooses an' cottages in the heart of the village. I first went there wi' Paw and Joe when it opened in 1969. We'd been fishin' oorsels that day, withoot much luck I hasten tae add. The museum's jist got bigger and bigger since then, a bit like the fish Paw caught that day gets bigger an' bigger wi' the story-tellin'.

Ye'll find there's something here for a' the femily. The museum is "broken up" into a range of galleries, makin' it easy tae find what ye want. There are literally tens of thousands of things tae see, from paintings and auld photographs tae a whole collection of actual historic boats. There's a big ane ca'd "Zulu" that's 78 ft long. Find oot aboot how yer Anstruther ancestors actually caught fish. Marvel at the photies of "the silver darlings". . . no' the bonnie fisher-lassies fae the local dances, but the name given by folk tae the millions o' herring that once used tae be landed. There's naturally a memorial room to remind ye o' the "real price of fish", the hundreds of brave fisher-folk who have lost their lives in the dangerous waters around the Scottish coast.

While ye're there, what better way tae finish aff a day at the fishing museum then a visit tae the finest fish and chip shop in the country. And that's official (or is that oFISHal?). It's the Anstruther Fish Bar, UK winner of Seafish Fish & Chip Shop of the Year 2008/2009. It's been winning awards for years and a fish supper there will tell ye why. And it's only a stone's throw fae the museum richt on the harbour front. Sit in an' eat or take an' oot on yer day oot an' sit at the harbour's edge.

So there ye go, sling yer hook an' get doon tae the Neuk!!

i
Scottish Fisheries Museum,
KY10 3AB. Tel: 01333 310628
www.scotfishmuseum.org
Anstruther Fish Bar KY10 3AQ.
Tel: 01333 310518
www.anstrutherfishbar.co.uk

Falkland Palace

THE PALACE is in the town of Falkland in Fife, nestling at the foot of the Lomond Hills. Built by James IV and James V between 1450 and 1541, it was a country retreat of the Stuart monarchs of Scotland for over 200 years and much enjoyed by Mary, Queen of Scots.

Entering the Palace through the Gatehouse, visitors come to the courtyard, enclosed on two sides by the South Range and the now ruined East Range, accidentally destroyed in 1654 when Cromwell's troops were garrisoned at the Palace, which originally housed the Royal Apartments. The architecture of the building and restoration works carried out by the 3rd Marquis of Bute in the 19th century can be easily examined from here.

The Gatehouse, completed in 1541, contains the private quarters of the Keepers of Falkland Palace, a hereditary position of which the present holder is Ninian Crichton Stuart of Falkland.

The Chapel Royal is the most significant surviving original interior of the Palace and dates from the reign of James V. The oak entrance screen and painted ceiling are of national importance and a set of 17th century Flemish tapestries tell the story of Joseph and Benjamin. The

Tapestry Gallery forms the processional route from the King's Apartments to the Chapel Royal. The gallery is hung with 17th century "Verdure" tapestries. Look out for the goat with the eyes that follow you as you walk by!

Gardens

The orchard is in its original 17th-century site and contains a large selection of fruit trees, including apple, pear, plum and cherry. The herbaceous borders in the main garden provide a colourful setting for the Palace.

Falkland Palace,
KY15 7BU
Tel: 0844 493 2186
www.nts.org.uk

St Andrews Links Trust, 9XL. Tel: 01334 466
www.standrews.org.uk
Secret Bunker, KY16 8Q
Tel: 01333 310301
www.secretbunker.co.uk
St Andrews information:
www.saint-andrews.co
www.visit-standrews.c

The Sunday Post 28

Days Out: *Scotland's Secret Bunker*

Just 7 miles outside St Andrews you can find Scotland's best kept secret. At ground level it looks just like any other farmhouse, but 100 feet under the ground beneath it is hidden an enormous former government control centre. It consists of two floors, each the size of a football pitch. If there had been a nuclear war, this is where Scotland would have been governed from.

The bunker contained everything that was needed to survive a nuclear attack. Around 300 people could live there, protected by 15-ft thick concrete walls and a 3-ton door, and it even had its own cinema.

It was built in the 1950s and nobody knew it was there. You can now explore the bunker and discover what it was like to live with the threat of nuclear war.

It's a visit you will not forget – and make sure you don't get trapped in at closing time . . . The Secret Bunker is open from March to the end of October and it is now well sign-posted so that you can find it.

St Andrews Castle, KY16 9AR
Tel: 01334 477196
www.historic-scotland.gov.uk
St Andrews Cathedral, KY16 9QL
Tel: 01334 472563
www.historic-scotland.gov.uk
St Andrews Aquarium,
KY16 9AS. Tel: 01334 474786
www.standrewsaquarium.co.uk

Could I no' hae met a Prince when I was visitin' St Andrews?

Wills & Daph

ST ANDREWS
by Maw Broon hersel'

ST ANDREWS, the home of GOLF, or so they tell me. It's ane o' my favourite places and it's like nae place else in Scotland. Sadly there's nae railway station here, and if ye dinna come in yer ain car, ye need either tae get a bus or get the train tae Leuchars Station and catch the local bus.

Ye jist canna come tae St Andrews and no' see the golf course, but me I stick tae the putting greens. And what's mair, if ye do want tae play, ye'll need mair than a few bawbees for yer round. That's what happens when ye have the maist famous golf course in the world richt in the toon. But it is worth a look-see.

Whatever else ye dae, dinna miss the impressive CASTLE and visitor centre (ye'll kick yersel' if ye miss this). Dinna drop intae the bottle-nose dungeon, mind, cos it's impossible tae get oot. And then there's the ruined CATHEDRAL. The teeth o' the ruins jist soar up intae the sky. It must have been some place afore it was knocked aboot a bit. Goodness knows what the heating bills must hae been like. But it's lovely tae sit there in the gardens wi' a nice flask o' tea and a sandwich an' let yer mind wander.

There's TWA beaches at St Andrews, the East and the West Sands. Now there's the perfect spot tae unwind an' let yer bairns run aboot efter a visit tae a' the wee shops. And St Andrews has some lovely wee shops . . . golf shops, woollen shops, gift shops, whisky shops (Granpaw and Paw were in there near a' day), a lovely cheese shop and ane selling the best ice cream ye've ever tasted.

If ye're in the toon in early August dinna miss the Lammas Fair and in April there is the KATE KENNEDY PROCESSION . . . and there's the ST ANDREWS AQUARIUM that yer bairns will love, richt on the sea shore.

St Andrews is famous for anither Kate. It's whaur Prince William met Kate Middleton while they were baith at the Uni. Daph thinks if she had went to St Andrews Uni then mebbe she would hae met a prince. You should hae stuck in at those hard sums Daph!

So, jist a wee taster of what's tae see oot there on the east coast. An' ye dinna hae tae be handicapped trauchlin' a' that golf equipment aboot tae hae a real day oot.

THE WEST SANDS

On The Beach

WE DO LIKE TAE BE BESIDE THE SEASIDE
by Maw Broon

The Broon family DO like tae be beside the sea. For me, it's a great day oot and I can lie back an' read a book while a'body does their different things. The Bairn will sit for hours makin' castles wi' the Twins, Horace rakes aboot in pools for sea creatures, Granpaw and Paw sit wi' their coolbox and occasionally roll up their trooser legs and hae a paddle (I suspect Granpaw, the auld rogue, does this mair often when there's a bonnie lassie aboot). Hen an' Joe, like a' big bairns, like horsin' aboot in the waves and Maggie and Daphne jist sit lookin' bonnie an' fryin' themselves in sun oil.

Now, there's a' manner o' whit folk are callin' AWARD beaches – there's Blue Flag beaches, Yellow Flag beaches – and they're the places tae look oot for. The sand is clean and the water is safe for bathin'. There were only six o' the best Blue Flag beaches in Scotland in 2008 and maist o' them were on the East coast, which was a surprise tae me, as I've been on many bonnie bonnie stretches o' sand up and doon the West for years. No' that I dinna like the winners on the East ye ken, Aberdour, St Andrews an' the like. Ye'll find a list o' thae spots under SEASIDE AWARDS or whatever on yer computer (even we have ane now).

So, Yellow or Blue, ye pays yer money an' takes yer choice. Here's the top six BROON FLAG beaches dotted up an' doon the West coast that mak' a great "day oot". Sorry if I've no' listed yer favourite.

THE EAST SANDS

LIFE GUARD AT BROUGHTY FERRY

The Broon flag beaches

1) **Islay. Laggan Beach**, not far from the ferry port at Port Ellen, stretches for miles and miles nearly all the way to Bowmore. There's birds of all shapes and sizes swooping about and with the waves making music on the sand, it's heaven. Start at a wee place called Kintra in the big sand dunes. (Another Islay favourite is Machir Bay. It's breathtaking.)
2) **Calgary Beach, Isle of Mull**. About 11 miles from Tobermory, an absolute must.
3) **Sanna Sands**. It's at the west end of the Ardnamurchan peninsula. Stand at the water's edge and just look out into the Minch.
4) **Sandaig Bay**, near Glenelg. This is where Gavin Maxwell wrote the book about the otters, *The Ring of Bright Water*. There's a memorial to one of his pet otters, Edal. Even though it's called Sandaig, it's not very sandy, but it's a wonderful spot. There's a short walk down from the road, but it's worth the effort.
5) **Achmelvich Bay**, north of Lochinver. Stunningly beautiful. Watch the setting sun turn the Sutherland mountains pink. You will feel proud to be Scottish.
6) **Sandwood Bay**. In the far North West, on the road to Durness, turn off to Kinlochbervie and follow the coast road until you reach the car park. Sandwood Bay is then a few miles walk. You should take a map, but the walk is not difficult. It is wild and not for swimming, but it's one of the most beautiful bays in the world. Watch the big booming breakers hammer down on the sands. Magic.

Seaside Award Beaches in Scotland
www.keepscotlandbeautiful.org

Cycling

CYCLING - USING THE NATIONAL CYCLE NETWORK
By Horace

The national cycle network is now over 12,700 miles long with over 2100 miles in Scotland. It has been developed by the UK charity, Sustrans, that works to encourage and enable people to travel on foot, bike or public transport for more journeys we make every day as well as for homegrown adventures and great days out.
The Sustrans website - www.sustrans.org.uk - has a free online map service to discover how to get around every day on foot or by bike. Search for local or national routes, plot journeys, or find what the local area has to offer from schools, supermarkets and local landmarks to car clubs, bus stops and bike shops.

See the www.routes2ride.org.uk website for details, downloadable maps and leaflets of routes such as:

Aviemore to Carrbridge
Ayrshire Coast Cycleway - Irvine and Ayr
Bowling to the Falkirk Wheel
Clyde Walkway - Glasgow to Uddingston
Cunninghame Cycleway - Kilmarnock to Ardrossan
Edinburgh to the Forth Road Bridge
Esk Valley Cycleway - Musselburgh to Dalkeith
Forest and Loch - Aberfoyle to Callander
Garnock Valley Cycleway - Irvine and Kilbirnie
Inverness to Dingwall
Lochwinoch Loop Line - Paisley Canal to Glengarnock
Moray Coast Ride - Portgordon to Cullen
Ports of Tay Ride - Leuchars to Dundee
Up the Tay - Perth to Dunkeld
Water of Leith - Balerno to Edinburgh

i
www.routes2ride.org.uk/scotland
www.sustrans.org.uk

NATIONAL CYCLE NETWORK FACTS

- Across the UK it carries 1 million walking and cycling journeys every single day and passes within 1 mile of over 55% of the UK population.
- Almost 3,000 volunteers help Sustrans maintain and promote the Network with 397 rangers in Scotland.
- The Network hosts the largest collection of outdoor art and sculpture in the UK – over 2,000 pieces from over 300 artists over the last 20 years. Key pieces to see in Scotland are: 'The Bedrock Bike' now near Howwood on Route 7 – an enormous bike made from granite millstones, the result of a find on the Airdrie to Bathgate railway by the construction team; and 'Legs' – six giant pairs of brilliant blue legs offering a striking view from the nearby road on the Hillend Loch route.
- The highest point on the Network in Scotland is the Drumochter Pass in the Highlands – part of Route 7 – at a heady 1515 feet.
- 17% of the Network in Scotland is in urban areas – and 25% is totally traffic free.
- One of the most popular routes in Scotland is the 'Lochs and Glens North' route – 217 miles of challenging and spectacular route from the centre of Glasgow, through The Trossachs, past Lochs Lomond, Venachar and Tay, over Glen Ogle and the Drumochter Pass, through the Cairngorms, past Culloden Battlefield, and ending in the capital of The Highlands – Inverness.
- Historic Scottish sites you can see on the Network include the Forth Rail Bridge, Skara Brae, St Andrews, the Caledonian, Crinan, Forth & Clyde and Union canals, Burns Heritage Centre, Scott's Ship RSS Discovery, Culloden Battlefield, Clava Cairns and Edinburgh, Dunnottar, Brodick and Caerlaverock Castles.
- The flattest route for those wanting a leisurely easy ride is the ten miles from Johnstone to Kilbirnie in Ayrshire.
- Test your head for heights as you cross the Cullen Viaduct on the Aberdeen to John o' Groats route – part of National Route 1 – or on the spectacular Glen Ogle viaduct on Route 7.
- The newest route on the Network in Scotland is under construction – an almost entirely traffic-free path that will run from Oban to Ballachulish, linking to Fort William.
- The Network in Scotland even goes international – Route 1 is part of the North Sea Cycle Route, which travels down through Norway, Sweden, Denmark (through Odense – the Danish "cycling capital"), Germany, The Netherlands, Belgium, across to England and up to Shetland. A staggering 6,000 km through eight different countries and the longest signed cycle route in the world.

Local Delicacies

NARDINI'S ICE CREAM
LARGS

ARBROATH SMOKIE
(FAE IAIN R SPINK)

FISH TEA - SEASIDE SCOTLAND

DUNDEE CAKE
DUNDEE

KILLIE PIE
KILMARNOCK

BRIDIE (FLAKY PASTRY)
EVERYWHERE

LORNE SAUSAGE
EVERYWHERE

TABLET
EVERYWHERE

SCOTCH PANCAKES
EVERYWHERE

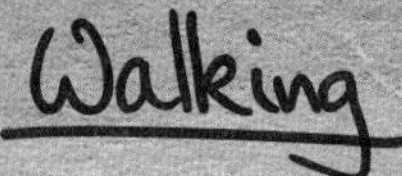

WALKING DAYS OOT
by Horace

There are many bonny places where you can have a great walking day oot. We're not talking about climbing mountains, although a lot of folk like to do just that, but about more gentle walking near some of Scotland's beauty spots - walks that you can enjoy without having to worry too much about wearing special gear or having a' they fancy gadgets to guide you. Mind you, oor Joe is a bit of gadget man and he loves the chance to try out his GPS and fancy new poles!

Scotland's hills and mountains and coastal areas offer some of the best walking countryside in the world with walks that can vary from gentle strolls along a river bank to challenging hillwalks that demand fitness and navigation skills. There are walks in Scotland to suit all levels of ability.

If you enjoy some of the walks we have suggested in *Days Oot*, you may want to move on to something a bit more challenging. One way to do this is to look for a rambling or hillwalking club near you where you can be part of a group outing with proper leaders. Some clubs even train you in the skills you will need to be safe on longer or more challenging walks and help you to build up your fitness levels so that you can cope with climbing mountains not just hills!

Here are a few tips about safe walking from the Mountaineering Council of Scotland

1. Before setting out on any walking trip, check the weather forecast on national and local radio or TV or online. Scotland's weather is very changeable. Even on warm sunny days bad weather might be on the way. So if the wind strengthens, clouds thicken and visibility decreases or the temperature falls, consider whether you should revise your plans.
2. Choose a walk which is appropriate to you and your parties' experience, fitness, navigation skills, knowledge of the area and the prevailing weather conditions.
3. If you are going on a more challenging walk let a responsible person know where you are going and when you expect to return, then inform them when you get back.
4. Children don't have the same levels of stamina as adults, so take children on routes that take account of this and which allow for a safe and easy retreat. Be prepared to turn back if someone in your group is tiring or getting cold.
5. What to take:

- Warm, wind- and waterproof-clothing is essential. Even if you are only walking on short routes in warm weather be prepared for sudden changes in the weather and carry clothing such as a waterproof jacket and a warm sweater.
- Always carry a copy of the route even if you are walking near a visitor centre where tracks or paths are signposted. On any longer walks and those on higher ground always carry a map and compass and know how to use them.
- Also carry equipment that can be used in an emergency such as a mobile phone (which will only work if there is a signal), torch, whistle and a simple First Aid kit. The emergency signal is six blasts on the whistle or six flashes with the torch.
- Your footwear should provide good ankle support and have a firm sole with a secure grip. Hillwalking boots are strongly recommended.
- Your party will also need adequate food and drink for the planned distance, and taking a little more than you need is always a good idea in case you get delayed.

www.mcofs.org.uk

The Mountaineering Council of Scotland's Associate Member, www.walkhighlands.co.uk has a great website with graded walks throughout Scotland. These vary from short walks in the lowlands to expeditions into remote and high country. You should be able to find information and inspiration here to help you take the first steps in your Scottish walking journey!

Hill Facts

There are currently 283 Munros, 221 Corbetts, and 224 Grahams in Scotland. Regardless of height, all will be challenging in some way, and some include difficult terrain or craggy elements that might involve rock climbing, so always follow the advice of the Mountaineering Council of Scotland. The Sgurr Dearg Munro on Skye has the "Inaccessible Pinnacle" as its highest point, a rocky outcrop only accessible by rock climbing. A real challenge for Munro baggers. A few hills are more suitable for beginners than others, but you can't judge this by height alone. It is best to consult specialist books on the Scottish mountains for detailed advice.

The Munros

There are 283 Munros, that is, Scottish mountains of 3,000 feet / 914.4 metres or higher that can be regarded as "separate mountains". They are given this status by the Scottish Mountaineering Club (SMC). The original list of Munros was drawn up in 1891 by Sir Hugh Munro (1856–1919) in the Scottish Mountaineering Club Journal. The most well-known Munro is Ben Nevis, the highest mountain in the British Isles, with an altitude of 4,409 feet (1,344 metres).

The Corbetts

Bristol-born J (John) Rooke Corbett (1876 –1949) climbed all of Scotland's Munros: the fourth person to do so and the first Englishman. In addition, he also climbed all of Scotland's hills over 2,000 feet. He listed all those hills of height between 2,500 feet (762 metres) and 3,000 feet (914.4 metres) and which had at least 152 metres (500 feet) of "ascent" or "prominence" on all sides. When he died, this list was passed to the SMC by his sister. The list of Corbetts has changed a little over the years as a result of changes in height measurements but the present list contains 221 Corbetts.

The Grahams

The Grahams is the name given to all the mountains in Scotland which are between 2,000 and 2,499 feet (610 and 761 metres) with a drop of at least 150 metres (490 ft). Previously, Scottish hills in this height range were known as the Elsies. It's short for Lesser Corbetts (or LCs). Alan Dawson, in The Relative Hills of Britain, first published a list of these hills in the early nineties and, at around the same time, Fiona Torbet (neé Graham) published her own list. Fiona went missing in 1993, and was, in 1994, found to have been murdered. The Grahams are named in her memory. The original list of Elsies, and the new list of Grahams, were combined into this single list of 224 mountains which is maintained by Dawson.

The West Highland Way

From lowland moors, lochside paths, country parks and bluebell woods to challenging mountainous terrain, the West Highland Way has something for walkers of all abilities. This waymarked trail of 154km (96 miles) joins Milngavie to the foot of Ben Nevis at Fort William, that's 154km (96 miles). It will take around seven days to accomplish the whole route but can be enjoyed in separate sections according to ability.

Milngavie to Carbeth – 5 miles (8 km)
Carbeth to Drymen – 7 miles (11.2 km)
Drymen to Balmaha – 8 miles (12.8 km)
Balmaha to Rowardennan – 7 miles (11.2 km)
Rowardennan to Inversnaid – 7 miles (11.2 km)
Inversnaid to Inverarnan – 7 miles (11.2 km)
Inverarnan to Crianlarich – 6 miles (9.6 km)
Crianlarich to Tyndrum – 6 miles (9.6 km)
Tyndrum to Bridge of Orchy – 7 miles (11.2 km)
Bridge of Orchy to Inveroran – 2 miles (3.2 km)
Inveroran to Kingshouse – 10 miles (16 km)
Kingshouse to Kinlochleven – 9 miles (14.4 km)
Kinlochleven to Fort William – 16 miles (24 km)

(i) Mountaineering Council of Scotland
www.mcofs.org.uk

Scottish Mountaineering Club
www.smc.org.uk

Mountain weather information
www.mwis.orvg.uk
www.metoffice.gov.uk/loutdoor/mountainsafety

www.routes2ride.org.uk/scotland

www.sustrans.org.uk

www.west-highland-way.co.uk

www.walkhighlands.co.uk

MILE MARKER
N THE WEST HIGHLAND WAY

BLUEBELL WOODS NEAR
MILLAROCHY BAY

Kintyre

KINTYRE
By Hen Broon

Going to CAMPBELTOWN in Kintyre may seem a long way to go for a day oot but the journey itself is a braw outing (especially when I'm not driving). Me, Joe and Horace went for a day trip. Beautiful scenery and plenty of places to stop off for a quick cup of tea – or an oyster! LOCH FYNE OYSTER BAR at Cairndow is just across the loch. I couldnae resist them and had a wee plate. Visit the ARDKINGLAS GARDENS in Cairndow to see Britain's tallest tree. Taller than me even!

Other places you will pass include Inveraray Castle, Inveraray Jail, Crarae Gardens, Lochgilphead, Ardrishaig and the Crinan Canal, and finally West Loch Tarbert before you reach the peninsula of Kintyre and a short drive down its west coast to Campbeltown. With ISLAY and JURA and GIGHA lying off Kintyre's shoreline, keep a lookout for seals, seabirds, otters and dolphins.

Campbeltown is on the shores o' CAMPBELTOWN LOCH. Campbeltown has a long history of whisky distilling and whisky is still produced in the town. Ye can visit SPRINGBANK DISTILLERY and enjoy a dram after the tour. see page 99

This town was once one of the wealthiest in Scotland – ye can see that by a' its fancy Victorian and Edwardian buildings. The town has a wee museum, built in 1899. Horace was fair charmed by the wee Art Deco cinema on the waterfront, the oldest surviving purpose-built cinema in Scotland – and it's still showing films.

On the way back we took the route to CARRADALE to visit oor Maggie's pal, Aggie. (It was a one-track, windy road with passing places. Michty, I was regretting the oysters.) One time in Carradale, me and Joe hiked up DEER HILL. Ye get great views at the top. Now I come tae think o' it though, I never saw any deer. We had a rerr cuppa wi' hame made cakes in the visitor centre and then a wee dram at the CARRADALE HOTEL afterwards. This time, though, it was a flying visit. Aggie made us a wee spot o' supper and we were on oor way hame again, talking a' the road hame, aboot having a longer stay the next time.

ⓘ Loch Fyne Oyster Bar, PA26 8BL
Tel: 01499 600482
www.lochfyne-restaurants.com

Springbank Distillery, PA28 6EX
www.springbankwhisky.com

Carradale Hotel, PA28 6RY
www.carradalehotel.com

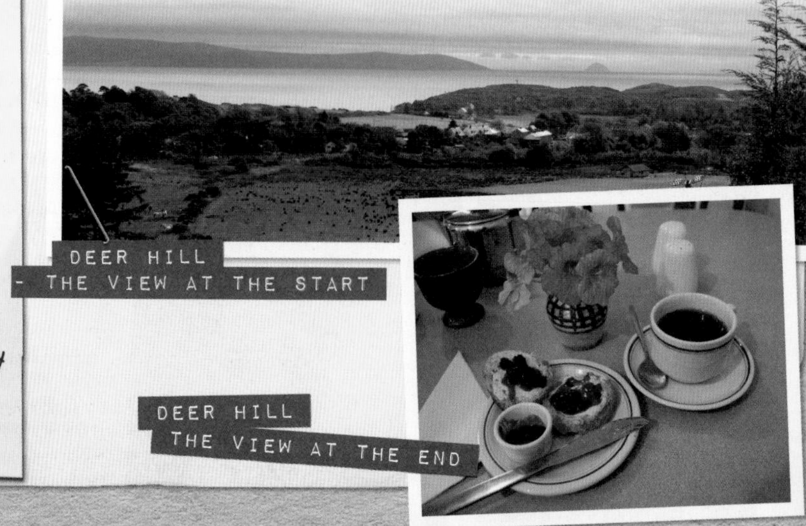

DEER HILL – THE VIEW AT THE START

DEER HILL THE VIEW AT THE END

Mull of Kintyre Music Festival
Campbeltown hosts an annual Mull of Kintyre Music Festival in August which includes acts by local bands and some by well-established groups, as well as a Kintyre Songwriter's Festival earlier in the year in May.

(i) Mull of Kintyre Music Festival,
PA28 6AZ
www.mokfest.com
Tel: 01586 552056
mokfest@hotmail.co.uk

Bellochantuy

Beaches
While there are many beautiful beaches in Kintyre, the miles of sand between Machrihanish and Westport provide one of the best surfing beaches in the UK. Facilities are limited at Westport and most surfers base themselves in Machrihanish, where there is good camping available. There's also a beautiful beach at Bellochantuy with caravan and camping facilities nearby. This beach is renowned for its gorgeous sunsets.

A Kintyre Way marker

Kintyre Way
The way-marked Kintyre Way criss-crosses the Kintyre peninsula for 87 miles (140 km), stretching from Tarbert at the north end to Southend in the south. With 4 to 7 days of walking, different sections offer serious hiking and gentle rambles as you walk past castles, abbeys, prehistoric remains, beaches, moorland and on forestry tracks with glorious views over Arran and towards Ireland.

(i) The Kintyre Way
www.kintyreway.com
info@kintyreway.com

(i) Kilmartin House Museum,
PA31 8RQ
Tel: 01546 510278
www.kilmartin.org

Scottish Scene 23

Dunadd Fort

KILMARTIN GLEN is one of Scotland's richest prehistoric landscapes, with more than 150 prehistoric monuments within a six-mile radius of the village of Kilmartin, Argyll not far from Kintyre.

Many of the sites are looked after by Historic Scotland, and include carvings, stone circles, cairns . . . and Dunadd Fort, which was a stronghold of Dalriada, the kingdom of the ancient Scots.

On top of the hill at Dunadd, two footprints, a boar and an ogham inscription have been carved into the natural rock. Some think that the carved footprints is linked to the coronation of the kings of Dalriada.

The award–winning Kilmartin House Museum was established to investigate and interpret this internationally important archaeological landscape.

To the Islands

The Scottish islands are some o' the most beautiful places on earth. Even the tiniest o' them has its awn character an' charm. For Grandpaw it has tae be Islay (see page 160), for Joe it's Skye (see page 166), for Daphne it's Arran (see page 152) and for Maw it's Iona (see page 164). Aye, we all have oor favourites. But how tae get there? It's CalMac ye need.

CALMAC FERRIES

Dramatic sunsets, spectacular scenery and a traditional Scottish island welcome are just a few of the things that the network makes possible, whether a trip is a visit to one island or an island-hop round a few.

CalMac sails to 24 destinations on Scotland's West Coast. From Arran in the south to Lewis in the north, the network covers some of the most beautiful and dramatic places in Scotland.

CalMac currently operates a fleet of around 31 ferries to provide passenger, vehicle and shipping services to the islands off the West Coast of Scotland and in the Clyde estuary.

Vast numbers of people get away from it all by ferry with Caledonian MacBrayne and discover a different world, their ferries carrying more than 5 million passengers, 1 million cars, 94,000 commercial vehicles and 14,000 coaches each year.

ⓘ

Caledonian MacBrayne
www.calmac.co.uk

Islands the ferries go to

Arran	Eigg	Muck
Barra	Gigha	Mull
Bute	Harris	Raasay
Canna	Iona	Rum
Coll	Islay	Skye
Colonsay	Lewis	Tiree
Cumbrae	Lismore	The Uists

Here are some island ideas suggested by Caledonian MacBrayne:

Go dolphin spotting
All of the islands are full of beautiful wildlife. Sail to islands such as Arran, Mull or Coll and look out for the mix of wildlife along the way.

Get wet and wild
Tiree is great for windsurfing. Try kayaking in Skye or Uist. Experience outdoor adventure on Raasay.

Go back in time
Discover the history of the islands: Callanais stones on Lewis or whisky heritage on Islay are just a few ideas.

Seek out beautiful buildings
Why not visit the likes of Kisimul Castle on Barra, Kinloch Castle on Rum or Mount Stuart on Bute.

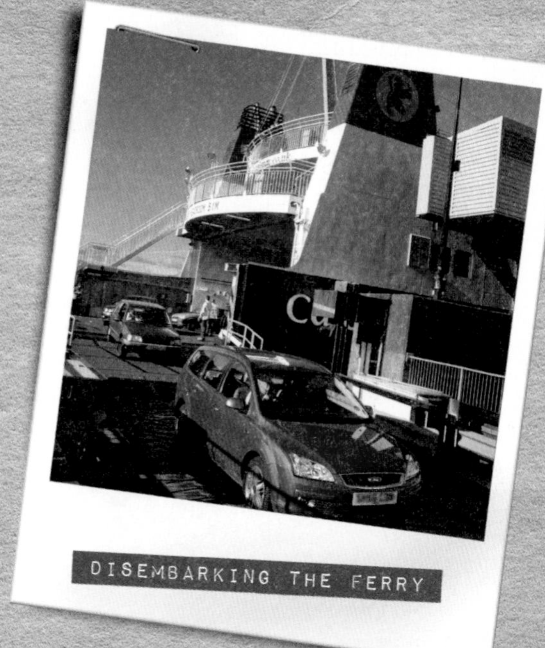

DISEMBARKING THE FERRY

We Think Horace is barking!

The Scots Magazine 23

Who are Caledonian MacBrayne?

CALEDONIAN MACBRAYNE started life in 1851 as a steamer company called David Hutcheson & Co and had three partners – David Hutcheson, Alexander Hutcheson and David MacBrayne. The fleet, which David Hutcheson & Co inherited, comprised eight paddle steamers and two track boats on the Crinan Canal. The main sphere of operation, called the Royal Route because Queen Victoria had travelled on part of it only four years earlier, was from Glasgow through the Crinan Canal to Oban and Fort William and then on through the Caledonian Canal to Inverness.

An excursion steamer was based at Oban for Mull, Staffa and Iona and a further vessel sailed all the way round the Mull of Kintyre to Skye. The company, however, extended its operation in 1855 by building new boats for the demanding all year round service to Mull, Skye and Lewis and by extending sailings to Stornoway inaugurated its first service to the Outer Isles.

Throughout the late 1870s and 80s the MacBrayne empire continued to expand with a mail ship to Islay, Harris and North Uist from Skye, and from Oban to Barra and South Uist. It then modified its sailings as the railways came to the coast, and carried on providing its services to the islands.

In 1964 the government provided finance for three new car ferries to link Skye to the Outer Isles, Skye with Mallaig and Mull with Oban and Morvern. Five years later the state-owned Scottish Transport Group was formed to operate not only MacBrayne's but also the Caledonian Steam Packet Company on the Clyde. Soon after they were amalgamated and renamed Caledonian MacBrayne Ltd. The CalMac vessels soon sported the red CSP lion in the yellow disc in the centre of the red funnel. The Head Office was established in Gourock. In February 2001 Caledonian MacBrayne celebrated their 150th Anniversary.

ISLAND HOPPING

By Joe Broon

Just a few miles fae the mainland there are some amazing communities tae be met, sights tae be seen and events to take part in. Ye'll get the maist friendly welcome in Scotland. Music festivals, sport, art, windsurfing, stone-skimming, castles, hills, pubs (aye, after a day's hiking you need a cosy pub tae come back tae) and some plants and animals that you dinna see onywhere else.

See seals, dolphins, porpoises, whales, basking sharks, otters, red deer, highland coos and ponies. You'll mibbie hae the chance to see the aurora borealis – the Northern Lights. It's braw. Horace says it's somethin' tae dae wi' solar flares and particles in the atmosphere but ah jist ken it's a bonnie thing to watch – especially if you are watchin it wi' a bonnie lassie!

THE AURORA BOREALIS OR NORTHERN LIGHTS

Most Isles can be reached by the CalMac ferry. For ithers ye need tae be a bit mair canny – but it's a' part o' the adventure! Sometimes ye need tae ring a claxon or flash a light tae summon the local ferry.

The islands often have awfy wee populations – because o' that ye'll find a lot o' islanders have mair than ane job. Aye, they're very clever and practical people, yer islanders.

Now, it is possible tae be a daytripper tae many o' the islands, but think aboot staying for a few days holiday tae get a right proper taste o' island life because it wid be a richt shame tae miss oot seeing the isles that only have public transport aince a day (or less).

Wi a wee bit o' planning ye can still island hop even if ye are staying over and as well as self-catering, hotels and B&Bs, there are many camping areas available, inexpensive hostel-type accommodation in some areas, bothies and even a Mongolian yurt (that's a big roond tent ... on the Small Isles of Muck and Eigg).

You'll find a community-run website for nearly a' the isles. Ah think that's awfy clever. How many mainland towns can you say that of? Auchentogle disnae hae ane. Mibbie that can be Horace's next project.

Island Hopscotch® Tickets

ISLAND Hopscotch® tickets allow you to travel – at your own pace – on a selection of pre-planned routes around the Scottish Islands. There are 25 options to choose from. Tickets are valid for one journey on each route and can be used in either direction. They are valid for one month from the date of your first journey.

Advance booking may still be necessary on certain routes. See www.calmac.co.uk for details.

Travel to:
- Bute and Cowal
- Bute, Cowal and Kintyre
- Arran and Kintyre
- Mull and Morvern
- Mull, Ardnamurchan and Skye
- Barra, Uists, Harris and Lewis
- Uists, Harris and Lewis
- Uists and Skye
- Skye, Uists, Harris and Lewis
- Skye, Harris, Lewis and Uists
- Skye, Harris and Lewis
- Harris and Uists
- Barra, Uists and Skye
- Arran, Kintyre and Islay
- Islay and Colonsay
- Coll and Tiree
- Barra and Uists
- Mull and Ardnamurchan
- Mull, Morvern and Skye
- Barra, Uists, Harris and Skye
- Uists, Skye, Harris and Lewis
- Barra, Uists, Skye, Harris and Lewis
- Islay
- Barra and Uist

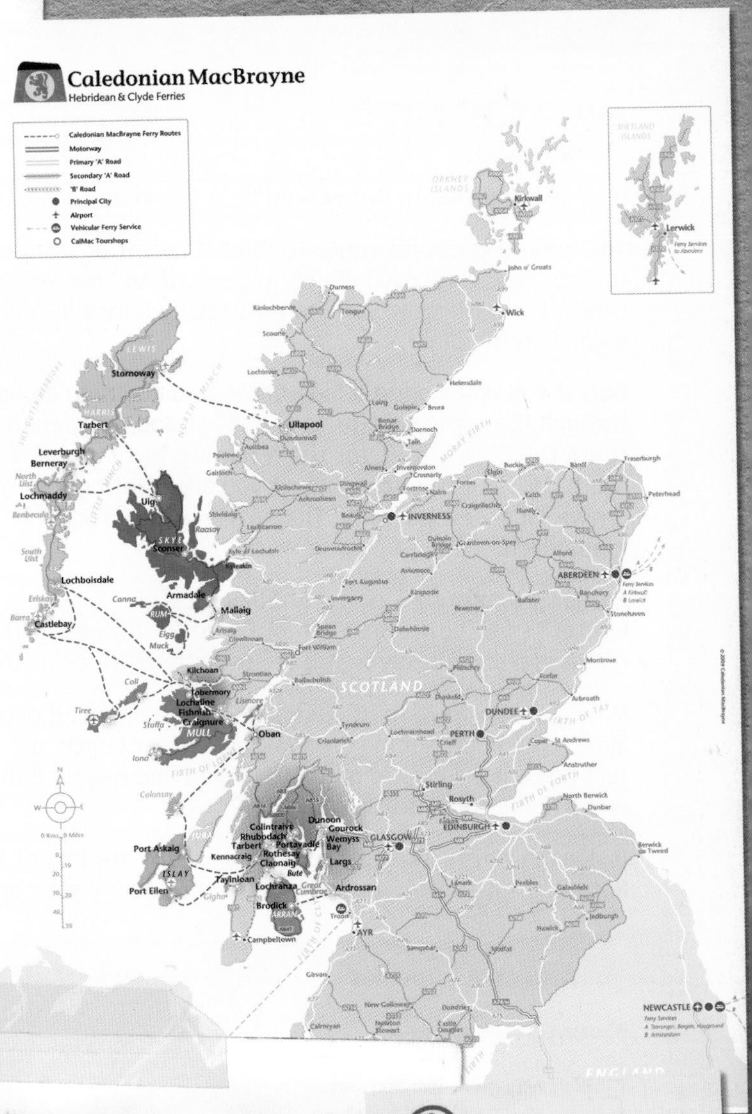

Caledonian MacBrayne
Hebridean & Clyde Ferries

- Caledonian MacBrayne Ferry Routes
- Motorway
- Primary 'A' Road
- Secondary 'A' Road
- 'B' Road
- Principal City
- Airport
- Vehicular Ferry Service
- CalMac Tourshops

Caledonian MacBrayne
www.calmac.co.uk

Bute

A DAY OOT TAE BUTE
by Horace

If ye like, getting to Bute could be a grand day oot in itsel'.

The main and easiest route to Bute is by car or train to the ferry from Wemyss Bay to Rothesay. The crossing only takes half an hour with sailings every 45 mins at peak times. From Glasgow you are potentially only a 90-minute journey away from Bute (on a good-traffic day!).

But, if you don't mind a long drive, you could go along the shores of Loch Lomond, through the Arrochar Alps to the "Rest and Be Thankful". Reach Loch Fyne and head south to COLINTRAIVE for the 5-minute ferry-crossing to RHUBODACH on Bute. It's no short-cut - but it is stunning. If you are wanting to visit Loch Fyne or Inveraray Castle anyway it's well worth it. The crossings are frequent. ROTHESAY is about 7 miles from Rhubodach.

Rothesay was once a prime holiday location. Glaswegians would head "doon the watter" - i.e. down the Firth of Clyde for a week at the seaside. Fashions change for holidays but Rothesay is still well worth a visit or a stay.

Maw and Paw have fond memories of the big band dancing at ROTHESAY PAVILION. Maw remembers seeing Jack Milroy, Jimmy Logan and Johnny Beattie when they were just boys! It's a classic of 1930s design and has recently been refurbished. Check the website for current listings.

It doesn't have to be just a day oot, there are lots of B&Bs along the shoreline in Rothesay - it's lovely to wake up to that bonny view across the watter.

Mount Stuart

FROM April to October don't miss a visit to stately Mount Stuart. The house is the seat of the Stuarts of Bute, derived from the hereditary office "Steward of Bute" held since 1157. The family are descendants of Robert the Bruce whose daughter Marjorie married then Walter Stewart, 6th High Steward of Scotland, in 1315. Their son, King Robert II of Scotland, became the first Stuart King.

ⓘ

Mount Stuart, PA20 9LR
www.mountstuart.com
Tel: 01700 503877

ROTHESAY CASTLE

www.isle-of-bute.com

Rothesay Pavilion,
PA20 0AU
Tel: 01700 504250

www.isle-of-bute.org.uk/pavilion

Cumbrae – Millport

ON a summer's day why not go for a pleasant day out in sunny Millport (it's sunny sometimes!), another stop on the trip "doon the watter". Millport has faded over the years but retains quite a bit of old-fashioned seaside charm. It's the main (the only) town on the Isle of Great Cumbrae. Take the ferry from Largs this time. Why not enjoy a bit of cycling, have a game of crazy golf, an ice cream, a fish supper and get all nostalgic for seaside holidays gone by while you eat your Millport rock.

:owal Peninsula

:ROSS the Kyles of Bute, lies the Cowal Peninsula, with autiful villages Tighnabruaich, and Lochgoilhead.

Its main town is Dunoon, a delightful stop off if you've been avelling "doon the watter" on the Firth of Clyde.

Serious walkers could attempt the mountains around Loch ›ng, or for those who prefer a gentler hike Argyll Forest ırk is a perfect location

LOCHGOILHEAD

On Arran

DAPHNE

MY FAVOURITE DAY OOT
by Daphne Broon

Maw asked wid I write tae Uncle Doogie in Australia an' tell him aboot ma favourite day oot. She really wants Doogie tae come an' visit us, so we'll wait an' see. This is my idea o' a perfect day – me an' Maggie went wi' Joe and Hen on hire bikes while we were holidayin' on Arran wi' the gang.

I fair enjoyed the boat "crossin' fae Ardrossan" (that's a rhyme by the way!). Caledonian MacBrayne boats are the biz and the breakfasts are tae die for. Try the full Scottish fry-up! The boat lands at Brodick and ye can walk tae Brodick Castle and Gardens fae the boat, or get the bus if ye must. The bairns wanted tae hire bikes as weel, but Arran's a richt hilly place. Jist HOW hilly Hen didna mention until later.

We cycled fae Brodick tae the north o' the island past a wee place ca'd Corrie wi' a bonnie harbour facing across the Clyde. I should hae stopped there!! Three miles up the road the hill fae Sannox tae Lochranza wiz like biking over Ben Nevis wi' lumps on it. I pushed the bike a' the way UP the hill. Efter catchin' ma breath at the summit for aboot half an 'oor and twa sandwiches, the freewheel tae Lochranza was better than the Blackpool Pleasure Beach. Afore I kent where I was, I was sittin' in the Lochranza Distillery Visitor Centre. Dinna miss it. The range o' malts is fantastic. I bocht a miniature and rubbed it intae ma thighs tae stop the pain . . . and their scones and jam are pain free. I had six.

Lochranza Distillery
Visitor Centre, KA27 8HJ
Tel: 01770 830264
www.arranwhisky.com

Brodick Castle gardens – beautiful.

Caledonian MacBrayne:
Ardrossan, KA22 8ED
Tel: 01294 463470
Brodick, KA27 8AY
Tel: 01770 302166
www.calmac.co.uk

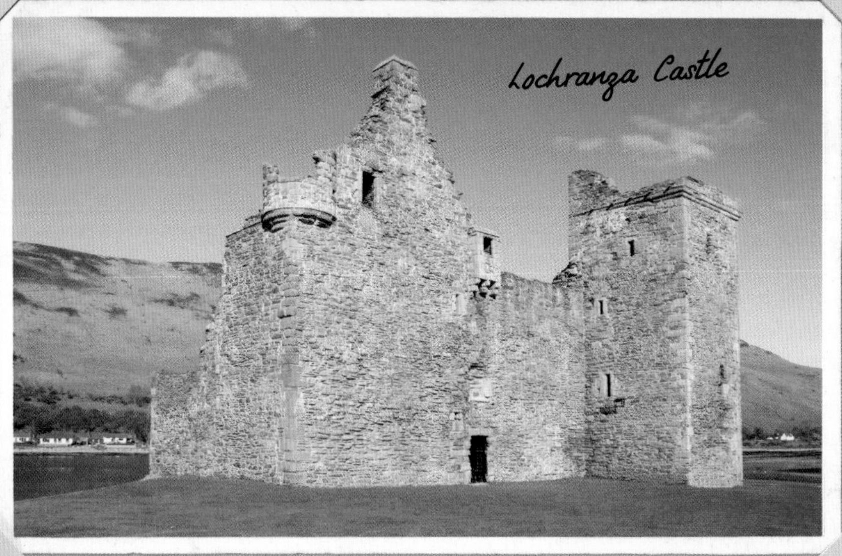
Lochranza Castle

Back on the bike, it was doon the west coast, wi' lovely views oot tae the Kintyre Peninsula. This no-sae-wee stretch o' road is as bonnie a spot as ye'll find. At Machrie, where ye can visit the Standin' Stanes (me, I could hardly stand masel' by this time), we turned east through the middle o' the island back towards Brodick.

Ye can cycle farther doon an' dae the hale circuit if ye're like Lance Armstrong or Hen Broon, but it's too far for the fuller figure (nae laughin'!). And of course, nae prizes for guessin' there's ANITHER muckle hill tae cycle. It's ca'd the String Road, but I remember it as the STING Road. I dinna ken whether it was the whisky wearin' aff or the muscle strain, but ma legs were on fire. But I made it tae the tap withoot gettin' aff . . . Hen gied me a tow!

Doon the brae again like the wind and it was intae the Arran Cheese Shop and the Arran Brewery, jist near the Castle where we'd started.

Standin' stanes at Machrie

i
Isle of Arran Brewery Visitor Centre, KA27 8DE
Tel: 01770 302353
www.arranbrewery.com
Island Cheese Company, KA27 8DD
Tel: 01770 302788
www.islandcheese.co.uk

On Arran – continued

Now, back wi' the family at the Castle, we had a rerr visit. The main rooms are on the first floor, so ye hae tae help aulder folk up the stairs. Granpaw was a star . . . he helped me a' the way up. Ma legs were like jelly fae the bikin'. The gardens are richt bonnie and we had a picnic on the grass wi' Maw's corned beef sandwiches, Dundee Cake and a flask o' coffee (wi' a wee smidgen o' a suggestion o' ten-year-auld malt!). There are heiland coos, woodland trails and the waterfalls. Ane o' the laddies fell in the burn, but that's normal on a Broons' day oot.

I was mair than pleased wi' MY day and although I was tired I'd dae it a' again ony day . . .on the back o' Sandy Bell's motorbike!! Hen wanted us a' tae go up Goatfell the next day but THIS auld goat was fell knackered and I spent the next day wi' Maggie at the AUCHRANNIE SPA RESORT. BLLLLLISS! There will also be a play barn with adventure playground, soft play area, ball pool and interactive games room available soon.

Est^d 1995

The Arran Malt

SINGLE MALT SCOTCH WHISKY

DISTILLED, MATURED AND BOTTLED IN SCOTLAND, ISLE OF ARRAN DISTILLERS LTD, ARRAN.

70cl e 46%Alc./Vol 46% Vol.

YEARS

Brodick Castle, Garden & Country Park, KA27 8HY. Tel: 0844 493 2152

Country Park Ranger
Tel: 0844 493 2155

www.nts.org.uk

Auchrannie Spa Resort, KA27 8BZ
Tel: 01770 302234

www.auchrannie.co.uk

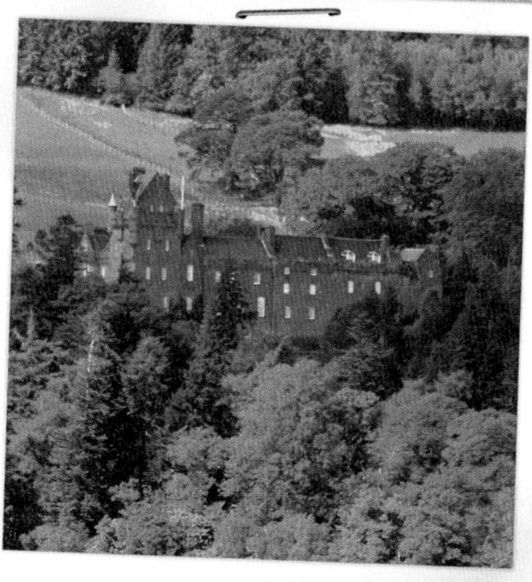

Brodick Castle

BRODICK Castle sits on sheltered land overlooking Brodick Bay. The Vikings used the site first, but the oldest parts of the castle now date from the 13th century. James IV granted the castle to his cousin, James Hamilton, in 1503, and made him Earl of Arran at the same time. The East Tower was built in 1588 and extended when the castle was occupied by Cromwell's troops in the 1650s. The 10th Duke of Hamilton greatly extended the castle in the 1840s and remodelled much of the inside in what was then a fashionable Jacobean style. The castle contains a precious collection of oil paintings and antique furniture once owned by the Dukes of Hamilton. The wonderful gardens were created in the last century and contain an internationally renowned collection of over 200 different rhododendron species. Beyond the gardens is the Brodick Country Park, with many woodland trails and an abundance of wildlife.

Goatfell

TOWERING above the castle are Arran's rocky mountains, the highest being Goatfell at 2,866 ft (874 metres). To climb it you need good boots and you need to stick to the paths unless you are an experienced mountaineer. From the summit you can see Ben Lomond, the island of Jura and across the Clyde to Ayr and even the coast of Ireland on a good day. The start of the walk up Goatfell starts opposite the Brodick Country Park.

The King's Cave

ALONG a pleasant three-mile walk from Blackwaterfoot along the coast of Arran you will see the King's Cave, one of a series of natural caves that local legend says were once the refuge of King Robert the Bruce (there are a few places around Scotland that are claimed to have been the hiding place of Bruce!). Bruce is said to have hidden here during the winter of 1306 following his murder of John Comyn at the altar of Greyfriars Abbey in Dumfries.

Bruce is said to have watched a spider repeatedly attempt to build a web on wet, slippery stone – an inspiration to continue his fight for the crown. The story was actually made up by Sir Walter Scott – in "Tales of a Grandfather" – and it was about Sir James Douglas, not Robert the Bruce – but it has made its way into Scottish legend.

To protect some fragile ancient carvings from vandalism, an iron gate now closes off the main cave but the walk along the coast to this spot is a lovely one. And whether the connection to Robert the Bruce is true or not, the ancient carvings show the caves were once inhabited by people with inscriptions in a runic alphabet known as Ogham.

A GREAT SPOT FOR A PICNIC
GOATFELL
FROM BRODICK BAY

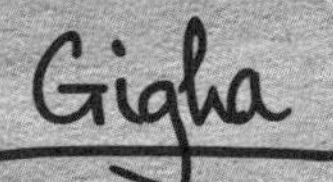

GIGHA – "PLEASE DO WALK ON THE GRASS"
by Maggie

Ye can expect a right warm welcome on this island. Granpaw would fit in right away. Daph and I went a wee day trip there when we were staying with my pal Aggie in Carradale.

Ye get the ferry fae TAYINLOAN, about 30 miles south of Tarbert on the Mull of Kintyre. It's good and regular even on stormy days. In fact, if ye're worried aboot weather it is actually a full three degrees warmer on the island than it is on the mainland. So if Campbeltown is driech and cold why not pop across to Gigha?

Gigha is a beautiful island for walks. Its pure white sandy beach is stunning.

The islanders are a canny lot. They bought the island themselves. And they bought three wind turbines second hand tae. They're called Faith, Hope and Charity. Between them, they make enough power for the island and a wee bitty extra to sell to the mainland, making Gigha about £80,000 per year. Every penny counts when your island is your means of making a living.

ⓘ

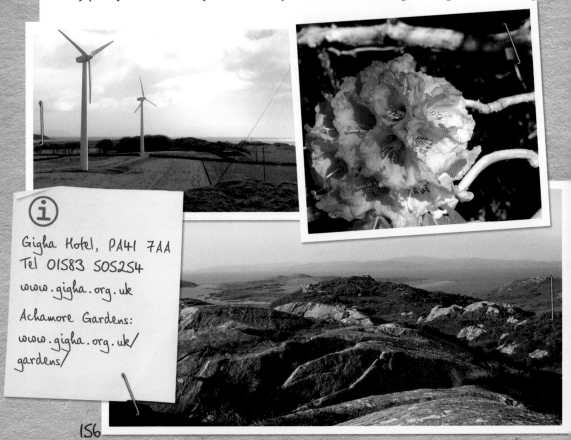

Gigha Hotel, PA41 7AA
Tel 01583 505254
www.gigha.org.uk

Achamore Gardens:
www.gigha.org.uk/gardens/

Gigha - continued
Gairdeners must visit ACHAMORE GARDENS - it's lovely. It has some unusual specimens. In fact it is lovely to visit even if ye ken nothin' aboot plants because of the warm sheltered areas, a walled gairden under restoration and a beautiful woodland walk that has bluebells in the spring. I really liked the sign "Please do walk on the grass. Please do touch and smell the flowers." Seems to sum Gigha up!

There's an honesty box asking for a £4.50 donation to see the gairdens. Do pay the admission as the lad that looks after them would struggle to keep them going withoot it.

Daphne and I are going tae go back and stay the nicht at the GIGHA HOTEL next time because we want to see the braw sunset or - if we can get up early enough - the sunrise. Hmm, Daph likes her bed, I think we're mair likely to see the sunset. The locals were very friendly and the hotel is where all the community meet up. We might even go on curry night!

Lismore

Ionad Naomh Moluag, Exhibition
Tel: 01631 760030
Cafe tel: 01631 760 020.
Tigh Iseabal Dhaibh
www.celm.org.uk

LISMORE - THE BIG GARDEN
By Hen

Can we squeeze this ane in Horace? I verra near forgot. Another lovely wee place is the Isle of LISMORE. It's is really close tae Oban and Mull and no too far frae equally lovely Iona. Me and Joe and Horace did a wee tour o' them one long weekend. The name Lismore comes frae Gaelic - Lios Mor - and means the big garden. Ye get there frae Oban on the car ferry or frae Port Appin on the passenger ferry. It's an easy place tae reach, and guid for a wee day trip. On the way look out for LISMORE LIGHTHOUSE, built by Robert Stevenson (Robert Louis Stevenson's faither). There's a heritage centre ca'd IONAD NAOMH MOLUAG (meaning "gathering place of St Moluag". Saint Moluag was a pal o' Saint Columba's I think, or he wis ages wi' him at least). The café there is lovely - hame cooking - and it seems tae be a guid meeting place fur the locals. And there's a traditional cottage you can look roon' tae, TIGH ISEABAL DHAIBH (you pronounce that ... er ... leave that one with me). Horace brought his binoculars and spotted a buzzard and a heron but we never saw the skylarks we were telt aboot. Next time maybe.
A lovely day oot!

Isle of Jura

PATH TO CORRYVRECKAN
Barnhill 4 Miles
Kinuachdrachd 5 Miles
Corryvreckan 7 Miles
NO MOTOR VEHICLES

THE ISLE OF JURA
By Paw

It's difficult to get tae but, michty me, the place is bonnie. The best way tae get there is tae catch the ferry frae Islay.

Ane village (Craighouse), ane shop, ane hotel, ane road - Jura has mair deer (6000) than folk (200 Diurachs, that's whit somebody fae Jura is cried). Ane distillery tae - making Isle of Jura single malt. A fine dram.

Walkers come here for the PAPS OF JURA which I'm telt is quite a climb. I widnae know - some o' us less adventurous walkers are content tae just look up at them. There are a few routes up them - ask a local expert. Mountains or not, it's a great island tae walk or cycle on the quiet single track road.

Me, Granpaw, Maw and The Bairn stayed in a nice B&B - the rest o' them had fun camping in the hotel field (The Twins telt Maggie adders lived in the heather and she didnae get a wink o' sleep).

Jura is lovely an' quiet (or at least it was till we turned up) and it's been a bit o' a writer's retreat in its time. George Orwell wrote 1984 here. I felt inspired tae dae a wee bit o' writin' masel. Poetry is my thing ....

Watch oot for the Corryvreckan
Dinna let its waters beckon.
For swimming near a whirlpool
Is only done by a silly auld fool.

THE CORRYVRECKAN WHIRLPOOL

Worthy of McGonnagle. The CORRYVRECKAN is the third largest whirlpool in Europe. We chartered a wee boat tae see it and I was quite taken with the gurgling, swirling water. I was fair hypnotised by it. Maw had to waft some corned beef pieces under my nose to bring me back.

We visited the JURA HOUSE WALLED GARDEN on the south shore of the island. Whit beautiful views to Islay and I even think I saw Kintyre.
Jura house has a real, active Victorian Kitchen walled garden. Granpaw kept saying his allotment is just as guid but he was fooling naebody. We went on a smashing woodland walk there.

Then there's the RED DEER - people are out-numbered 30 to 1 by red deer on Jura. We were telt that in October it's quite something tae hear the stags making their mating calls - it echoes all around the island. Thank goodness Hen and Joe just use the phone.

Jura – Getting There

The most common way of getting to Jura is from Islay. Jura is separated from its neighbour by a half-mile wide stretch of water known as the Sound of Islay. There's a ferry between the two islands that runs from Port Askaig, on the east coast of Islay, to Feolin, in the south-west corner of Jura.

From Port Askaig the Jura ferries run regularly all day till 6.30pm.

The Jura Passenger Ferry, run by www.islayseasafari.co.uk has in the past operated during summer months, from Tayvallich to Craighouse, but this will be subject to funding for 2011-2013. Regular flights depart from Glasgow Airport to Islay.

www.calmac.co.uk
www.jurapassengerferry.com

Jura Festivals and Events

The Whisky Festival: May
www.isleofjura.com

Fell Race: May
www.jurafellrace.org.uk

Ardlussa Sports Day: July
www.theisleofjura.co.uk

Jura Regatta: First weekend of August
www.isleofjura.com/island-life/regatta.aspx

Music Festival: September
www.juramusicfestival.com

i

ww.jurainfo.com
ww.juradevelopment.
.uk

Jura House

ura House Walled Garden is open all week rom 9am to 5pm. Jura House garden offers voodland, cliff and shore valks as well as a tea tent nd a "plants for sale" hop. There is a little dmission charge and arking is possible on the ther side of the road.

Jura Music Festival

JURA'S population nearly trebles over the weekend of the island's September music festival. Friday night sees local musicians playing in the main hall and bar. They'll be playing sessions all weekend. Saturday night's grand concert features professional traditional musicians from all over the world and concludes with a ceilidh lasting into the wee small hours. All weekend there are varied workshops: drumming, dancing, piping, fiddling, guitar etc. And kids can join in a 'play if you like' where they act out a Jura-themed story in the distillery cooperage. There's also a big marquee where the festival's non-traditional music is played.

Come and join in the fun!

ISLAY – IT'S NOT A' ABOOT WHISKY
By Granpaw

There are aboot 3,200 people living on Islay, the Queen o' the Hebrides. How dae ye get there? Sail tae Port Ellen or Port Askaig frae Kennacraig on Kintyre.

Now, ye ken, there's pages in this book aboot touring the DISTILLERIES on Islay. There's eight working distilleries so you can see why ye micht mention them aince or twice. Well there's a lot mair to do besides that – though I am awfy fond o' seein' the distilleries. Anyway ...

There's FEIS ILE – THE ISLAY FESTIVAL OF MALT AND MUSIC – aye, I ken, whisky again. This is a great festival, lasting a whole week and starting on the last weekend of May each year.

Mair music at the ISLAY JAZZ FESTIVAL – taking place in September in venues all over the island including Lagavulin distillery filling shed – whoops, whisky again. Some big names play here and it's not surprising that jazz-lovers come fae a' ower the world tae this festival. You can bet there will be Islay oysters for sale tae and hame baking! I don't mind the old-time jazz but ye canny beat a bit o' Jimmy Shand.

The ISLAY BOOK FESTIVAL – The first weekend o' September in Port Ellen Primary School. Famous authors come tae this wee festival and there's a braw spread o' hame baking available tae. I dare say they micht talk aboot the odd whisky book?

The ISLAY HALF MARATHON – This happens in early August and involves a 13-mile run from the village of Bowmore (there's a distillery there) out to Islay Airport and back. Afterwards there's a licensed dance held in Bowmore Hall.

There's a TOPE FISHING FESTIVAL – "Whit's a tope?" ye micht well ask. Well, I wisna sure either, so I looked it up in the dictionary and the verb means to drink excessively. No, despite Islay haeing eight distilleries, that's not what it means here. A tope is a wee shark. These wee beasties are visitors in Islay's waters and also Loch Indaal. Stormcats, boat builders at Lagavulin (there's a braw whisky fae there tae), organise it.

And – something for the young yins and no' a granpaw wi' rheumatic knees – ISLAY BEACH RUGBY, the only beach rugby tournament in the UK an it's open to boys and lassies. It happens on the second weekend of June.

PORT ELLEN LIGHTHOUSE

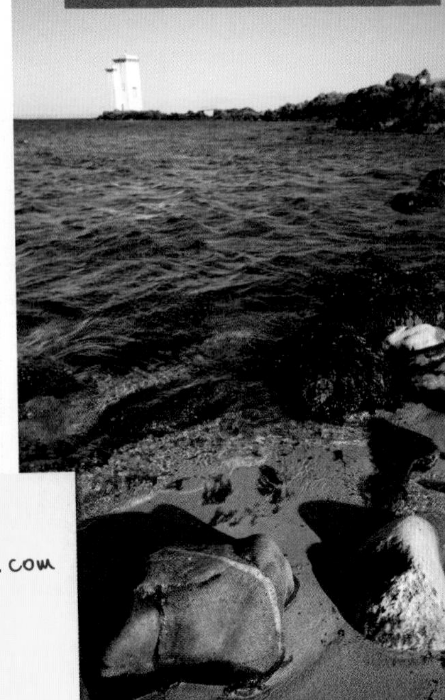

i Tope Fishing Festival
www.stormcats-islay.com

Islay Beach Rugby
islaybeachrugby.com

Feis Ile
www.theislayfestival.co.uk

Islay Jazz Festival
www.islayjazzfestival.co.uk
Box Office: 0845 1110302

Islay Book Festival
islaybookfestival.org.uk

Islay Half Marathon
www.islayhalfmarathon.co.uk

Museum of Islay Life,
PA48 7UA
www.islaymuseum.org

ISLAY –Things to Do and See

Activities:-
golf
cycling
mountain biking
fishing
horseriding
swimming – check locally for the safe swimming areas
arts and crafts – plenty of those to see and buy, lace, pottery, jewellery, batik prints – great stuff.
music
whisky tasting

Sights:-
stunning bays at Machir, Saligo and Sanaigmore
beautiful sunsets
beaches
cliffs
seals
dolphins
buzzards
eagles
Port Charlotte
Port Ellen
Portnahaven
Round Church at Bowmore
Viking farms
distilleries aplenty!

Islay Quilters
www.islayquilters.org.uk, PA44 7NZ
enquiries@islayquilters.org.uk

ISLAY QUILTERS
by Maw

I had a braw afternoon o' sewing, tea drinking and blethers wi' the lovely lassies at ISLAY QUILTERS who hae a workshop at ISLAY HOUSE SQUARE near BRIDGEND. This is a braw spot for arts and crafts on the island and it's also whaur ISLAY BREWERY is! It was a Thursday and a' the quilting lassies were in (they're volunteers, you know). While my lot were going roon' the distilleries I was quite comfy here. Their work is amazing - and a lot o' it is raffled for charity. I'd be proud to own ane o' thae quilts. Irene's shortbread wis braw tae! I bought masel some new knitting needles while I was there - a nice memento of Islay! It's open Monday to Saturday, 2pm till 4.30pm. Next time I'm bringing my ain sewing tae show them.

Caledonian MacBrayne:
Craignure, PA65 6AY
Tel: 01680 812343;
Oban, PA34 4DB
Tel: 01631 566688;
Tobermory, PA75 6NU
Tel: 01688 302017
www.calmac.co.uk

Duart Castle, PA64 6AP
Tel: 01680 812 309
www.duartcastle.com

THE BONNIE ISLE O' MULL
Joe Broon

Oh, it's hard tae pick a favourite day oot on Mull. Me an' Hen have cycled the ups and downs of Mull's wee roads that many times and never twa days the same.

Ye can get tae the island on ane o' three different Caledonian MacBrayne boats, and there's nae twa o' them the same. Ane comes intae Tobermory harbour from Kilchoan on the Ardnamurchan peninsula. That's my favourite. Anither crosses tae Fishnish from the mainland at Lochaline and the biggest boat surges over from Oban packed wi' cars and trippers tae Craignure, passin' majestic DUART CASTLE on the way. There's a wee railway runs from Craignure tae the castle. The bairns loved that. Granpaw loves the TOBERMORY DISTILLERY tour. Daphne loved seeing the real Mull on her MULL MAGIC WILDLIFE WALK.

Hen Broon
Joe's richt, it's hard tae pick one day better than anither. But if ye've lang legs like mine (and no' a lot o' folk do right enough) an' ye're a keen cyclist, the single track road from Tobermory past Dervaig, stunning Calgary beach, doon the west past Ulva and Loch na Keal then Salen on the Sound o' Mull and back up the road tae yer start point at Tobermory and a pint is the best bike day oot in the world. It really is. It's less than fifty miles, feels mair like a hunner an' goes up an' doon an' up an' doon.

I've been a' over the world (even tae John o' Groats nae less!) and this is my number one. Le Tour de Mull. Get yer yella jersey on, mes amis!!

by The Twins

Nae cyclin' for us. We just spent the day in Tobermory. The hooses on the sea front are a' painted in different bright colours. It's like a scene aff a chocolate box.

The Bairn was in her element, cos this is where the BBC "Balamory" series was filmed. A' the places from the series are easily picked oot. The harbour's packed wi' boats o' every shape and size, and on the pier is oor favourite fish an' chipper. Ye'll easily spot it. It's the van parked richt next tae the clock tower in the middle o' the main street. If ye canna spot that, jist look for the big queue, wi' oor cyclin' brothers at the end wi' their tongues hingin' oot.

Balamory – Tobermory

Tobermory Distillery,
PA75 6NR
01688 302645
Open Easter – Oct: by appointment
Mon – Fri 10am – 5pm
Groups: by arrangement

Mull Magic Wildlife Walks,
PA75 5QP
Tel: 01688 301213
Mob: 07923 153976
enquiries@mullmagic.com

Caledonian MacBrayne:
Fionnphort, PA66 6BL.
Tel: 01681 700559
Iona Abbey, PA76 6SQ.
Tel: 01681 700512
www.historic-scotland.gov.uk

Coming
ashore on Iona

IONA
by Maw Broon

Me and the lassies had only one thing on oor minds for oor trip tae Mull. Iona Abbey and then Fingal's Cave on the island of Staffa.

I'm no' much o' a history scholar, but I do know a wee bit aboot Iona. (I read it in stuff I picked up at Historic Scotland's reception kiosk actually.) The bonnie wee single track road fae Craignure tak's ye a' the way tae the Iona ferry at Fionnphort. It's only a wee crossing over the Sound of Iona but the wind can blaw a wee bit. I could hardly wait tae get across. Ye can see the Abbey fae the pier.

Iona Abbey stands near where St Columba landed in AD 563. That's no' the day nor yesterday. The place is steeped in history. It was the burial place o' early Scottish kings richt up tae MacBeth in 1057. History tells us that it was the 8th Duke o' Argyll, head o' Clan Campbell, who began the process o' rescuing what was a ruin aboot 1874. And it was Mrs Effie MacDonald that telt me the Campbell Duke's guid sense almost made her forgive the Campbells for chappin' up her great-great-great-great-great Uncle Lachie MacDonald in Glencoe in 1692. Anyway, what ye see here now on Iona is really a restoration of what was once here hundreds of years ago.

by Maggie Broon

I'd better tell ye the rest o' oor wee adventure cos Maw was that impressed she could hardly speak.

It's the boat trip fae Fionnphort tae Fingal's Cave on the island of Staffa. Ye cannae really describe it. It tak's yer breath away. The boat will land ye near the cave and ye have tae watch yer step and haud on tae the rails as ye teeter roond and intae the big cave. In some ways it's mair impressive than Iona Abbey inside.

Dinnae tak my word for it, just go and see for yersel' . . . and one ither thing, whatever ye dae, dinna miss a wee walk tae see the puffin colony on the north side o' the island while ye're there. It's hard tae believe thae birds are real . . . jist wee comics, like oor Bairn.

Aww! Look whit the Bairn drew. That's smashin'

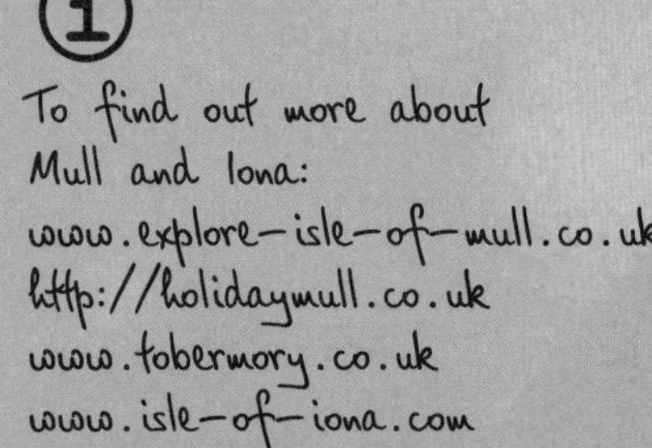

i
To find out more about Mull and Iona:
www.explore-isle-of-mull.co.uk
http://holidaymull.co.uk
www.tobermory.co.uk
www.isle-of-iona.com

Iona Abbey

OVER THE SEA TO SKYE
by Joe Broon

Gettin' there
There are several ways o' goin' over the sea tae Skye.

- Ye can sail in tae Uig fae Tarbert on Harris in the Western Isles on CalMac ferries.
- Ye can drive ower the Skye Bridge fae Kyle of Lochalsh tae Kyleakin.
- Ye can tak' "The Road tae the Isles" fae Fort William and CalMac-it fae Mallaig tae Armadale.
- Ye can dae what I always dae . . . fae Shiel Bridge on the main A87 Invergarry tae Kyle road, turn aff at signpost tae Glenelg over the steep pass o' the Mam Ratagan and cross tae Kylerhea on Skye on the wee "Glenachulish" ferry boat. It's the last wee ferry boat o' its kind in Scotland. There's a turntable that the lads push roond by hand so that yer car's aye facin' the richt way for drivin' aff . . . ye'll love this. Do NOT miss it.

There are hunners of books on Skye, so I'm just gonna give ye the driver's (that's me!) tips on oor family day oot birlin' roond Skye in ma wee mini bus.

The Cuillins – daunting!

The Auld Man of Storr

Glenelg to Kylerhea Ferry
www.skyeferry.co.uk
Information about Skye
www.skye.co.uk

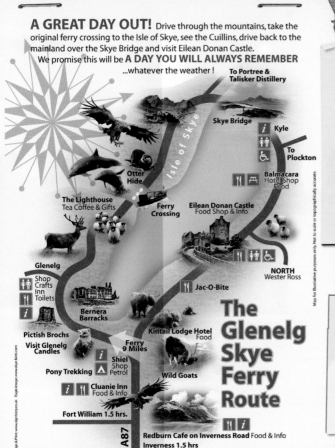

A GREAT DAY OUT! Drive through the mountains, take the original ferry crossing to the Isle of Skye, see the Cuillins, drive back to the mainland over the Skye Bridge and visit Eilean Donan Castle.
We promise this will be **A DAY YOU WILL ALWAYS REMEMBER** ...whatever the weather !

To Portree & Talisker Distillery
Skye Bridge
Kyle
To Plockton
Isle of Skye
Otter Hide
Balmacara Hotel Shop Food
The Lighthouse Tea Coffee & Gifts
Ferry Crossing
Eilean Donan Castle Food Shop & Info
Glenelg
Shop Crafts Inn Toilets
NORTH Wester Ross
Jac-O-Bite
Bernera Barracks
Pictish Brochs
Visit Glenelg Candles
Kintail Lodge Hotel Food
Ferry 9 Miles
Shiel Shop Petrol
Pony Trekking
Wild Goats
Cluanie Inn Food & Info
Fort William 1.5 hrs.
A87
Redburn Cafe on Inverness Road Food & Info
Inverness 1.5 hrs

The Glenelg Skye Ferry Route

Map for illustrative purposes only. Not to scale or topographically accurate.

Design & Print: www.signbizzy.co.uk Eagle image: www.skye-birds.com

Caledonian MacBrayne: Armadale, IV45 8RS Tel: 01471 844248; Mallaig PH41 4QD Tel: 01687 462403; Tarbert, HS3 3DG Tel: 01859 502444; Uig, IV51 9XX. Tel: 01470 542219
www.calmac.co.uk

Skye Serpentarium, IV49 9AQ
Tel: 01471 822533
www.skyeserpentarium.org.uk

Kylerhea to Staffin

There's an otter sanctuary at Kylerhea and if ye're lucky ye micht even spot ane o' the bonnie beasts fae the wee ferry itsel'. Even if there's nane there, the mannie on the ferry will tell ye ye've jist missed ane, lookin' the wrang way at the wrang time!! Aye, thae Highlanders!

Up the wee steep road now through Glen Arroch. Feartie passengers on the right side o' the bus. There's a big drap on yer left. We're now headin' through Broadford (the Reptile House, or Skye Serpentarium, for those that like creepy crawlies) then past Sligachan Hotel at the foot o' the Cuillin Hills. Sligachan's the place for climbers an' campers and midges.

We're goin' anti-clockwise roond the island now, cos we're anti-clocks as there's nae great hurry. Coffees an' lemonades an' munchies at the island's capital, Portree (see the bonnie harbour), and a chance for me tae stretch ma legs, afore on and on up the east coast tae Staffin, passin' the Storr Rock on yer left. Cameras oot!!

Dunvegan Castle & Gardens, IV55 8WF.
Tel: 01470 521206
www.dunvegancastle.com

Talisker Distillery, IV47 8SR.
Tel: 01478 614308
www.discovering-distilleries.com/talisker
Bella Jane boat trips,
IV49 9BJ. Tel: 01471 866244
www.bellajane.co.uk

Staffin to Dunvegan

Ye can drive a' the way roond the top o' the island and the views are wonderful, but I like tae cut across fae Staffin tae Uig on the ribbon road that climbs up beside "the Quirang". If ye've time, walk up tae see this great pile o' weird and wonderful rock spires. It's like the ruins o' the biggest cathedral in Scotland.

Intae Uig now, where the CalMac boat comes in efter its crossin' fae Harris and we're headed south again. Dinnae miss the right turn aff the A856 aboot four miles fae Portree on tae the A850 through Fairy Bridge to DUNVEGAN CASTLE. Dunvegan Castle and Gardens are open from April to October.

This is the home of Clan MacLeod. With pictures of the Chiefs of MacLeod fae the year dot . . . and there's mementoes of that man Bonnie Prince Charlie again and Flora MacDonald, who famously rowed the Bonnie Prince "over the sea to Skye" in song and legend. There's an interesting exhibit at the castle ca'd "The Fairy Flag" from the 7th century. Legend has it that it can only be unfurled three times in case of emergency. It's been unfurled twice already, presumably tae assist MacLeod o' whatever vintage frae bein' attacked by Flora's MacDonald lot. Clans were aye attackin' ane anither. So the flag has only one magic "assist" left. I can tell ye, the MacLeods were nearly bringin' it oot when they saw oor lot pilin' oot o' the mini bus and stormin' the restaurant.

The Cuillins

Then it's doon the road tae TALISKER DISTILLERY, the only ane on Skye. It's aboot here ye get the best roadside views o' the Cuillin Hills, the rock climbers' paradise. Back to Broadford now, retracing oor steps in time for one last Skye treat.

The tiny A881 road runs fourteen unhurried miles from Broadford to another world at Elgol, passing the jaw-droppin' view of the mighty Blaven Hill from a wee place called Torrin. A'body got aff the bus tae photograph this. Doon at the harbour at Elgol is possibly the best view in Skye, lookin' at the whole of the Cuillins like a big oil painting across the sea waters of Loch Scavaig. Sunsets are tae die for here. Ye can get closer on boats like the "Bella Jane", that will take ye right in under the mountains near Loch Coruisk. This is a day oot in itself.

And tae finish aff the rollercoaster day oot in the wee bus? We treated oorsels tae some Skye seafood at a local restaurant. The manager near choked when The Broons turned up for "a table for eleven". That's a lot o' fresh prawns, lobsters and crab legs and delicious wee things ca'd squatty lobsters. They rustled up the Bairn's favourite omelette. The manager's jaw dropped mind ye, when we asked if she had a "family room". We ran up a rerr wee bill, but as Granpaw hadna spent a ha'penny o' his pension since afore the Coronation, it was a painless treat. And as he's sae fond o' his malt, we a' had tae keep him company. Onyway, I'd been drivin' a' day. I deserved it.

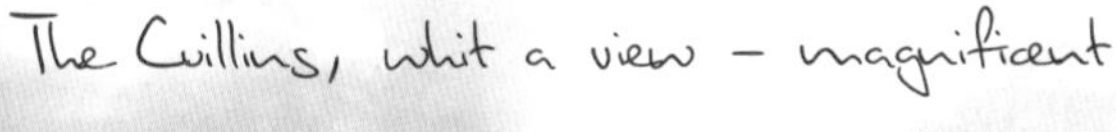
The Cuillins, whit a view – magnificent

Raasay

FOR some great walks, in a very different landscape to Skye, go to Raasay. Get there by ferry from Sconser on Skye. If you miss the ferry, get comfy at the Sconser Hotel till the next one (01478 650 333).

There is no public transport on Raasay. From the ferry it's a mile to the main village Inverarish.

The most distinct feature on Raasay is the flat-topped peak known as Dun Caan. If you get there nice and early you can make the 5/6-hour walk to the highest point of 1456 feet and back again in time to catch the last ferry. For more details see this great website: ***www.walkhighlands.co.uk/skye/isle-of-raasay.shtml***

The Slate Islands

Easdale, Seil, Luing, Lunga, Shuna, Torsay and Belnahua used to be famous, for almost three centuries, for slate mining. The slate for the University of Glasgow came from the quarries of Luing.

The last slate was cut in the 1950s. Now what once was quarry is now rock pool, and home to bird and plant life. Lunga, Shuna, Torsay and Belnahua are mostly uninhabited.

The easiest and most-used method to access these islands is to follow the A816 south from Oban. Cross the Clachan Bridge, also known as 'The Bridge over the Atlantic' to reach the Isle of Siel.

Seil

Next to the bridge there's the Tigh na Truish Inn (The House of Trousers). The name comes from the period after the 1745 Jacobite rebellion when kilts were banned. Kilted Islanders heading for the mainland are said to have stopped here to swap their kilts for trousers. The village of Balvicar is home to quaint old quarriers' cottages. Stock up at the local store.

Or head for Ellenabeich, the largest village on Seil. Parts of the film *Ring of Bright Water* were filmed here. What looks like a harbour is actually the remains of the slate quarry there. The village of Ellenabeich on the Isle of Seil houses the Slate Islands Trust Heritage Centre – where a restored cottage lets you see how the 19th-century slate workers used to live. Ellenabeich is the place to get a passenger ferry to Easdale Island.

Easdale

There are no roads and few paths on Easdale. The preferred mode of transport is the wheelbarrow. Easdale is the smallest permanently-inhabited island of the Inner Hebrides. It's less than 10 hectares in size and has a permanent population of about 70. The future could have been grim for Easdale. After the death of the slate industry its population in the 1960s was only 4 people. But Easdale has been repopulated, by descendants of the original quarry men and by others from around the world, and now has a vibrant community, a really nice pub (The Puffer Bar) and an award-winning community hall that hosts lots of events for an island of its size. Don't forget the quirkiest of festivals, the World Stone Skimming Championships held in September every year. Open to all entrants and taking full advantage of an environment made by the slate industry.

Luing

At Cuan, at the southern end of Seil, you can catch the car ferry to unspoilt and peaceful Luing. Famed for its sunsets, Luing is perfect for a day trip to truly get away from it all for a few hours. Watch for otters, hares, dolphins and seals which inhabit the land and shore of Luing. The Forestry Trust maintain trails and woodland paths around the island. Divers can look for the shipwrecks of the Sound of Mull. Why not rent a bicycle and see the 5 square miles of island that way.

Clachan Bridge: The Bridge Over The Atlantic

A COTTAGE ON EASDALE

EASDALE ISLAND
FERRY
TO CALL FERRY PRESS
BOTH BUTTONS IN SHED
PLEASE CHECK TIMETABLE
FOR FERRY SCHEDULE

EASDALE – THE WORLD STONE SKIMMING CHAMPIONSHIPS
by Granpaw

The World Stone Skimming Championships have been held in Easdale every September since 1997. There's a "pre-skim" party the nicht afore which is guid enough reason tae decide tae stay for the nicht. Just don't let a dram too many affect your stone skimming the next day. Me and Paw went for a day trip frae Oban.

Ane o' the competition rules is you've only tae use the Easdale slate for the skimming. Flat, round Easdale stones are just right for the job. There used tae be a big quarry on Easdale years ago. Now it's filled wi' water and is like a wee loch. They have the skimming there – and that flat, still water is perfect for it. Me and Paw entered the "Auld Tossers" competition. I was narrowly done oot o' the trophy (actually, it's a commemorative walking-stick) by an almichty twinge o' my sciatica. Paw's stones sunk withoot a bounce. Ah think the nerves got the better o' him. It wis a big crowd and he was only wearing his second-best bunnet.

Donald – the fella that organises it – he says it's getting mair and mair busy every year. Me and him had a wee dram thegither afore I caught the ferry back across to Ellenabeich tae get to ma digs in Oban. Nice lad. That ferry man's a character tae. It was a braw day oot wi' a great atmosphere for sic a wee totie place.

i

www.easdale.org

www.stoneskimming.com

COLONSAY – CEÒL CHOLASA

by Hen Broon

One summer, when I was staying on Islay, I went a day trip tae Colonsay and met some folk in The Colonsay Pantry. They raved aboot their September music festival CEÒL CHOLASA and I just had tae go. I had a word wi' Donald and Keith, the festival organisers, and me an' Joe got put on the list for tickets for the following year. The following year! Now, I'm only telling ye aboot this on the condition that ye dinna tell onybody aboot it. I want tae be able tae get tickets for Ceòl Cholasa again some time. So that's a secret jist a'tween us – understood? I dinna want a'body trying tae go.

You can sail tae Colonsay fae Oban but there's only ane ferry a day. There's nae ferries on a Saturday (there's only three ferries in the winter – aye, I did say it was remote). Ye micht need a wee overnight in Oban as the ferry leaves bright and early.

The festival was frae Thursday tae Sunday, so me an' Joe caught the early Oban tae Scalasaig ferry on the Thursday morning and we got there aboot noon. The boat was fu' o' folk – festival-goers, singers and musicians all together – on their way to the festival. Some were singing already. I had a great feeling aboot this trip.

We stocked up for oor tea at The GENERAL STORE in Scalasaig (I had phoned them to order a few wee tasty bites afore we arrived) and then we had a quick dram at the COLONSAY HOTEL before walking the 2 km tae oor digs. Whit bonnie! If ye've time for a big hike there's Kiloran Bay, COLONSAY HOUSE GARDENS and ye can tak' a walk ower The Strand to Oronsay, visiting the priory.

We had booked oorsels intae a wee hostel, THE COLONSAY ESTATE BACKPACKER'S LODGE. It was a fine wee place – an old gamekeeper's lodge. We stayed in bunk beds in the dormitory that sleeps 16. (Some fellas complained aboot some loud snoring but I never heard a thing and slept like a bairn.)

I took a big torch out wi' me so we could find oor way back after dark, but somehow, each nicht we managed to stay oot till the sun started coming up again. I dinna ken how that happened! The time passed so quick listening tae stories an' music; an' ceilidh dancin', singing an' sampling the rather fine gold-medal-winning IPA fae the COLONSAY BREWERY. A wee island wi its ain brewery. No wonder I felt at hame.

The festival was right cosy and friendly. Joe was wishing he'd brought his accordion. Musicians were jamming everywhere and folk were singing. I fair enjoyed the wee sing-song we had wi' a couple o' American lassies. Folk come frae a' ower the world tae this wee festival.

We stayed on for another day efter the festival ended. I sat amang the dunes on Balnarhard beach and I'm no' ashamed tae say, wi' a wee tear in my e'e, I wished I didna have tae go hame.

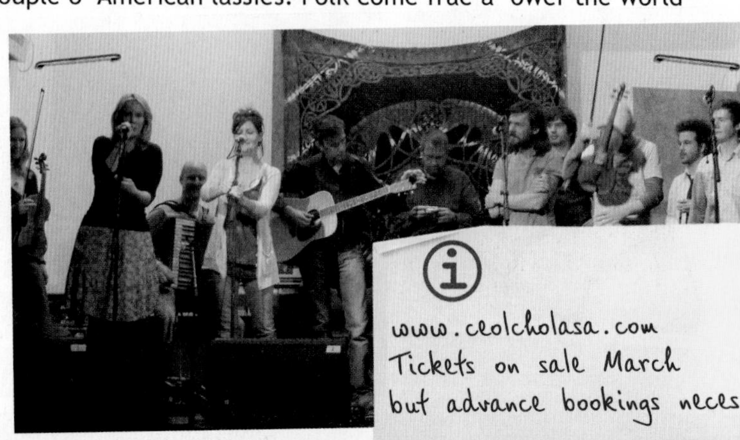

ⓘ

www.ceolcholasa.com
Tickets on sale March
but advance bookings necessar

Leann Cholbhasa

You all know the story of IPA – brewed to ensure by the time the beer reached India it was in perfect condition. Our IPA is from the same tradition: brewed to be at its very best by the time the ferry docks at Oban.
Seriously, this IPA is a truly refreshing ale that is ideal for a session – though like all ...

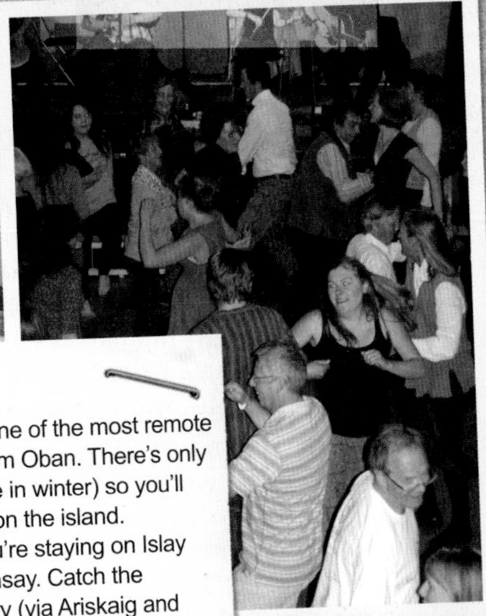

Colonsay House
www.colonsay.org.uk/gardens

lonsay Brewery, PA61 7YT
ww.colonsaybrewery.co.uk

lonsay General Store, PA61 7YR
ww.colonsayshop.net
l: 01951 200 265

Getting to Colonsay

Colonsay in the southern Hebrides is one of the most remote communities in Britain. You can sail from Oban. There's only one ferry a day, six times a week (three in winter) so you'll usually need to book accommodation on the island.
In the summer, on a Wednesday, if you're staying on Islay it's possible to be a daytripper to Colonsay. Catch the early morning Kennacraig to Oban ferry (via Ariskaig and Colonsay) at Port Askaig on Islay to Scalasaig on Colonsay. You then have all day to explore Colonsay until the ferry does it's return trip from Oban reaching Colonsay around 6pm.

Colonsay

FESTIVAL OF SPRING
For three weeks in May celebrate Colonsay's Festival of Spring. Wildflower, ornithology, archeological and conservation walks, classes in foraging for wild food as well as painting and poetry workshops: there are several events, talks, walks and classes on every day. With weekly passes at £25 it's the best value festival in Britain. Children under 12 have free entry when accompanied by an adult.

GOLF
Colonsay has a natural links course by Machrins bay, reputedly over 200 years old. To play this 18-hole course you must be a full member but he cost is only £220 for the year and membership can be purchased by anyone at the Colonsay Hotel. It is possible to play a 9-hole game on this course.

CYCLING
Cycling is the perfect way to get around on Colonsay since the roads are quiet and relatively flat. All the family can enjoy cycling around the island. Bikes can be rented from Archie MacConnell at Kilchattan. There a limited number for hire from the Colonsay Hotel and Estate office.

LOCAL PRODUCE
Honey, oysters and beer, now there's a balanced meal! Ask locally if there are oysters in season. Colonsay honey has a unique flavour made distinctive by the local wildflowers. Colonsay's honey producer Andrew Abrahams also runs beekeeping classes in May and June.
Colonsay has it's own microbrewery. During Festival of Spring you can tour it and beers can be purchased in the brewery shop. Also available online or on the mainland at Scottish branches of Peckhams.

(i) Accommodation
www.colonsay.org.uk
Festival of Spring
www.colonsayevents.co.uk
Tel: 07850 230000

D BIRDWATCHING HISTORY AND ARCHAEOLOGY
S AND LECTURES EXPERT WILDFLOWER WALKS
LKS FORAGING AND COOKING COURSES POETRY
ITALS CONCERTS PLAYS LANDSCAPE PAINTING
KSHOPS GOLF TOURNAMENTS KAYAKING TRIPS

TIREE WAVE CLASSIC
by The Twins (with spelling corrected by Horace)

Sailin', surfin', windsurfin'? All very exciting we're sure. But, whit aboot wave sailing? The maist challenging kind o' windsurfing. Now, nane o' us Broons are very guid swimmers let alane surfers but even though we wurnae actually getting oor ain feet wet – whit a thrill it was tae watch these lads and lassies riding the tops o' giant waves an' flying through the air. Tiree has a lot o' wind (a bit like Paw) – near-perfect conditions for the big waves needed for this extreme surfin! Every October they haud a competition – the Tiree Wave Classic. It's a week long and has been going since 1986. Windsurfers come frae a' ower the world tae go tae a wee Scottish island. Amazin'!

Hen was dying tae hae a shot but we reckon he wid hae been taller than some o' the sails. Joe swims like a brick so he never said onything. We were lucky, the day that we went tae Tiree it was quite blustery. If the weather is ower nice the waves urnae big enough and they cannae wave sail. The weather had been awfy nice for most of the week o' the competition. Some lads were saying that they had to play beach volleyball, five-a-side football and rounders in the sunshine instead. Sounds fun tae us.

We were happy to leave the surfin' up tae the experts – but it wis a grand sight tae watch the surfers' turns, moves and jumps. They made it look easy but we bet it wisnae. It was the awards ceremony in the hall that night and a really great band wis playing. We had a rerr time! But Maw took us and The Bairn back tae the guest house and the others stayed oot late. No fair!

Horace: We went on a Friday till the Saturday. We thought we were going tae miss the boat back because we couldn't find Maggie and Daph. My sisters – not known for their interest in sport – were tae be found at the hotel, talking enthusiastically with some young male surfers.

Tiree Wave Classic
www.tireewaveclassic.org

Tiree – Getting There

TIREE'S gaelic name is Tir fo Thuinn, "Land below the waves". With its beautiful, long white beaches that attract surfers from all over the world the name is very appropriate.

It takes about 4 hours to sail from Oban to Tiree. There's just one ferry a day in summer (except for a Thursday where a day trip with a 6-hour stay on the island is possible, arriving back in Oban at 10pm). Most days it's a very early departure from Oban, so an overnight stay in Oban is recommended (and perhaps after the day trip too if you've far to travel). Tiree is a small island and summer accommodation – from B&Bs, hotels and hostels to stunning beach houses – can be in high demand so book early.

It's not surprising that it's popular, Tiree is one of the sunniest places in Britain with warm temperatures influenced by the Gulf Stream. Winter on Tiree can be several degrees warmer than on the mainland and summer nights are generally warm and pleasant – with enough wind to make it midge free!

You can also fly to Tiree, landing on the beach!

Coll

www.isleoftiree.com
www.visitcoll.co.uk

COLL
by Joe

Sail to Coll from Oban. In the winter, the CalMac Ferry goes to Coll on a Tuesday, Thursday, Saturday and Sunday. In summer there's a ferry every day and two on a Thursday so you can go on a day trip to Coll from Oban. On a Thursday the boat also goes to Barra.

What are ye going tae find on tiny Coll?
Shops? No.
Street lights? No.
Tourist information? No.
Accommodation? Not much.
Public transport? No.
Roads? Well, aye, but they're pretty rough.
Mobile phone coverage? No.
Peace and quiet? Oh aye.
Tranquillity? Definitely.
Beauty? By the bucket load.
Nature? Plenty o' that.

You can properly get away from it all on Coll. Wi a faimily o' eleven ye don't get much o' chance for peace an' quiet, privacy and time tae yersel. Coll was right up ma street for a day trip. I took a book, a packed lunch, my hiking gear, a camera and ma Ordnance Survey map (Explorer Map 372, Coll and Tiree). Peace!

THE SMALL ISLES

You can sail to the Small Isles from the port of Mallaig. Always check the CalMac website for details.

There's an informative community paper for Mallaig, Morar, Arisaig, Lochailort, Glenfinnan Glenuig, Knoydart and the Small Isles: www.westword.org.uk

The coast around the Small Isles offers ideal opportunities for whale, dolphin and seal watching. Minke whales are a regular feature in the waters between July and September. Dolphins of several species, and particularly porpoises, are also seen on a regular basis. You'll probably see seals around the islands too.

MUCK

Tiny but beautiful Muck is only two miles long by one mile wide and home to about 38 people. Muck is very secluded and has only recently been powered by a community-owned wind farm.

Gallanach Bay provides a beautiful safe harbour for water sports. And you can stay in a yurt (www.isleofmuck.com)!

EIGG

In 1997, Eigg became the first Scottish community to buy their own island. There is a growing population presently around 80 people.

You can get the ferry from Mallaig to Eigg – there's only one ferry a day so there can be no day trippers but it's a beautiful island for a quiet retreat.

Laig Beach and the Singing Sands

On the north-west side of the island the Singing Sands are well named. The grains of sand sort of squeak as you scuff your feet over them. It's a beautiful spot to paddle and take in the stunning view.

The Lodge and Gardens

This neo-colonial building stands in the woods 15 minutes above the pier surrounded by exotic plants. There are carved Celtic stones at the entrance to the building. The gardens are open to the public.

Feis Eige

A festival of traditional music and culture taking place in July (www.isleofeigg.net/activities/feis/feis.htm, 01687 4824 10 or write to Cuagach, Isle of Eigg , PH42 4RL)

RUM

Rum is a very special place. Only recently it has become much more accessible by ferry so it would be daft not to visit.

Spot wild goats, otters, red throated divers, sea eagles, Rum ponies and many red deer!

Accommodation

Kinloch Castle – an astounding building to visit, and you can stay there! In the Youth Hostel. Book early and ask for a four poster! There have been a lot of renovations happening there though, so phone or email to see if they're finished (01687 462037, kinlochcastle@snh.gov.uk).

You can camp too but watch out for lots of midges!

There are also two bothies, at Dibidal and Guirdal, run by the Mountain Bothy Association. Follow the bothy code!

CANNA

A tiny place (the island is only five miles by one mile in area) with a tiny community (fourteen permanent residents on Canna including seven children) but with a lot of heart.

It has a bird sanctuary and nine scheduled monuments, with links to the Neolithic, Columban and Viking eras.

Surprisingly, there's a restaurant on Canna, called Gille Brighde – which means Oystercatcher.

If you are looking for seclusion and beautiful views Canna is the place. Day tripping is not possible and there are no shops.

Accommodation

The island has B & B accommodation at Tighard Guest House (01687 462474) and at The New House (01687 462175), a bunkhouse and self-catering cottages (www.nts.org.uk/Holidays), or why not hire a great big tent (01687 460166, www.cannafolk.co.uk)?

The Outer Hebrides

BENBECULA, NORTH UIST AND SOUTH UIST
By Paw

Bonnie Prince Charlie landed in BENBECULA (is there ony Scottish island he didnae hide on?) and sailed tae Skye wi' Flora Macdonald in 1746. This lovely island is a guid wee spot for loch fishing, sea angling an' relaxing. It's connected by causeways to the Uists so it's a guid base for visiting the Uists. I had a holiday here when I wis a boy and me Granpaw did plenty o' fishing a' ower these islands. Me and him went back there recently for an auld boys' weekend. Brought back a lot o' memories.

Another way to get to the Uists is tae head for SOUTH UIST on the ferry frae Oban or Barra. South Uist has Highland Games in July with plenty o' family events, the famous tug-of-war and a dance at night. But all summer there is plenty going on, especially if you like live music and ceilidhs. There are a lot o' talented musicians livin' in these pairts.

You can get the Cal Mac ferry tae NORTH UIST frae Uig on Skye or Leverburgh on Harris. Or get there frae South Uist ower the causeways. North Uist has its share o' bonny beaches, beautiful "machair" land (that's a Gaelic word for a fertile, grassy plain) and there's thoosands o' wee lochs and rolling moors too and plenty o' wildlife and rare birds for twitchers like oor Horace.

A couple of nearby smaller islands are worth visiting: ye can get tae the ISLE OF VALLAY at low tide (there's a spooky abandoned mansion there) and Prince Charles's favourite island BERNERAY is easy tae reach by causeway. You can also get the ferry there frae Harris.

An' it's no' just wildlife – there's an arts centre in Lochmaddy ca'ed TAIGH CHEARSABHAGH. There's films, poetry readings, an' a' that stuff for your arty types. Me, I enjoyed a nice cuppa in the café and the braw view across the Lochmaddy Lagoons tae Harris.

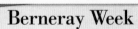

A BEACH IN NORTH UIST

A GREAT SPOT FOR A PICNIC

Berneray Week

Berneray Week is held in July in the Community Hall of this tiny island, just two miles by three, and with a population of around 130. Berneray is connected to the Uists and Benbecula by a causeway. Its week-long summer festival of activities has included Gaelic songs, local food, traditional music, ceilidhs, sports activities for children, Gaelic lessons, a 10k race, boat trips, a treasure hunt, kite flying and a beach barbecue! It's very much a community festival but visitors are very welcome to this friendly island!

www.isleofberneray.com.
Berneray Development Group,
The Nurse's Cottage, Tel: 01876 525001

i

www.visit-uist.co.uk

Taigh-chearsabhagh Arts Centre
taigh-chearsabhagh.org
01876 500293 Reception,
Post Office & Shop
Tel: 01876 500240 (Office)
Tel: 01876 500450 (Café)

Barra and Vatersay

THE BARRA FACTS
by Paw Broon

Did ye ken ...?

- The islands of Barra and Vatersay in the Western Isles were gifted to public ownership by the landowner Iain MacNeil in 2004.
- In 2001, MacNeil had also donated the ancestral family seat, Kisimul Castle on Barra, to the nation for a bottle of whisky and £1 a year! That's my kind o' present!
- Someone fae Barra is cried a Barrach.
- The old film "Whisky Galore" was filmed there.
- Barra is an excellent place for cycling, Barra's main road loops twelve miles around the island.
- It's got a 9-hole golf course.
- There's a 13-mile "Barrathon" in July.

www.isleofbarra.com

www.kilda.org

Vatersay

VATERSAY – linked to Barra by a causeway – has about 100 inhabitants and is also the name of the only village on the island.

Vatersay has some rare wildlife – look for the corncrake and Bonnie Prince Charlie's flowers. There are also the ruins of an Iron Age Fort. The abandoned village of Eorasdail is a very interesting visit and the Annie Jane memorial of 1853 is a reminder of how the islands can suffer from the raging storms that surround them. Three hundred and fifty crew died and are buried on Vatersay.

Getting to Barra and Vatersay

A CalMac vehicle ferry sails from Oban on the mainland and from Lochboisdale on South Uist. On a Thursday in summer you can get there from Tiree. Getting to Barra can sometimes be a challenge! Check the CalMac website for details.

22 *The Scots Magazine*

St Kilda

By Wendy Paine-Archer

ST KILDA didn't seem uninhabited to me – I'm not just talking about the conservation workers and MoD staff that live there – there seemed to be ghosts everywhere of a sad but remarkable past.

There's no easy way of getting to remote St Kilda. I went on an organised cruise to this beautiful UNESCO World Heritage site from Harris, which over several days took in the more remote sights of the Hebrides, and we dropped anchor at Village Bay for an overnight to admire flora, fauna and archeology.

The history of remote St Kilda – 41 miles west of Benbecula – is fascinating. There never was a person called Saint Kilda. No one knows for sure, but the name could be a distortion of Norse *sunt kelda* ("sweet wellwater") or from the Norse word *skildir*, meaning "shields". The St Kildans were always very isolated, cut off by distance, treacherous sea conditions and at the mercy of the weather.

The islanders would communicate with the rest of the world by lighting a bonfire on the summit of Conachair to attract the attention of passing boats. Or there was the "St Kilda mailboat": a message attached to a piece of wood, attached to a bladder of sheepskin. It was launched when the wind came from the north-west and left to fate whether it was delivered.

Boats brought trade, religion and tourism to St Kilda; but all took their toll on island life. The islanders adopted a very strict religious observance – and life was hard under this regime. Tourism brought new diseases that St Kildan's had never encountered before. Increased contact with the rest of the world brought a new money-based economy, but a deterioration of the islanders' self-reliance.

The population lost old skills and knowledge, and started to leave, until, in the 1920s, there were hardly any young men left on the island. Crops failed and a 'flu epidemic killed four of the few remaining young men. It was time to go. The entire population was evacuated in 1930.

The ghostly, ruined main street is now tended to and preserved by conservationists who live on the island. I could picture this harsh but beautiful spot occupied and full of life.

THE VATERSAY BOYS GIVE IT LALDY

Barra Fest
Tel: 01871 810088
feisbharraigh@googlemail.com
www.barrafest.co.uk

www.thevatersayboys.com

BARRA FEST
By Joe

Me and Hen saw The Vatersay Boys play at the Barras – Glasgow Barrowlands. It was a rerr night. We heard aboot them fae my pal Angus John who originally comes fae Barra – no' the Glasgow Barras, but the island. Angus John asked if we wanted to come and stay wi his faimily on Barra in the summer for the Barra Fest music festival and sample a bit mair of o' island music. We couldnae say no (his bonnie wee sister Katie micht hae had something tae dae wi that tae). We went from Oban to the Uists and stayed there a night – lovely place – and from there went to Barra.

BARRA FEST usually happens on the last Friday and Saturday of July. The group running it is a charity called Feis Bharraigh and all the workers at the festival are local volunteers. You can expect Celtic rock, folk music, local hospitality, a dram or twa and a great atmosphere. It's held in a marquee just five minutes ootside Castle Bay. It's a locally-run festival for the folk of Barra but we were made more than welcome and had a rerr time.

WIND-POWERED FUN

Barra Power Kiting,
HS9 5XN
www.barrapowerkiting.co.uk
Tel: 01871 810950

Barra Power Kiting

Why not use Barra's naturally windy weather to your advantage and try power kiting? Learn how to fly a kite and let wind power transport you along the beautiful secluded beach by buggy or board.

Lewis and Harris

ⓘ Hebridean Celtic Festival.
Three days in July.
Location: Several venues, Stornoway, Isle of Lewis
www.hebceltfest.com
Accommodation: 01851 703088

Lewis and Harris

You need three or four days to properly appreciate Lewis and Harris.

Lewis is the largest island of the Western Isles or Outer Hebrides. It's main town is Stornoway and it's a lively, vibrant place with a great music scene and all sorts of events to keep you amused an entertained. It regularly plays host to the **Royal National Mod.**

Sundays are special on Lewis. There's a strong religious influence on the island from the Presbyterian Free Church. There's a limited Sunday ferry service from Ullapool, and some of the larger pubs and hotels in Stornoway might be open, but most things are closed on Sunday. This will make your stay on Lewis on a Sunday quite a contrast with the commercial bustle of the mainland.

Sunday is then the perfect day to take things slowly. Maybe visit the **Calanais (or Callanish) Standing Stones** or the beautiful beaches. Use the quiet Lewis Sunday to take things down a gear and appreciate the stunning scenery. Hiring a car is probably a good idea as there is no public transport on Sunday.

A highlight of the summer on Lewis is definitely the **Hebridean Celtic Festival**, with a world-famous line up and great atmosphere. Book your accommodation early – this festival is popular!

The **Isle of Harris** is joined to the Isle of Lewis, and Tarbert is its main port. You can get there by ferry from Uig on Skye or from Berneray in North Uist or by car from Lewis. The Isle of Harris has some of the cleanest most beautiful beaches in Europe. It has a 9-hole golf course. Harris is also known for Harris tweed, but this is mostly now made in Lewis.

www.visithebrides.com
www.hiddenlewis.org.uk
www.isle-of-lewis.com
www.stornoway-lewis.co.uk
www.acgmod.org

HARRIS IS A MORE
MOUNTAINOUS AREA THAN LEWI

To get to Lewis you catch the CalMac ferry from ULLAPOOL on the mainland. Why not check out this great arts and crafts town while you are there:

www.ullapool.co.uk
www.loopallu.co.uk
www.ullapoolbookfestival.co.uk
www.ullapoolguitarfestival.com

(i) Calanais Standing Stones, HS2 9DY
Tel: 01851 621422
www.historic-scotland.gov.uk/places

The Scots Magazine 43

Calanais, Lewis

CALANAIS comprises a late Neolithic stone ring and associated lines of standing stones. Excavations have revealed that the ring was set up between 2900 and 2600 BC, making it earlier than the main circle at Stonehenge. It has a unique arrangement, with lines of stones radiating in four directions from the ring. The layout of the site, along with many others across the British Isles, appears to have an association with astronomical events, the precise nature of which is unknown.

Between 1000 BC and 500 BC, the stones were covered by peat, and it was not until 1857, when the peat was cut, that their true height was once again revealed. In the landscape around the ring are at least 11 other stone circles and settings that hint at how important the area was to prehistoric peoples The existence of Bronze Age monuments in the area imply that Calanais remained an active focus for prehistoric religious activity for at least 1500 years.

14 *Scotland's History*

The Blackhouse, Arnol, Lewis

Not prehistoric, but near Calanais, and a unique survivor of an old way of life. For hundreds of years it was the custom in Lewis for man and beast to be housed under the same roof. This thatched blackhouse, built around 1880, is the sole representative of a way of life once so common but now altogether gone. In a blackhouse, animals and people lived in the same building and there was no chimney. Having animals 'living in' had its advantages. It made the house warmer and meant fewer buildings were needed. The smoke rising from the peat fire into the roof also had hidden benefits. It killed bugs, and the smoke-laden thatch made excellent fertiliser for the fields.

The blackhouse has a living room, a bedroom, a byre for the animals and a barn. The peat fire in the centre of the living room was the centre of family life and was never allowed to go out.

Arnol Blackhouse, HS2 9DB.
Tel: 01851 710395
www.historic-scotland.gov.uk

Orkney

ORKNEY

by Horace

There is a lot to see and do in Orkney. I actually went on a day trip there while I was staying wi' Auntie Betty in Inverness, but I only saw a tiny bit o' whit there is to see. It would be guid to stay for a fortnight. I don't hae space to list a' the archaeological sites in Orkney. It's a place where you can see history laid bare on the land. The Italian Chapel on Lamb Holm shows its wartime history. The Earl's Palaces in Birsay and Kirkwall are whit's left o' the time when the Stewarts ruled Orkney from 1564 to 1615. Kirkwall's St Magnus Cathedral, est. 1137, is fae the time o' of the Norse rule. Pictish carvings and Neolithic standing stones like the Ring of Brodgar an' sic like, show there was life on Orkney earlier than 3000BC! It's a shame it's still a mystery as to whit they mean and wha put them there. The famous Neolithic village at Skara Brae was covered up for thoosands o' years until a big storm uncovered it in 1850. It's amazing. Goodness knows what is still to be discovered!

Orkney – Getting There

Day trips are possible from Inverness (a bus connects with the John O' Groat's Ferries). A day trip might not do it justice though. The www.visitorkney.com website gives a very detailed description of all the things to see on each of the inhabited islands.

You can sail there from Aberdeen (it takes 6 hours) and Scrabster (in Thurso Bay in Caithness and the ferry takes 90 mins), Gills Bay (three miles west of John O' Groats 1hr) or John O' Groats in Caithness (40 mins).

NorthLink Ferries provide the service from Aberdeen (3 or 4 sailings per week depending on season) and Scrabster (3 or 4 sailings per day depending on season).

Pentland Ferries have 3 or 4 sailings per day (depending on season) from Gills Bay and St. Margaret's Hope.

John O' Groats Ferries provides a May – September passenger only service to Burwick on South Ronaldsay.

You can fly there from Glasgow, Edinburgh, Aberdeen, Inverness and Sumburgh.

Orkney Ferries operate between the islands.

www.jogferry.co.uk
Tel: 01955 611 353
www.northlinkferries.co.uk
Tel: 0845 6000 449
www.pentlandferries.co.uk
Tel: 01856 831 226
www.orkneyferries.co.uk
Tel: 01856 872044

There are 70 islands making up the islands of Orkney. Mainland Orkney is home to most of the population (numbering around 20,000). In the north you have north islands of Shapinsay, Gairsay, Stronsay, Wyre, Rousay, Egilsay, Eday, Sanday, Westray, Papa Westray and North Ronaldsay; and the south islands of Graemsay, Hoy, Burray, Flotta and South Ronaldsay are also populated. Burray and South Ronaldsay are connected to mainland Orkney by a causeway. Orkney's capital is Kirkwall. Kirkwall has the magnificent St Magnus Cathedral, founded by Earl Rognvald Kolson in 1137. Beautiful Stromness is its second biggest town.

The Italian Chapel, Lamb Holm

Stromness

Things to do in Orkney (A shorter list would be things you can't do!)

walking
cycling
fishing
sailing
climbing
kayacking
diving
golf
windsurfing
kite surfing
birdwatching
sightseeing
shopping ...

Orkney Festivals and Events

The Folk Festival – an impressive line up play at concerts, ceilidhs, dances, pub sessions etc over four days – May.
The St Magnus Festival – orchestras, choirs, dance etc. – June.
Stromness Shopping Week – a family-oriented festival with games, competitions, music and dancing – July.
The agricultural shows – a showcase of the best of Orkney farming produce. The County Show is the largest of the shows – early August.
The Orkney International Science Festival – September.

i Birdwatching
RSPB Orkney,
KW16 3AG
Tel: 01856 850176
www.rspb.org.uk

i www.visitorkney.com
Kirkwall Visitor Information, KW15 1GU
Tel: 01856 872856
info@visitorkney.com

Stromness Visitor Information,
KW16 1BH
Tel: 01856 850716
stromness@visitorkney.com

Skara Brae, Orkney

The Neolithic village of Skara Brae was discovered in the winter of 1850. Wild storms ripped the grass from a high dune known as Skara Brae, and exposed the best-preserved Neolithic village in northern Europe. Skara Brae was inhabited before the Egyptian pyramids were built, and flourished for centuries before construction began at Stonehenge. It is some 5,000 years old. The structures of this semi-subterranean village survive in amazingly impressive condition.

All the houses are well-built of closely-fitting flat stone slabs. They were set into large mounds of household refuse and linked by covered passages. Each house comprised a single room with 'fitted' stone furniture made up of a dresser, where prized objects were probably stored and displayed, two box-beds, a centrally placed hearth and small tanks set into the floor, perhaps for preparing fish bait.

Many items have been excavated, including gaming dice, hand tools, pottery and jewellery. Most remarkable are the richly carved stone objects, perhaps used in religious rituals. The villagers were farmers, hunters and fishermen and, as no weapons have been found, they probably lived a peaceful life until the village was abandoned around 2500 BC. No one knows why. Some argue that it was because a huge sandstorm engulfed their houses, others that its decline was more gradual.

i
ara Brae, KW16 3LR.
.: 01856 841815
w.historic-scotland.gov.uk/
ces

ORKNEY BEACH WITH VIEW OF HOY

EARL'S PALACE IN KIRKWALL

Shetland

SHETLAND – BETWEEN WEATHERS
by Hen Broon

So whit's the weather like in Shetland? Well, "varied" is as good an answer as ony. Ask any Shetlander and they'll tell you that Shetland has plenty o' weather! The time I went it was, well, refreshing shall we say.

Photographers like Joe will find it has braw light, when it's "between weathers", or "atween wadders" to use the local lingo, which is how Shetlanders describe yon days that are clear and mild.

Shetland is on the same latitude as Anchorage in Alaska, St Petersburg and southern Greenland. However, it's a lot milder than you might think thanks to the (slightly) warming effect of the northern end of the Gulf Stream – though that wind can be somethin' else!

There's plenty tae dae in Shetland especially if ye like music but there is one big event that is famous throughout the world. On the last Tuesday o' January every year they haud the largest fire festival in Europe – Lerwick's "UP-HELLY-AA".

Shetland has a Scandinavian heritage – that means Vikings! This is celebrated by the islands' fire festivals. Did ye ken there are umpteen Up-Helly-Aas in Shetland? Lerwick's is the biggest. Women aren't allowed tae tak' part in the torchlit procession in Lerwick, Daphne says this is a right cheek. But they are allowed in the other fire festivals. I was lucky enough tae see the Lerwick ane many years ago. The procession is stunning – the torches look like a river of fire. The Viking costumes are amazing. The beards impressive! And the burning of the Viking Galley – help ma boab! The torches are thrown into the galley tae set it alight and the Guizers (that's the fellas who are a' dressed up) sing "The Norseman's Home".

The Norseman's Home
(Traditional song)

The Norseman's home in days gone
Was on the rolling sea,
And there his pennon did defy
The foe of Normandy.
Then let us ne'er forget the race,
Who bravely fought and died,
Who never filled a craven's grave,
But ruled the foaming tide.
The noble spirits, bold and free
Too narrow was their land,
They roved the wide expansive sea
And quelled the Norman band.
Then let us all in harmony,
Give honour to the brave
The noble, hardy, northern men,
Who ruled the stormy wave.

Lerwick Up Helly Aa, the largest of the islands' fire festivals – last Tuesday of January.

Shetland Folk Festival, four days, beginning of May.

Bergen – Shetland Race – End May.

The Shetland Nature Festival – July.

Fiddle Frenzy – August.

Shetland Blues Festival – September.

Sailing

Each year in May over 50 Norwegian yachts arrive to compete in the Shetland-Bergen Race and participants in the Annual Round-Britain Yacht Race enjoy a short rest in Shetland before sailing south again. In addition, many hundreds of pleasure craft from all over the world visit Shetland each year.

Peerie Willie Guitar Festival – September.

Shetland Accordion and Fiddle Festival – October

Food Festival – November.

www.uphellyaa.org
www.shetlandfolkfestival.com
http://shetland-race.no/
www.shetlandnaturefestival.co.uk
www.shetlandfiddlefrenzy.com

A VIKING LONGBOAT VISITS LERWICK

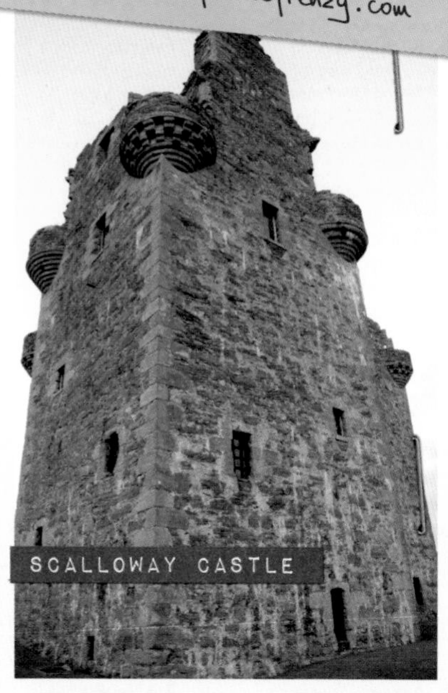

SCALLOWAY CASTLE

SAILING BOATS IN LERWICK

www.shetlandtourism.com
visit.shetland.org
www.shetlandblues.info
www.shetlandfoodfestival.co.uk
www.shetlandaccordionandfiddle.com

PICTURE CREDITS

The Broons Comic Strips copyright © 2011 DC Thomson & Co Ltd
Design and artwork by Hugo Breingan with Waverley books
"Wind-powered Fun", page 179 by Matthew Scott.

Photographic Credits:

• **Adam Jones**: Barra Power Kiting 178. • **Adrian T Jones/Shutterstock**: Anstruther 133. • **Alex Smith/Cairngorm Reindeer Centre**: reindeer 92. • **Alf Thomas/Shutterstock**: Portnahaven 161. • **Allen Furmanski/Shutterstock**: Jarlshof 84. • **Anne Ward**: Fish tea 140, top hat 140, Tunnocks 140, Zavaroni's 140, Rothesay Pavilion 150, Easdale Ferry sign 170, stone skimming sign 170, stones 170. • **Awe Inspiring Images/Shutterstock**: Bowmore Church 161. • **Ben Mullay**: Up Helly Aa 184. • **Bermrunner/Shutterstock**: Forth Road Bridge 20. • **Bill McKelvie/E Abraham**: Forfar Bridie montage 140. • **Bill McKelvie/ Shutterstock**: Greenock 40, Bothwell 122, Castle Campbell 122, Hermitage 122, Wallace Monument 126, Dunadd Fort 144. • **Bill Spiers/Shutterstock**: Lochgoilhead 150. • **BMCL/Shutterstock**: Greyfriars Bobby 10. • **Bowmore Single Malt Whisky**: visitor centre 101. • **Brendan Howard/Shutterstock**: Inverewe Garden 114. • **Brian A Jackson/Shutterstock**: Auld Man of Storr 166. • **Burn Stewart Distillers**: Tobermory Distillery 163. • **c./Shutterstock**: Canongate Kirk 13, Glasgow Cathedral 49. • **Caledonian MacBrayne**: ferry and map 147. • **ceolcholasa@yahoo.co.uk**: Ceol Cholasa 172, 173. • **Chad Bontrager/Shutterstock**: Dryburgh Abbey 29. • **Chasmac/Shutterstock**: Chatelherault 56. • **Chivas Brothers**: Aberlour Bottle 96. • **Chris Hawker/ Shutterstock**: Oban 65. • **Chris Jenner/Shutterstock**: Royal Yacht Britannia photo 18. • **Christophe Jossic/Shutterstock**: Dancer at Bathgate games 108. • **Christy Nicholas/Shutterstock**: Italian Chapel Orkney 182, Stromness Orkney 182. • **Collpicto/Shutterstock**: Duthie Park 50. • **Colonsay Brewery**: Colonsay IPA 172. • **Colonsay Festival of Spring**: leaflet 172. • **Corel**: Melrose Abbey 119, Dunvegan Castle 168, Calanais 181. • **Corrie Cook**: puff pastry bridie 140. • **Cream o' Galloway**: 32. • **Culture and Sport Glasgow (Museums)**: Riverside Museum 49. • **DC Thomson & Co Ltd**: Brodick postcard 152, Lochranza Castle 153, b/w cannon picture 8, pipers 25, Mackintosh furniture, tea things 47, Willow Tearoom 52, pipers 66, piper 87, whisky selection 95, Bruichladdich 102, Desperate Dan 116, rhino 130, postcard St Andrews 136, lifeguard 137, Tobermory 163, Iona 164, Iona Abbey 164, Cuillins 166, Cuillins 168, Ben Nevis and Fort William 68, flower 50, mapping 72, 73, Nessie 76, Black Watch 81, osprey 82, Dundee Botanical Garden 50, lily pads 50, Laphraoig 100, Isle of Arran distillery 154, Ardbeg 100. • **David Harding/Shutterstock**: tent 88, **David Hughes/Shutterstock**: Loch Fyne 63, **David Woods/ Shutterstock**: Strathisla 96, science centre 49, Peak of Buachaille Etive 66, Mount Stuart 150. • **Deep Sea World**: leaflet 20. • **Diageo**: Cardhu 96, Lagavulin pagodas 100, Lagavulin stills 101, Caol Ila 102, Oban 103, Talisker 103. • **Dianne Godden/Shutterstock**: Beach in North Uist 177. • **Domhnall Dods/ Shutterstock**: Loch Faskally 112, Pipes and drums 120. • **Donald Melville**: skimming group 170. • **Duirnish Light/ Shutterstock**: Scottish Parliament debating chamber 15. • **Dundee Women's Trail**: leaflet 116. • **Eleanor Abraham**: bere bannock 140, butteries 140, Scotch pancakes 140, square sausage 140, bluebells 142, Kintyre way marker 144, scones 144, Deer Hill 144. • **Eamonn McGoldrick/Sustrans**: Forth Rail Bridge 139. • **Edeltraud/Shutterstock**: cartoon 134. • **Edinburgh City of Literature**: leaflet 18. • **Edinburgh International Festival**: Tattoo program 1966 8, leaflet 120. • **elesuc/Shutterstock**: Inveraray Castle 63. • **Elnur/Shutterstock**: Edinburgh pipers 108. • **Ewan Chesser/Shutterstock**: seal 22, elephant 130, giraffe 130, lemur 130. • **Feis Bharraigh**: Band at Barra Fest 178, Vatersay Boys 178. • **Gail Johnson/Shutterstock**: Floors Castle 29, Arnol Black House, lewis 181. • **Glasgow School of Art**: School of Art leaflet 52. • **Gordon and MacPhail**: Benromach 98. • **Gordon McCreath**: Killie pie 140. • **Hallam Creations/Shutterstock**: Drummond Garden 114. • **Heartland/ Shutterstock**: Holyrood 16, Culloden Memorial Cairn 81. • **Henk Bentlage/Shutterstock**: Gannet 27, **Historic Scotland**: Edinburgh Castle 8, 78, **Hugo Breingan**: Edinburgh Tour bus 14, Preston Mill 42, Squirrel 56, Peregrine falcon 82, Puffin 82, Snowy Owl 82, Golden eagle carc 87, Distilleries postcard elements 94, Puffin 164. • **Iain Frazer/Shutterstock**: Loch Ness at Fort Augustus 76, Eigg and Rum from Arisaig 176. • **Iain Macilwain, www.broombankphotography.com**: Glengyle 99, Springbank 99. • **Iain McGillivray/Shutterstock**: Grey Mare's Tail 60. • **Iain R Spink/Bill Robertson**: Arbroath Smokies 140. • **Ian D Walker/Shutterstock**: book signing/Edinburgh Festival 120. • **Inveraray Jail**: leaflet 63. • **Isle of Arran Distillers**: 154. • **Isle of Arran Foods**: 154. • **Isle of Gigha Heritage Trust**: gardens 156, Gigha turbines 156, View north from Creag Bhan 156. • **Jaime Pharr/ Shutterstock**: Peat Oven 102, Paps of Jura 158. • **Jean Morrison/Shutterstock**: Big Wheel M&D's 56, John Knox's house 12, Forth Rail Bridge Pic 20, Falkland Palace 133. • **Jeff Banke/Shutterstock**: Urquhart Castle 79. • **jennyt/Shutterstock**: Canna Cliffs 176. • **Joe Gough/Shutterstock**: St Kilda 178, : Harris 180. • **John A Cameron/Shutterstock**: Morar Panorama 74. • **John Braid/Shutterstock**: Falls of Bruar 111. • **John Carter/ Dialogue Marketing**: Tiree 174, Tiree Wave Classic 174. • **John Waller/Shutterstock**: Maid of the Loch 58, Falls of Clyde 60. • **Jonathan Noden-Wilkinson/Shutterstock**: Coll 175. • **Jule_Berlin/Shutterstock**: Beach with view of Hoy 183, Earl's Palace Kirkwall 183. • **Julie T Photography/Shutterstock**: Dunure Castle 34. • **Kato Inowe/ Shutterstock**: Osprey catching fish 82. • **Keith Brame/Sustrans**: Pic 1 138. • **Kilchoman Distillery**: Kilchoman cask 101. • **Kinnaird Head lighthouse museum**: Kinnaird Head Lighthouse 30. • **Kristofer Keane/Shutterstock**: Eilean Donan 124. • **Lance Bellers/Shutterstock**: Culloden Memorial Cairn detail 81. • **Liz Small**: New Lanark 42, Kelvingrove park 47, Lord Kelvin 47. • **Luca Grandinetti/Shutterstock**: Strathpeffer pipe band 108. • **Lucid PR**: Hebridean Celtic Festival, Stornoway 180. • **Luke Hejtman/Shutterstock**: Skara Brae 183. • **Marianna Raszkowska/Shutterstock**: Ailsa Course Turnbury 34. • **Mark Mechan**: West Sands 134, tablet 140. • **Matt Hart/Shutterstock**: Port Ellen Lighthouse 161. • **Matthew Scott**: Barra Power Kiting art 179. • **Monkey Business Images/Shutterstock** Cullen Skink 140. • **Morag Fleming/Shutterstock**: Edinburgh Tattoo 120, **Mountain Bothy Association, and Neil Stewart**: Mark Cottage Bothy 90, **Museum of Rural Life**: Museum of Rural Life 44, West Kittochside Farm 44. • **National Trust for Scotland**: bookmarks 2, 3, Smails press 28. • **Nelson Monument**: leaflet 20. • **Nigel Paul Monckton/Shutterstock**: Loch Lomond 58, : Tent 70. • **Paul Butchard/Shutterstock**: Huntly 122, : Linlithgow 122. • **Paul Macrae**: Rothesay castle 150. • **Penny Grearson**: Bellochantuy 144. • **Peter Guess/Shutterstock**: Solway Firth 32. • **postcards**: Mallaig harbour 72, Helensburgh 73, Aberdeen 106, Brig o doon 38, Holyrood 15. • **Pseudolongino/Shutterstock**: Kelvingrove Museum 47. • **Richard M Lee/Shutterstock**: Dundee Cake 140. • **Richard Southall/Shutterstock**: Jura red deer 158. • **Robert Burns Birthplace Museum/National Trust for Scotland**: Museum Map 38. • **Roger Pilkington/Shutterstock**: Scottish Parliament outside 15. • **Roman Kruchuk/Shutterstock**: Northern lights 148. • **Ron Steenvoorden, www.jurainfo.com**: Jura House walled garden 158, sign 158, whirlpool 158. • **Ronald Sumners/Shutterstock**: Stirling Castle 126. • **Royal Highland Show**: food show 25, tractor 25, Royal Highland Show: picnic 25. • **Royal Yacht Britannia**: leaflet 18. • **Rubiphoto/Shutterstock**: Culzean Castle 36,. • **Ruth Black/Shutterstock**: stone 108. • **Ruth Fleming, Mull Magic**: walkers, walking boots 163. • **S Duffet/Shutterstock**: GOMA 54. • **S J Watt/ Shutterstock**: Osprey Centre Aviemore 82. • **S. Cooper Digital/Shutterstock**: Red Kite 32, Young Golden Eagle 82. • **Sander van der Werf/Shutterstock**: Kilchurn Castle 64. • **Scotch Whisky Expericence**: leaflet 10. • **Scott Monument**: leaflet 20. • **Scottish Mining Museum**: leaflet 26. • **Scottish Parliamentary Corporate Body**: Committee Room 16, Garden Lobby 16, MSP Window Seat 16. • **Shutterstock**: view from Ben Nevis 70, Machrie standing stones 153, Brodick castle 155. • **Speyside Cooperage**: workshop 96. • **Stefan Nielsen/Shutterstock**: Royal Highland Show: cows 25. • **Stephen Finn/Shutterstock**: Edinburgh Festival performer 120, Goatfell from Brodick bay 155, The King's Cave 155, Kisimul Castle, Barra 178, **Stephen Meese**: St Conan's Church 65. • **Sternstunden/Shutterstock**: Jacobite steam train on Glenfinnan viaduct 74. • **Stock Cube/Shutterstock**: Heart of Midlothian 10, Viking and Fire 84, Falkirk Wheel 128. • **Susan Macmillan**: West Highland Way marker 142. • **Sustrans**: 138, 139, **Tamara Kulikova/Shutterstock**: Caerlaverock 122. • **Tenement House/National Trust for Scotland**: leaflet 48. • **Terry Kettlewell/Shutterstock**: Ben Nevis, Glen Nevis 70, Falkirk Wheel 128. • **Tim Groot Kerk/ Shutterstock**: Palm House Edinburgh 50. • **Tsw photography/Shutterstock**: Clachan Bridge 170. • **TTphoto/Shutterstock**: Kinloch Castle Rum 176, Sailing boats at Lerwick 185, Viking boat 185. • **Uriel M Ulam/Shutterstock**: Hill house 52, Hunterian Museum 30. • **Valentines**: Isle of Mull 162, Culloden 81, Balmoral 105, Bridge of Dee 105, Crathie Church 105. • **Whyte and Mackay**: Isle of Jura 103. • **Whytock/Shutterstock**: Lismore Lighthouse 157. • **www. signbizzy.co.uk and www.skyeferry.co.uk**: Glenelg Skye Ferry leaflet 166.

MAP OF SCOTLAND

NICOLSON MAPS
2011

KEY TO MAP PAGES

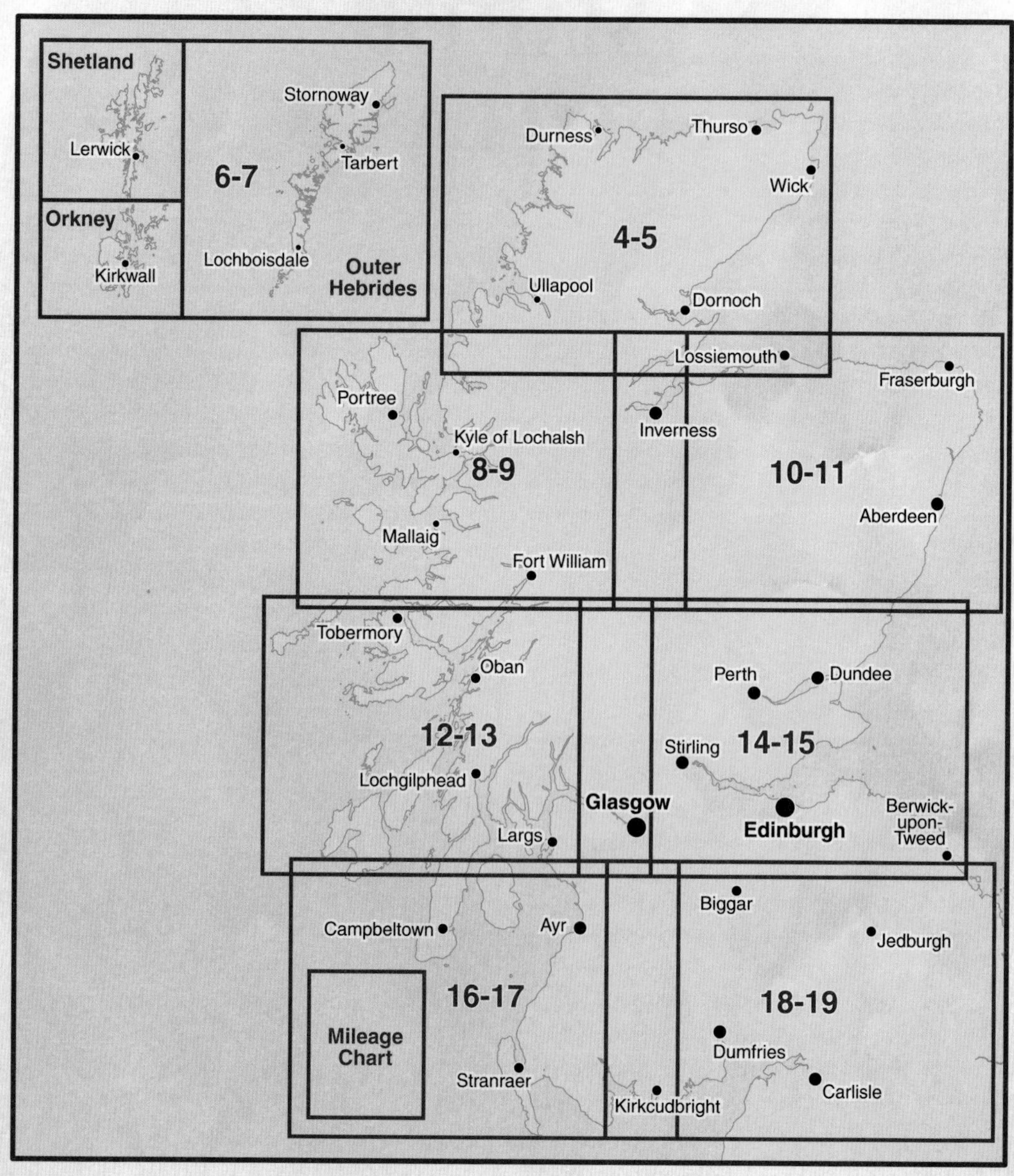

Shetland
Lerwick
Orkney
Kirkwall
6-7
Stornoway
Tarbert
Lochboisdale
Outer Hebrides
4-5
Durness
Thurso
Wick
Ullapool
Dornoch
Lossiemouth
Fraserburgh
Portree
Kyle of Lochalsh
8-9
Mallaig
Fort William
Inverness
10-11
Aberdeen
Tobermory
Oban
12-13
Lochgilphead
Largs
Glasgow
Perth
Dundee
Stirling
14-15
Edinburgh
Berwick-upon-Tweed
Campbeltown
Ayr
Mileage Chart
16-17
Stranraer
Kirkcudbright
Biggar
Jedburgh
18-19
Dumfries
Carlisle

KEY TO MAP SYMBOLS

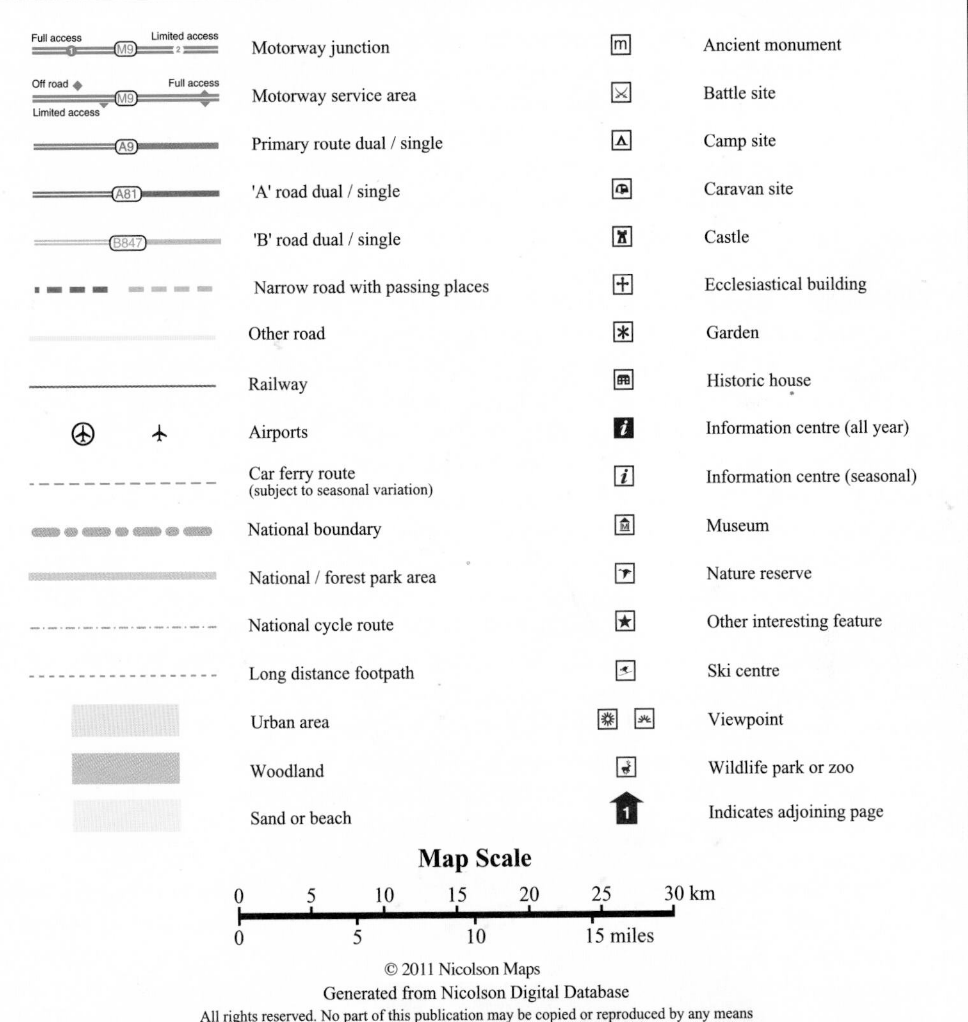

The representation of a road, track, footpath or place of interest does not guarantee a public right of access. Every effort has been made to ensure that this map is correct at the time of printing, the publisher, however, accepts no responsibility for errors or omissions, changes in the detail given or for any loss or expense thereby incurred.

Nicolson Maps, 3 Frazer Street, Largs, Ayrshire, KA30 9HP. Tel: 01475 689242, Fax: 01475 675500
E-mail: sales@nicolsonmaps.com Web: www.nicolsonmaps.com

© Nicolson Maps
E
F
G
16
15
14
13
12
Cape Wrath
Clo Mor
Balnakeil Bay
Faraid Head
Inshore
Durness
Smoo Cave
Achiemore
Sandwood Loch
Balchrick
Oldshoremore
Kinlochbervie
Portnancon
Loch Eriboll
Hope
Eriboll
Polla
Loch Hope
Achriesgill
Loch Inchard
Loch Laxford
Rhiconich
Fanagmore
Handa Island
Laxford Bridge
Scourie
Badcall
Loch Stack
Achfary
Loch More
Kinloch
Alltnacaillich
Dun Dornaigil Broch
Allnabad
Strathmore
Old Man of Stoer
Point of Stoer
Oldany Island
Eddrachillis Bay
Kylestrome
Unapool
Loch Glencoul
Loch Merkland
Loch Fiag
Culkein
Balchladich
Clashnessie
Stoer
Eas a' Chual Aluinn Waterfall
Ardvreck
Achmelvich
Baddidarach
Lochinver
Assynt Visitor Centre
Loch Assynt
Inchnadamph
The Minch
Rubha Coigeach
Inverkirkaig
Enard Bay
Loch Veyatie
Cam Loch
Loch Shin
Reiff
Altandhu
The Achiltibuie Garden
Achiltibuie
Loch Sionascaig
Inverpolly National Nature Reserve
Ledmore
Elphin
Knockan Cliff
Loch Urigill
Loch Lurgainn
Summer Islands
Priest Island
Culnacraig
Drumrunie
Cassley
Cassley Waterfall
Oykel
Rosehall
Oykel Bridge
Doune
Altass
Achnahanat
Isle Martin
Ardmair
Greenstone Point
Opinan
Gruinard Bay
Achgarve
Badluarach
Little Loch Broom
Loch Broom
Ullapool
Mellon Charles
Laide
Coast
Badcaul
Blarnalearoch
Leckmelm
Croick Church
Croick
Cove
Aultbea
Melvaig
Midtown
Loch Ewe
Dundonnell
Letters
Lael Forest Garden
Strathcarron
Carron
Inverewe
Tournaig
Dundonnell House
Inverlael
North Erradale
Poolewe
Fionn Loch
Loch na Sealga
Big Sand
Gairloch
Longa Island
Gair Loch
Loch Maree
Corrieshalloch Gorge
Braemore Junction
Loch Vaich
Loch Glascarnoch
East
Port Henderson
Kerrysdale
Lochan Fada
Loch Glass
Redpoint
Talladale
Wester Ross
Aultroy Visitor Centre
Beinn Eighe Nature Reserve
Kinlochewe
Loch Fannich
9
Achanalt
Grudie
Garve
A838
A894
B801
B869
A837
A835
A832
B8021
B8057
B8056

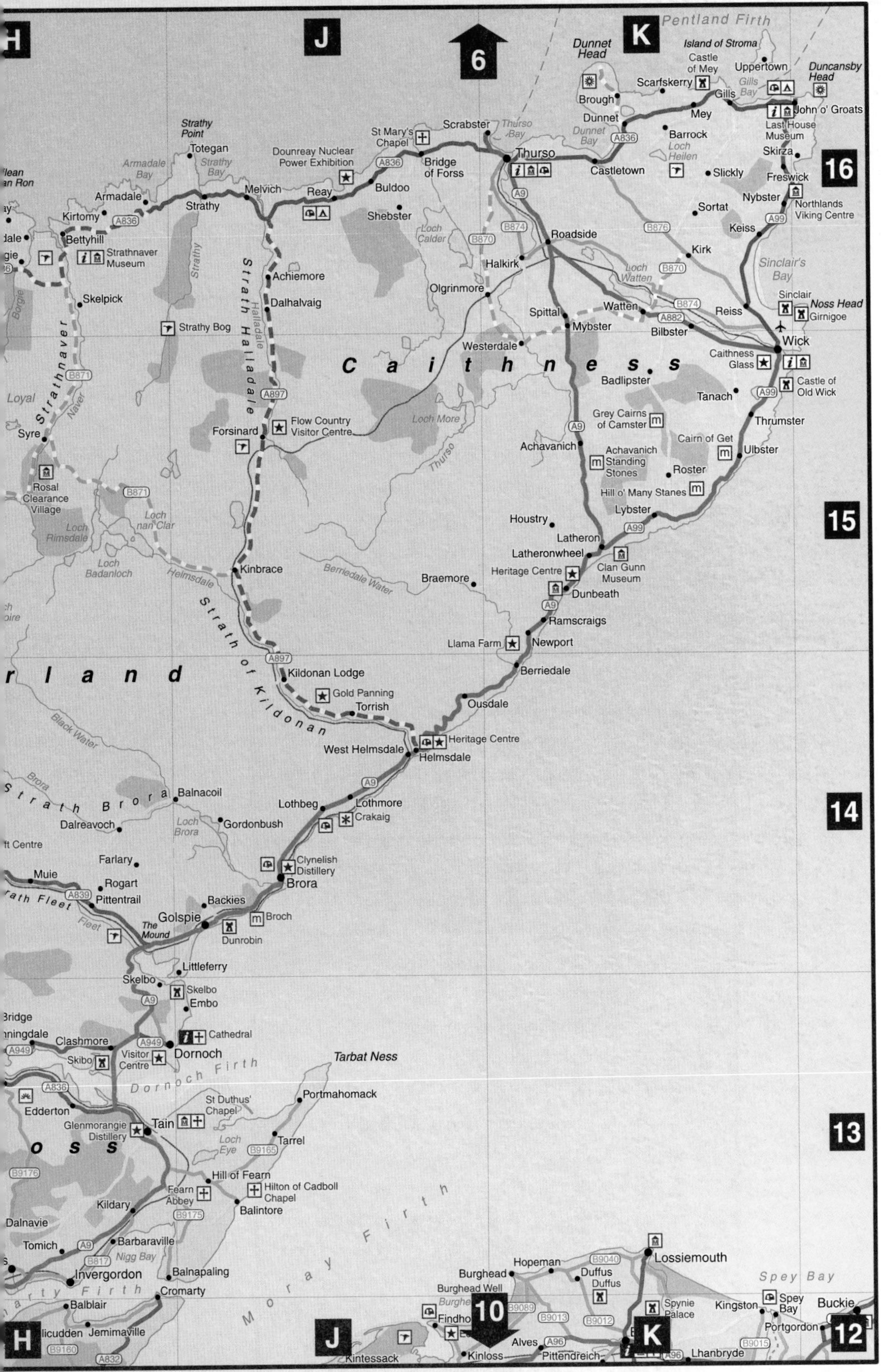

H
J
6
K
Pentland Firth
Dunnet Head
Island of Stroma
Castle of Mey
Uppertown
Duncansby Head
Scarfskerry
Gills
Gills Bay
Brough
John o' Groats
Dunnet
Mey
Last House Museum
Strathy Point
Scrabster
Thurso Bay
Dunnet Bay
Barrock
Totegan
St Mary's Chapel
A836
Loch Heilen
Skirza
Dounreay Nuclear Power Exhibition
Thurso
Castletown
Slickly
16
Armadale Bay
Strathy Bay
Bridge of Forss
Freswick
A836
Melvich
Buldoo
Reay
A9
Nybster
Armadale
Strathy
Sortat
Northlands Viking Centre
Kirtomy
A836
Shebster
A99
Loch Calder
B874
B876
Keiss
Bettyhill
Roadside
Strathnaver Museum
B870
Halkirk
Kirk
Sinclair's Bay
Loch Watten
B870
Achiemore
Olgrinmore
Skelpick
Dalhalvaig
Sinclair
Noss Head
Girnigoe
B874
Reiss
Spittal
Watten
A882
Strathy Bog
Mybster
Bilbster
Strath Halladale
Strathnaver
Naver
Westerdale
Wick
Caithness Glass
Caithness
Badlipster
Castle of Old Wick
B871
Tanach
A897
A99
Loyal
Flow Country Visitor Centre
Loch More
Grey Cairns of Camster
Thrumster
Forsinard
Syre
A9
Cairn of Get
Thurso
Achavanich
Achavanich Standing Stones
Ulbster
Roster
Rosal Clearance Village
B871
Hill o' Many Stanes
Loch nan Clar
Lybster
Houstry
15
Loch Rimsdale
A99
Latheron
Latheronwheel
Clan Gunn Museum
Loch Badanloch
Helmsdale
Kinbrace
Berriedale Water
Braemore
Heritage Centre
Dunbeath
A9
Strath of Kildonan
Ramscraigs
Llama Farm
Newport
A897
Kildonan Lodge
Berriedale
Gold Panning
Torrish
Ousdale
Black Water
Heritage Centre
West Helmsdale
Helmsdale
Brora
A9
Strath Brora
Balnacoil
Lothbeg
Lothmore
Crakaig
14
Dalreavoch
Loch Brora
Gordonbush
Farlary
Clynelish Distillery
Muie
Rogart
Brora
A839
Pittentrail
Backies
Golspie
Broch
Strath Fleet
Fleet
The Mound
Dunrobin
Littleferry
Skelbo
Skelbo
A9
Embo
Cathedral
Clashmore
A949
Dornoch
Visitor Centre
Skibo
Tarbat Ness
Dornoch Firth
A836
Portmahomack
Edderton
St Duthus' Chapel
Glenmorangie Distillery
Tain
13
Tarrel
Loch Eye
B9165
B9176
Hill of Fearn
Fearn Abbey
Hilton of Cadboll Chapel
Kildary
B9175
Balintore
Moray Firth
Dalnavie
Barbaraville
Tomich
A9
Nigg Bay
B817
Lossiemouth
Hopeman
B9040
Burghead
Duffus
Duffus
Spey Bay
Invergordon
Balnapaling
Burghead Well
Cromarty Firth
Cromarty
10
Spynie Palace
Kingston
Spey Bay
Buckie
Balblair
B9089
B9013
B9012
Portgordon
Jemimaville
Findhorn
B9015
12
H
J
K
B9160
A832
Kintessack
Kinloss
Alves
A96
Pittendreich
A96
Lhanbryde

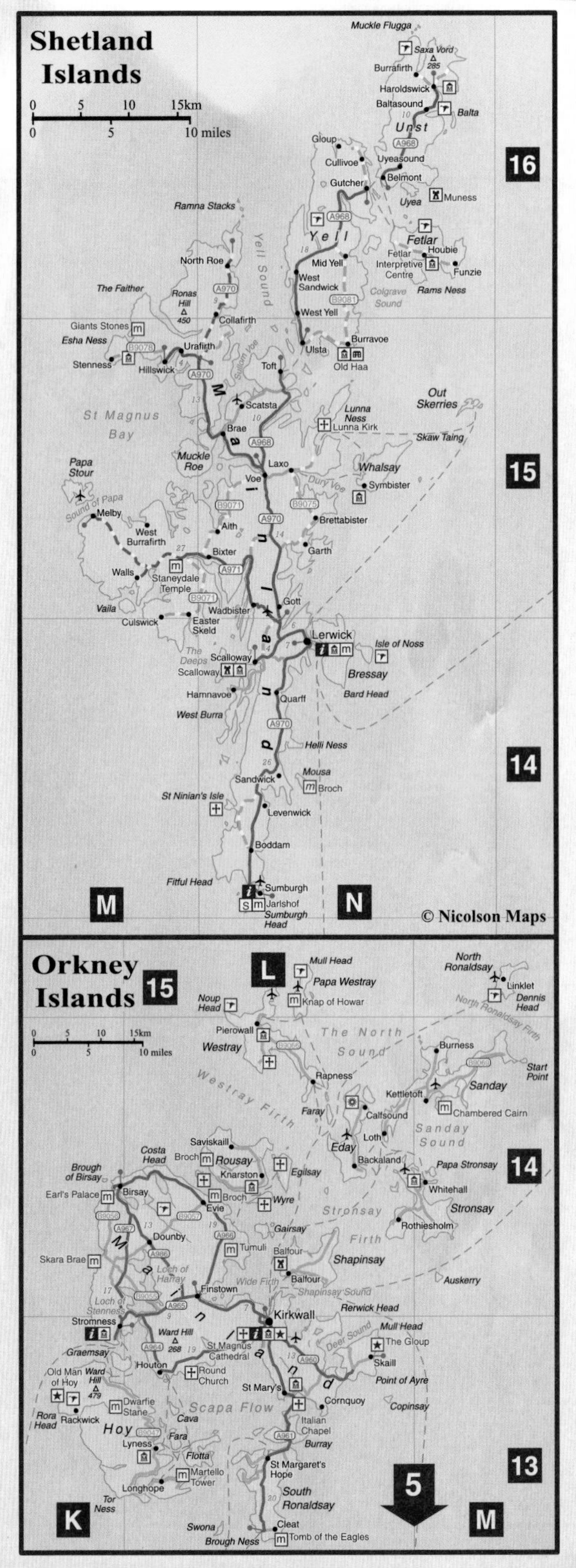
Shetland Islands
0 5 10 15km
0 5 10 miles
Muckle Flugga
Saxa Vord
285
Burrafirth
Haroldswick
Baltasound
Balta
Unst
A968
Gloup
Cullivoe
Uyeasound
Gutcher
Belmont
Uyea
Muness
Yell
Fetlar
Houbie
Fetlar Interpretive Centre
Funzie
Mid Yell
West Sandwick
Colgrave Sound
Rams Ness
B9081
West Yell
Burravoe
Ulsta
Old Haa
Ramna Stacks
Yell Sound
North Roe
A970
The Faither
Ronas Hill
450
Collafirth
Giants Stones
Esha Ness
B9078
Urafirth
Stenness
Hillswick
Sullom Voe
Toft
Scatsta
St Magnus Bay
Brae
A968
Out Skerries
Lunna Ness
Lunna Kirk
Skaw Taing
Papa Stour
Muckle Roe
Laxo
Whalsay
Voe
Dury Voe
Symbister
Sound of Papa
Melby
B9071
B9075
Brettabister
West Burrafirth
Aith
Garth
Bixter
Walls
Staneydale Temple
A971
Vaila
B9071
Wadbister
Gott
Culswick
Easter Skeld
Lerwick
Isle of Noss
The Deeps
Scalloway
Bressay
Bard Head
Hamnavoe
Quarff
West Burra
A970
Helli Ness
Mousa
Broch
Sandwick
St Ninian's Isle
Levenwick
Boddam
Fitful Head
Sumburgh
Jarlshof
Sumburgh Head
Mainland
M
N
16
15
14
© Nicolson Maps
Orkney Islands
15
L
0 5 10 15km
0 5 10 miles
Mull Head
Papa Westray
Knap of Howar
North Ronaldsay
Linklet
Dennis Head
North Ronaldsay Firth
Noup Head
Pierowall
Westray
B9066
The North Sound
Burness
Rapness
Start Point
Sanday
Westray Firth
Kettletoft
Calfsound
Chambered Cairn
Faray
Eday
Loth
Sanday Sound
Saviskaill
Costa Head
Broch
Rousay
Backaland
Papa Stronsay
Brough of Birsay
Knarston
Egilsay
Whitehall
Earl's Palace
Birsay
Broch
Wyre
Stronsay
Evie
B9057
Stronsay Firth
B9056
A967
Dounby
A966
Gairsay
Rothiesholm
Tumuli
Balfour
Skara Brae
A986
Loch of Harray
Shapinsay
Wide Firth
Balfour
Auskerry
Finstown
Shapinsay Sound
Loch of Stenness
B9055
A965
Kirkwall
Rerwick Head
Stromness
Ward Hill
268
Deer Sound
Mull Head
The Gloup
Graemsay
A964
St Magnus Cathedral
A960
Skaill
Old Man of Hoy
Ward Hill
479
Houton
Round Church
Point of Ayre
St Mary's
Cornquoy
Copinsay
Rora Head
Rackwick
Dwarfie Stane
Scapa Flow
Cava
Italian Chapel
Hoy
A961
Fara
Burray
Lyness
Flotta
St Margaret's Hope
Martello Tower
Longhope
South Ronaldsay
Tor Ness
Swona
Cleat
Brough Ness
Tomb of the Eagles
Mainland
14
13
5
K
M

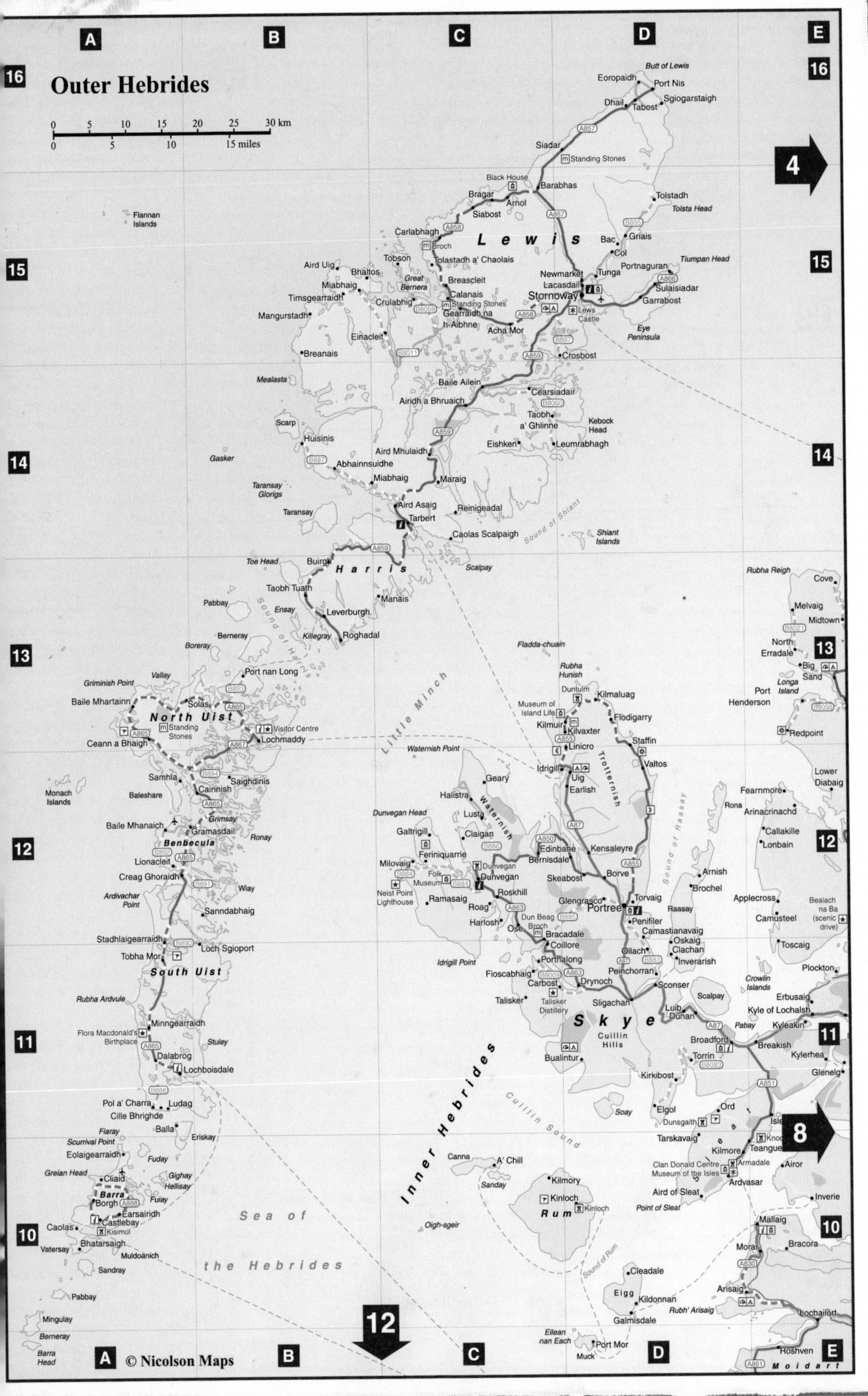

A
B
C
D
E
16
Outer Hebrides
0 5 10 15 20 25 30 km
0 5 10 15 miles
Butt of Lewis
Europaidh
Port Nis
Dhail
Tabost
Sgiogarstaigh
A857
Siadar
Standing Stones
4
Black House
Bragar
Arnol
Barabhas
Siabost
Tolstadh
Tolsta Head
Flannan Islands
Carlabhagh
A858
Broch
Lewis
Bac
Griais
B895
Col
Tobson
Tolastadh a' Chaolais
Aird Uig
Bhaltos
Great Bernera
Breascleit
Newmarket
Tunga
Portnaguran
Tiumpan Head
15
Miabhaig
Lacasdail
Sulaisiadar
Timsgearraidh
Crulabhig
Calanais
Standing Stones
Stornoway
Lews Castle
Garrabost
Mangurstadh
B8059
Gearraidh na h-Aibhne
A858
Acha Mor
Eye Peninsula
Einacleit
B897
B8011
Breanais
A859
Crosbost
Mealasta
Baile Ailein
Cearsiadair
B8060
Airidh a Bhruaich
Taobh a' Ghlinne
Kebock Head
Scarp
A859
Huisinis
Eishken
Leumrabhagh
Aird Mhulaidh
14
Gasker
B887
Abhainnsuidhe
Miabhaig
Maraig
Taransay Glorigs
Aird Asaig
Reinigeadal
Taransay
Tarbert
Sound of Shiant
Shiant Islands
Caolas Scalpaigh
A859
Toe Head
Buirgh
Harris
Scalpay
Rubha Reigh
Cove
Taobh Tuath
Pabbay
Manais
Melvaig
Ensay
Sound of Harris
Leverburgh
Midtown
B8021
Berneray
Killegray
Roghadal
North Erradale
13
Boreray
Fladda-chuain
Big Sand
Longa Island
Valtay
Port nan Long
Rubha Hunish
Griminish Point
B893
Duntulm
Kilmaluag
Port Henderson
Baile Mhartainn
Solas
A865
Museum of Island Life
North Uist
Flodigarry
B8056
Standing Stones
Kilmuir
Visitor Centre
Kilvaxter
Redpoint
Ceann a Bhaigh
A865
Lochmaddy
A855
A867
Linicro
Staffin
Waternish Point
Little Minch
Idrigill
Valtos
Uig
Lower Diabaig
Samhla
B894
Geary
Trotternish
Earlish
Saighdinis
Cairinish
Fearnmore
Monach Islands
Baleshare
Halistra
Rona
Arinacrinachd
A865
Waternish
Dunvegan Head
Lusta
Sound of Raasay
Grimsay
Callakille
Baile Mhanaich
Gramasdail
Galtrigill
Ronay
Claigan
Benbecula
A850
Lonbain
12
B892
B886
Edinbane
Kensaleyre
A865
Feriniquarrie
Bernisdale
Lionacleit
A855
Milovaig
Dunvegan
Arnish
Creag Ghoraidh
B884
Folk Museum
Dunvegan
Skeabost
Borve
B891
B884
Wiay
Neist Point Lighthouse
Brochel
Ramasaig
Roskhill
Torvaig
Applecross
Bealach na Ba (scenic drive)
Ardivachar Point
Glengrasco
Roag
A863
Portree
Raasay
Sanndabhaig
Camusteel
Dun Beag Broch
B885
Penifiler
Harlosh
Ose
Bracadale
Camastianavaig
Stadhlaigearraidh
B890
Coillore
Oskaig
Toscaig
Loch Sgioport
Ollach
Clachan
Tobha Mor
Portnalong
A87
B883
Inverarish
Idrigill Point
South Uist
Fioscabhaig
A863
Peinchorran
Plockton
B8009
Carbost
Drynoch
Crowlin Islands
Sconser
Rubha Ardvule
Talisker
Talisker Distillery
Sligachan
Scalpay
Erbusaig
Luib
Kyle of Lochalsh
Dunan
Minngearraidh
Skye
A87
Pabay
Kyleakin
Cuillin Hills
Flora Macdonald's Birthplace
Broadford
11
Stuley
Breakish
A865
Bualintur
Torrin
Dalabrog
B8083
Kylerhea
Lochboisdale
Kirkibost
Glenelg
B888
A851
Pol a' Charra
Ludag
Cullin Sound
Soay
Cille Bhrighde
Elgol
Ord
Eriskay
Balla
Dunsgaith
Fiaray
Inner Hebrides
Scurrival Point
Tarskavaig
8
Eolaigearraidh
Kilmore
Teangue
Fuday
Canna
A' Chill
Armadale
Airor
Clan Donald Centre Museum of the Isles
Greian Head
Cliaid
Gighay
Hellisay
Sanday
Kilmory
Ardvasar
Barra
Borgh
A888
Fulay
Kinloch
Aird of Sleat
Inverie
Earsairidh
Rum
Kinloch
Point of Sleat
Castlebay
Sea of
Kisimul
Mallaig
Caolas
Oigh-sgeir
10
10
Vatersay
Bhatarsaigh
Morar
Bracora
Muldoanich
A830
the Hebrides
Sound of Rum
Sandray
Cleadale
Eigg
Arisaig
Pabbay
Kildonnan
Rubh' Arisaig
Mingulay
12
Galmisdale
Lochailort
Berneray
Eilean nan Each
Port Mor
Barra Head
Muck
Roshven
A
© Nicolson Maps
B
C
D
E
A861
Moidart

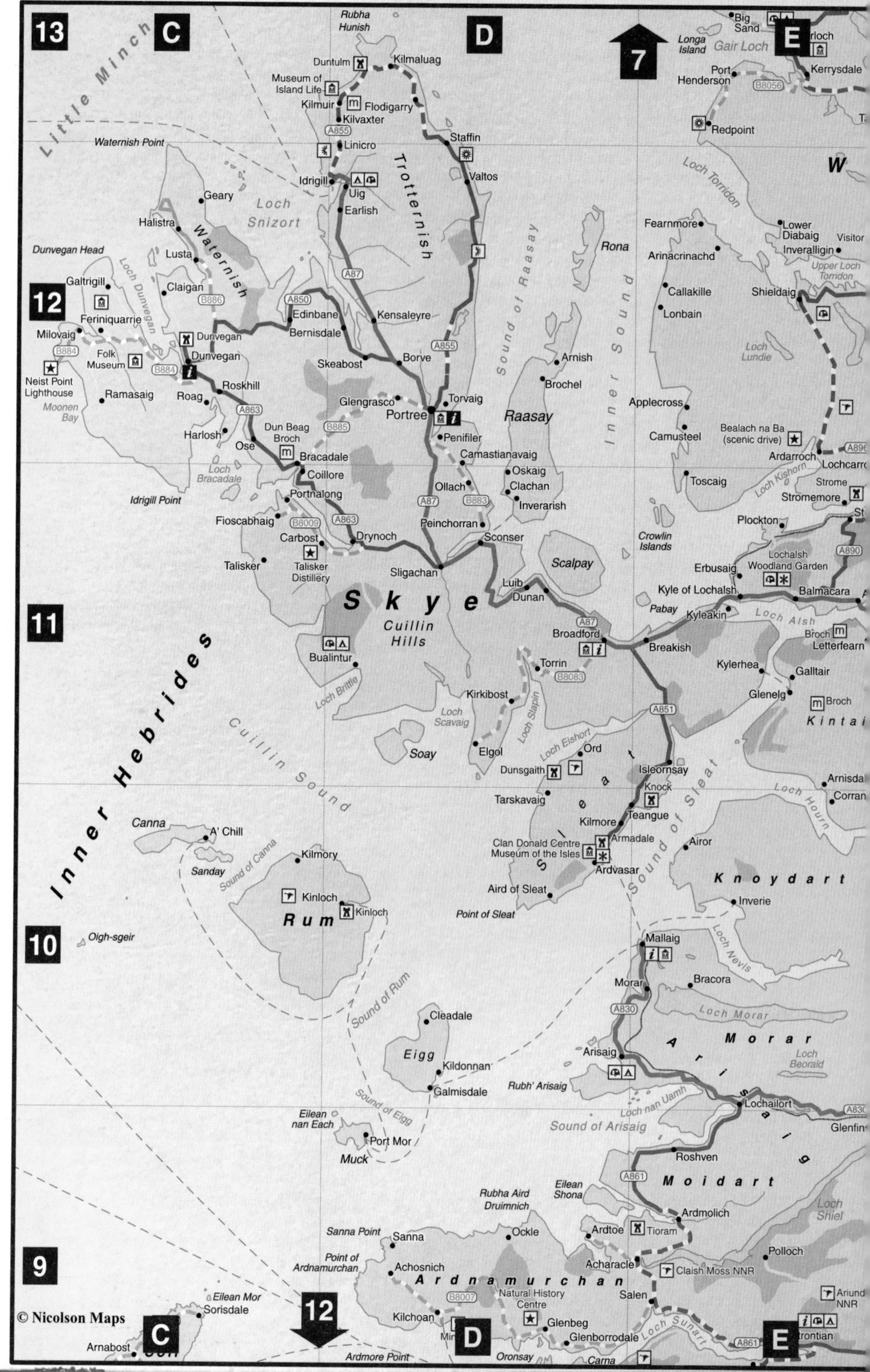

13
C
D
E
7
12
11
10
9
12
Little Minch
Rubha Hunish
Duntulm
Kilmaluag
Museum of Island Life
Kilmuir
Flodigarry
Kilvaxter
A855
Linicro
Staffin
Waternish Point
Idrigill
Uig
Valtos
Earlish
Geary
Loch Snizort
Trotternish
Halistra
Waternish
Dunvegan Head
Lusta
Loch Dunvegan
Galtrigill
Claigan
B886
A87
A850
Edinbane
Feriniquarrie
Kensaleyre
Bernisdale
Milovaig
Dunvegan
B884
Folk Museum
Skeabost
Borve
A855
Neist Point Lighthouse
Roskhill
Ramasaig
Roag
A863
Glengrasco
Torvaig
Portree
Moonen Bay
Dun Beag Broch
B885
Harlosh
Penifiler
Ose
Bracadale
Camastianavaig
Loch Bracadale
Coillore
Oskaig
Ollach
Clachan
Portnalong
Idrigill Point
B883
Inverarish
Fiscabhaig
B8009
A863
Peinchorran
Carbost
Drynoch
Sconser
Talisker
Talisker Distillery
Sligachan
Skye
Cuillin Hills
Bualintur
Loch Brittle
Inner Hebrides
Cuillin Sound
Loch Scavaig
Kirkibost
Soay
Elgol
Loch Slapin
Torrin
B8083
Broadford
A87
Luib
Dunan
Scalpay
Raasay
Sound of Raasay
Rona
Arnish
Brochel
Inner Sound
Crowlin Islands
Pabay
Kyleakin
Breakish
Loch Eishort
Ord
Dunsgaith
Isleornsay
Knock
Tarskavaig
Teangue
Kilmore
Armadale
Clan Donald Centre Museum of the Isles
Ardvasar
Aird of Sleat
Point of Sleat
Sleat
Sound of Sleat
A851
Canna
A' Chill
Sanday
Sound of Canna
Kilmory
Kinloch
Rum
Oigh-sgeir
Sound of Rum
Cleadale
Eigg
Kildonnan
Galmisdale
Sound of Eigg
Eilean nan Each
Port Mor
Muck
Mallaig
Morar
A830
Bracora
Loch Nevis
Inverie
Knoydart
Loch Morar
Morar
Loch Beoraid
Arisaig
Arisaig
Rubh' Arisaig
Loch nan Uamh
Sound of Arisaig
Lochailort
A830
Glenfinnan
Roshven
A861
Moidart
Eilean Shona
Rubha Aird Druimnich
Ardmolich
Loch Shiel
Sanna Point
Sanna
Ockle
Ardtoe
Tioram
Point of Ardnamurchan
Achosnich
Ardnamurchan
Acharacle
Claish Moss NNR
Polloch
B8007
Natural History Centre
Salen
Kilchoan
Glenbeg
Glenborrodale
Loch Sunart
A861
Ariundle NNR
Strontian
Mingary
Eilean Mor
Sorisdale
Arnabost
Coll
Ardmore Point
Oronsay
Carna
© Nicolson Maps
Big Sand
Longa Island
Gair Loch
Port Henderson
B8056
Kerrysdale
Redpoint
Loch Torridon
Fearnmore
Lower Diabaig
Visitor
Inveralligin
Upper Loch Torridon
Arinacrinachd
Callakille
Shieldaig
Lonbain
Loch Lundie
Applecross
Bealach na Ba (scenic drive)
Camusteel
Ardarroch
Lochcarron
Loch Kishorn
Toscaig
Strome
Stromemore
Plockton
Lochalsh Woodland Garden
A890
Erbusaig
Kyle of Lochalsh
Balmacara
Loch Alsh
Broch
Letterfearn
Kylerhea
Galltair
Glenelg
Broch
Kintail
Arnisdale
Loch Hourn
Corran
Airor

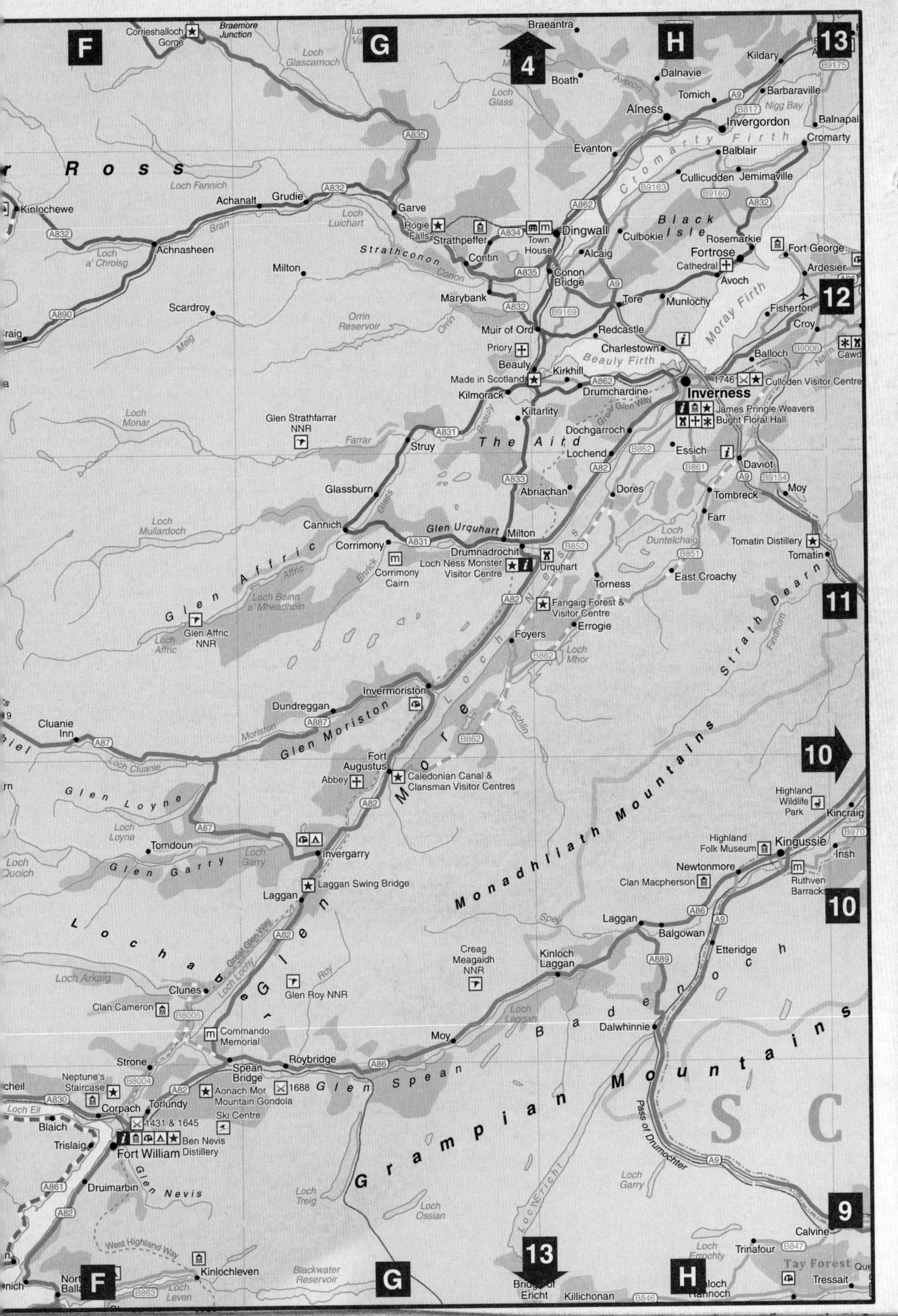
F
G
H
13
4
Corrieshalloch Gorge
Braemore Junction
Loch Glascarnoch
Braeantra
Boath
Loch Glass
Dalnavie
Averon
Kildary
Tomich
Barbaraville
Nigg Bay
Alness
Invergordon
Balnapaling
Cromarty
Cromarty Firth
Evanton
Balblair
Cullicudden
Jemimaville
Ross
Loch Fannich
Achanalt
Grudie
Kinlochewe
Garve
Loch Luichart
Bran
Rogie Falls
Strathpeffer
Town House
Dingwall
Culbokie
Black Isle
Rosemarkie
Fort George
Achnasheen
Loch a' Chroisg
Alcaig
Fortrose
Cathedral
Ardersier
Strathconon
Conon
Contin
Conon Bridge
Avoch
Milton
Marybank
Tore
Munlochy
Moray Firth
Fisherton
12
Scardroy
Orrin Reservoir
Orrin
Muir of Ord
Redcastle
Croy
Meig
Priory
Charlestown
Beauly
Beauly Firth
Balloch
Cawdor
Nairn
Kirkhill
Made in Scotland
Drumchardine
1746
Culloden Visitor Centre
Inverness
Kilmorack
Great Glen Way
Loch Monar
Glen Strathfarrar NNR
Kiltarlity
James Pringle Weavers
Bught Floral Hall
Beauly
Farrar
Struy
The Aird
Dochgarroch
Lochend
Essich
Daviot
Glassburn
Glass
Abriachan
Dores
Tombreck
Moy
Loch Mullardoch
Farr
Cannich
Glen Urquhart
Milton
Loch Duntelchaig
Glen Affric
Corrimony
Drumnadrochit
Tomatin Distillery
Tomatin
Affric
Enrick
Corrimony Cairn
Loch Ness Monster Visitor Centre
Urquhart
Torness
East Croachy
Loch Beinn a' Mheadhoin
Loch Affric
Glen Affric NNR
Farigaig Forest & Visitor Centre
Errogie
Strath Dearn
11
Findhorn
Foyers
Loch Mhor
Loch Ness
Invermoriston
Dundreggan
Glen Moriston
Moriston
Cluanie Inn
Fechlin
10
Loch Cluanie
Fort Augustus
Abbey
Caledonian Canal & Clansman Visitor Centres
Glen Loyne
Loch Loyne
More
Highland Wildlife Park
Kincraig
Monadhliath Mountains
Tomdoun
Invergarry
Glen Garry
Loch Garry
Loch Quoich
Highland Folk Museum
Kingussie
Insh
Newtonmore
Clan Macpherson
Ruthven Barracks
Laggan Swing Bridge
Laggan
Spey
Lochaber
Glen Mor
Great Glen Way
Laggan
Balgowan
Etteridge
Creag Meagaidh NNR
Kinloch Laggan
Loch Arkaig
Loch Lochy
Glen Roy NNR
Roy
Clunes
Clan Cameron
Loch Laggan
Dalwhinnie
Badenoch
Commando Memorial
Moy
Strone
Spean Bridge
Roybridge
Glen Spean
Neptune's Staircase
1688
Aonach Mor Mountain Gondola
Grampian Mountains
Corpach
Torlundy
Loch Eil
Blaich
1431 & 1645
Ski Centre
Trislaig
Fort William
Ben Nevis Distillery
Pass of Drumochter
Glen Nevis
Druimarbin
Loch Treig
Loch Ossian
Loch Ericht
Loch Garry
9
Calvine
West Highland Way
Kinlochleven
Blackwater Reservoir
Loch Leven
Bridge of Ericht
Killichonan
Loch Errochty
Trinafour
Tay Forest
Tressait
Kinloch Rannoch
North Ballachulish
A835
A832
A890
A834
A862
A9
A831
A833
A82
A887
A87
A86
A889
A830
A861
B9175
B817
B9163
B9160
B9169
B862
B9006
B9154
B861
B852
B851
B970
B8004
B8005
B847
B846
B863

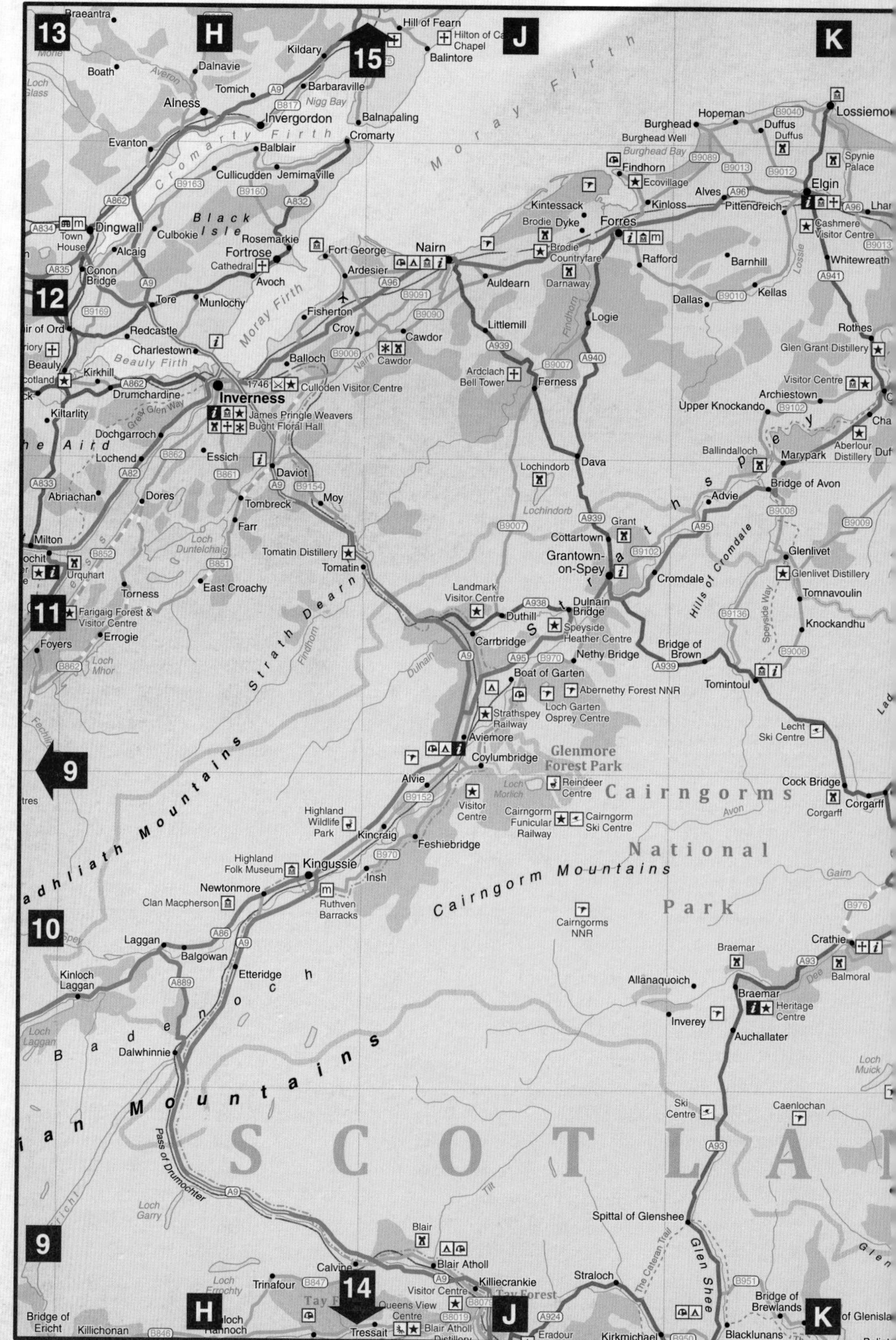

13
H
J
K
15
Braeantra
Hill of Fearn
Hilton of Cadboll Chapel
Balintore
Kildary
Dalnavie
Boath
Averon
Loch Glass
Tomich
A9
Barbaraville
B817
Nigg Bay
Alness
Invergordon
Balnapaling
Cromarty
Moray Firth
Cromarty Firth
Evanton
Balblair
B9163
Cullicudden
Jemimaville
B9160
A832
A862
Black Isle
Dingwall
Town House
A834
Culbokie
Rosemarkie
Alcaig
Fortrose
Cathedral
Fort George
Nairn
Ardesier
A835
Conon Bridge
A9
Avoch
A96
12
Tore
Munlochy
Moray Firth
B9091
Fisherton
B9169
Croy
B9090
Cawdor
Redcastle
Charlestown
Beauly Firth
Beauly
B9006
Balloch
Kirkhill
A862
Drumchardine
1746
Culloden Visitor Centre
Inverness
James Pringle Weavers
Bught Floral Hall
Kiltarlity
Great Glen Way
Dochgarroch
The Aird
Lochend
B862
Essich
B861
Daviot
A82
A833
A9
B9154
Abriachan
Dores
Tombreck
Moy
Farr
Loch Duntelchaig
Milton
B852
B851
Tomatin Distillery
Tomatin
Urquhart
East Croachy
Torness
11
Farigaig Forest & Visitor Centre
Errogie
Foyers
B862
Loch Mhor
Strath Dearn
Findhorn
Dulnain
9
Monadhliath Mountains
Auldearn
Darnaway
Brodie
Dyke
Brodie Countryfare
Kintessack
Forres
Rafford
Findhorn
Ecovillage
Burghead Bay
Kinloss
Burghead
Burghead Well
Hopeman
B9040
Duffus
B9089
B9013
B9012
Lossiemouth
Spynie Palace
Alves
A96
Pittendreich
Elgin
Cashmere Visitor Centre
Barnhill
Whitewreath
A941
Dallas
B9010
Kellas
Lossie
Logie
Littlemill
A939
A940
B9007
Ardclach Bell Tower
Ferness
Rothes
Glen Grant Distillery
Visitor Centre
Archiestown
Upper Knockando
B9102
Ballindalloch
Marypark
Aberlour Distillery
Bridge of Avon
Advie
B9008
B9009
Dava
Lochindorb
Lochindorb
A939
B9007
Grant
Cottartown
A95
Grantown-on-Spey
B9102
Cromdale
Hills of Cromdale
Glenlivet
Glenlivet Distillery
Tomnavoulin
Knockandhu
B9136
Speyside Way
Landmark Visitor Centre
A938
Duthill
Dulnain Bridge
Carrbridge
Speyside Heather Centre
A95
B970
Nethy Bridge
Bridge of Brown
A939
B9008
Tomintoul
Strathspey
A9
Boat of Garten
Abernethy Forest NNR
Loch Garten Osprey Centre
Strathspey Railway
Aviemore
Lecht Ski Centre
Coylumbridge
Glenmore Forest Park
Alvie
Loch Morlich
Reindeer Centre
B9152
Visitor Centre
Cairngorm Funicular Railway
Cairngorm Ski Centre
Cairngorms National Park
Cock Bridge
Corgarff
Avon
Highland Wildlife Park
Kincraig
Feshiebridge
B970
Highland Folk Museum
Kingussie
Insh
Newtonmore
Ruthven Barracks
Clan Macpherson
Cairngorm Mountains
Gairn
B976
Cairngorms NNR
10
Spey
Laggan
A86
Balgowan
A9
Kinloch Laggan
Etteridge
A889
Crathie
A93
Braemar
Balmoral
Dee
Allanaquoich
Braemar
Heritage Centre
Inverey
Auchallater
Loch Laggan
Badenoch
Dalwhinnie
Loch Muick
Grampian Mountains
Pass of Drumochter
Ski Centre
Caenlochan
SCOTLAND
A93
A9
Truim
Loch Garry
Tilt
Spittal of Glenshee
9
Blair
Glen Shee
The Cateran Trail
Calvine
Blair Atholl
Loch Errochty
Trinafour
B847
14
A9
Killiecrankie
Straloch
Visitor Centre
Tay Forest
B951
Queens View Centre
Bridge of Brewlands
Tay Forest
B8019
Bridge of Ericht
Killichonan
B846
Loch Rannoch
Tressait
Blair Atholl Distillery
A924
Eradour
Kirkmichael
B950
Blacklunans
Kirkton of Glenisla

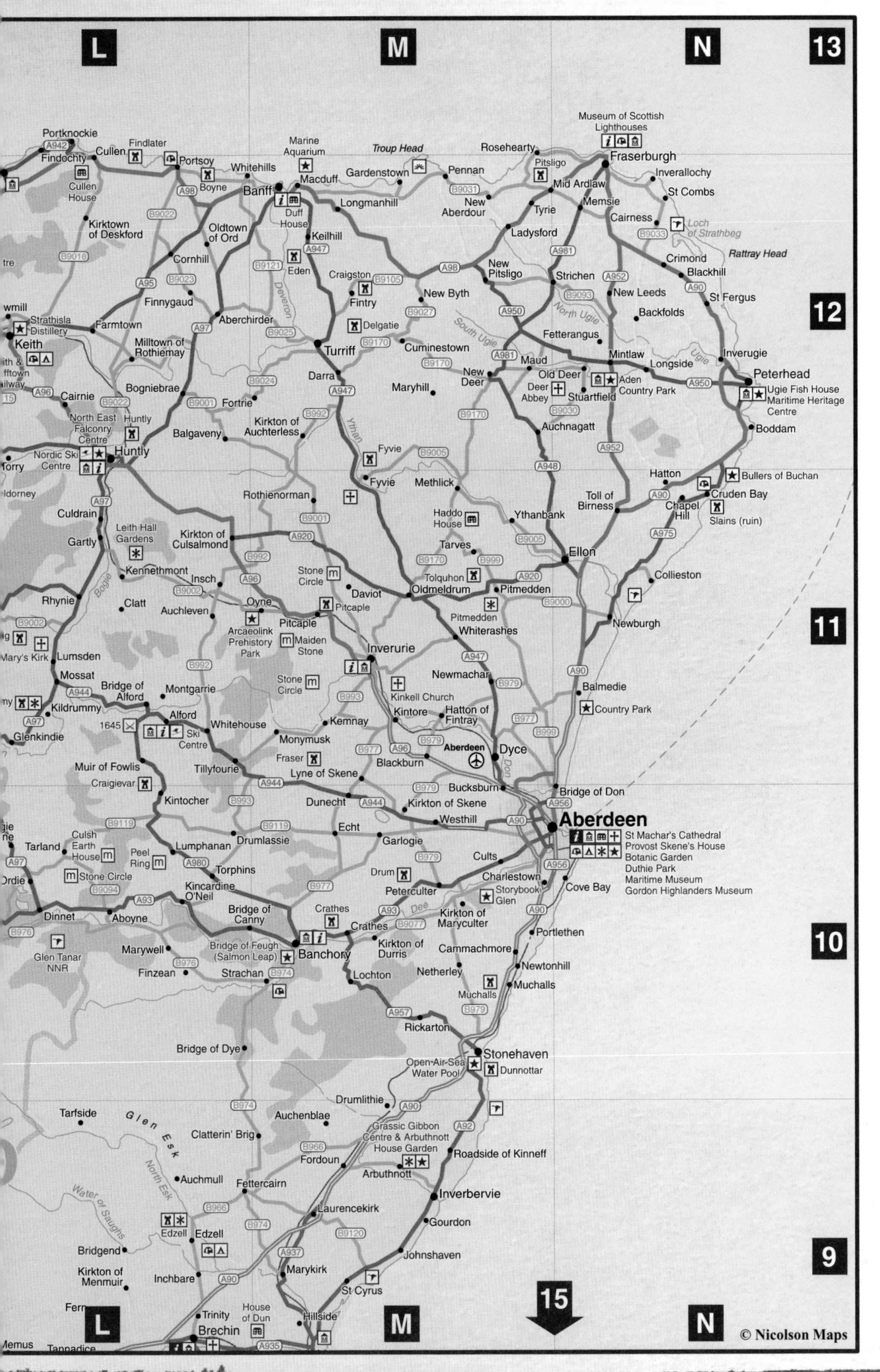
L
M
N
13
12
11
10
9
15
Museum of Scottish Lighthouses
Portknockie
Findlater
Marine Aquarium
Troup Head
Rosehearty
Pitsligo
Fraserburgh
Findochty
Cullen
Portsoy
Whitehills
Macduff
Gardenstown
Pennan
Mid Ardlaw
Inverallochy
Cullen House
Boyne
Banff
Duff House
Longmanhill
New Aberdour
Tyrie
Memsie
St Combs
Kirktown of Deskford
Oldtown of Ord
Keilhill
Ladysford
Cairness
Loch of Strathbeg
Cornhill
Eden
Craigston
New Pitsligo
Strichen
Crimond
Rattray Head
Blackhill
Finnygaud
Fintry
New Byth
New Leeds
St Fergus
Strathisla Distillery
Farmtown
Aberchirder
Deveron
Delgatie
South Ugie
North Ugie
Backfolds
Fetterangus
Keith
Milltown of Rothiemay
Turriff
Cuminestown
Maud
Mintlaw
Longside
Inverugie
Ugie
Darra
New Deer
Old Deer
Aden Country Park
Peterhead
Ugie Fish House
Maritime Heritage Centre
Cairnie
Bogniebrae
Fortrie
Maryhill
Deer Abbey
Stuartfield
North East Falconry Centre
Huntly
Kirkton of Auchterless
Auchnagatt
Boddam
Balgaveny
Ythan
Nordic Ski Centre
Fyvie
Hatton
Bullers of Buchan
Methlick
Toll of Birness
Cruden Bay
Rothienorman
Chapel Hill
Slains (ruin)
Culdrain
Haddo House
Ythanbank
Leith Hall Gardens
Kirkton of Culsalmond
Gartly
Tarves
Ellon
Kennethmont
Insch
Stone Circle
Daviot
Tolquhon
Pitmedden
Collieston
Bogie
Rhynie
Clatt
Oldmeldrum
Auchleven
Oyne
Pitcaple
Pitmedden
Whiterashes
Newburgh
Arcaeolink Prehistoric Park
Maiden Stone
Inverurie
Lumsden
Newmachar
Mossat
Bridge of Alford
Montgarrie
Stone Circle
Kinkell Church
Balmedie
Kildrummy
Kintore
Hatton of Fintray
Country Park
Alford
1645
Ski Centre
Whitehouse
Kemnay
Glenkindie
Monymusk
Aberdeen
Dyce
Fraser
Blackburn
Muir of Fowlis
Tillyfourie
Lyne of Skene
Don
Craigievar
Bucksburn
Bridge of Don
Kintocher
Dunecht
Kirkton of Skene
Westhill
Aberdeen
Culsh Earth House
Echt
Tarland
Drumlassie
Garlogie
St Machar's Cathedral
Provost Skene's House
Botanic Garden
Duthie Park
Maritime Museum
Gordon Highlanders Museum
Peel Ring
Lumphanan
Cults
Stone Circle
Torphins
Drum
Charlestown
Kincardine O'Neil
Peterculter
Storybook Glen
Cove Bay
Dinnet
Aboyne
Bridge of Canny
Crathes
Dee
Kirkton of Maryculter
Crathes
Portlethen
Glen Tanar NNR
Marywell
Bridge of Feugh (Salmon Leap)
Banchory
Kirkton of Durris
Cammachmore
Finzean
Strachan
Lochton
Netherley
Newtonhill
Muchalls
Muchalls
Rickarton
Bridge of Dye
Stonehaven
Open-Air Sea Water Pool
Dunnottar
Drumlithie
Tarfside
Glen Esk
Auchenblae
Grassic Gibbon Centre & Arbuthnott House Garden
Clatterin' Brig
Fordoun
Roadside of Kinneff
North Esk
Arbuthnott
Auchmull
Fettercairn
Inverbervie
Water of Saughs
Laurencekirk
Gourdon
Edzell
Edzell
Bridgend
Johnshaven
Marykirk
Kirkton of Menmuir
Inchbare
St Cyrus
House of Dun
Trinity
Hillside
Brechin
Tannadice
A942
A98
A95
A97
A96
A947
A98
A981
A952
A90
A950
A981
A920
A948
A975
A944
A93
A980
A957
A92
A937
A935
A956
B9022
B9018
B9023
B9121
B9105
B9025
B9027
B9170
B9093
B9024
B9001
B992
B9005
B9000
B979
B977
B999
B993
B9119
B9094
B976
B974
B966
B9120
B9002
B9031
B9033
B9030
B9077
© Nicolson Maps

B
C
D
9
8
7
6
5
Eilean Mor
Sorisdale
Coll
Arnabost
Ballyhaugh
Arinagour
Arileod
B8070
Gunna
Caolas
Balevullin
Tiree
B8069
Gott Bay
Scarinish
Barrapol
Crossapol
B8067
Hynish Bay
Hynish
Callach Point
Calgary
Calgary Bay
Treshnish Point
Treshnish Isles
Lunga
Gometra
Staffa
Fingal's Cave
Staffa NNR
Little Colonsay
Inch Kenneth Chapel
Ulva
Eorsa
Kilchoan
Mingary
Natural History Centre
Salen
Glenbeg
Glenborrodale
Loch Sunart
Ardmore Point
Oronsay
Carna
Glencripesdale NNR
Tobermory
Aros Park
Drimnin
Morvern
Dervaig
Heritage Centre
Loch Frisa
Sound of Mull
Killundine
B849
Fiunary
Loch Arienas
Kilninian
B8073
Fanmore
A848
Aros
Lochaline
Loch Tuath
Salen
Lagganulva
Killiechronan
Fishnish
Gruline
A849
Loch na Keal
Loch Ba
Torosay
Lochdon
Mull
Balnahard
B8035
Strathcoil
Loch Spelve
Loch Scridain
Abbey
Iona
Sound of Iona
Fionnphort
Heritage Centre
A849
Pennyghael
Lochbuie
Loch Uisg
Loch Buie
Bunessan
Ross of Mull
Carsaig
Soa Island
Erraid
Ardalanish
Ardchiavaig
Malcolm's Point
Rubh' Ardlanish
Firth of Lorn
Ellenabeich
An Cala
Torran Rocks
Garvellachs
Lunga
Sound of Luing
Gulf of Corryvreckan
Corryvreckan Whirlpool
Kiloran Bay
Kiloran
Kiloran
Kilchattan
B8087
Colonsay
Scalasaig
Garvard
Oronsay
Priory
Lealt
Jura
Ardlussa
Tayvallich
Loch Righ Mor
Tarbert
Loch Tarbert
Keillmore
Sound of Jura
Nave Island
A846
Bunnahabhain Distillery
Bunnahabhain
Paps of Jura
Ardnave
Loch Gruinart
Caol Ila Distillery
Sanaigmore
Killinallan
Port Askaig
Feolin Ferry
Ardfernal
B8018
Sound of Islay
Finlaggan
Keills
Keils
Small Isles
Loch Gorm
B8017
Ballygrant
Isle of Jura Distillery
Craighouse
Islay
A846
Kilchoman Distillery
Kilchoman
Bruichladdich Distillery
Blackrock
Jura House
Rubha na Traille
Machir Bay
Bridgend
Sculptured Stones
Bruichladdich
Loch Indaal
Kilchiaran
Bowmore
Bowmore Distillery
Rhinns of Islay
Port Charlotte
Ardpatrick Point
Nereabolls
A846
B8016
Portnahaven
A847
Laggan Bay
Glenegedale
16
Gigha
Ardminish
Sound of Gigha
Rhinns Point
Ardbeg Distillery
Laphroaig Distillery
Achamore
© Nicolson Maps

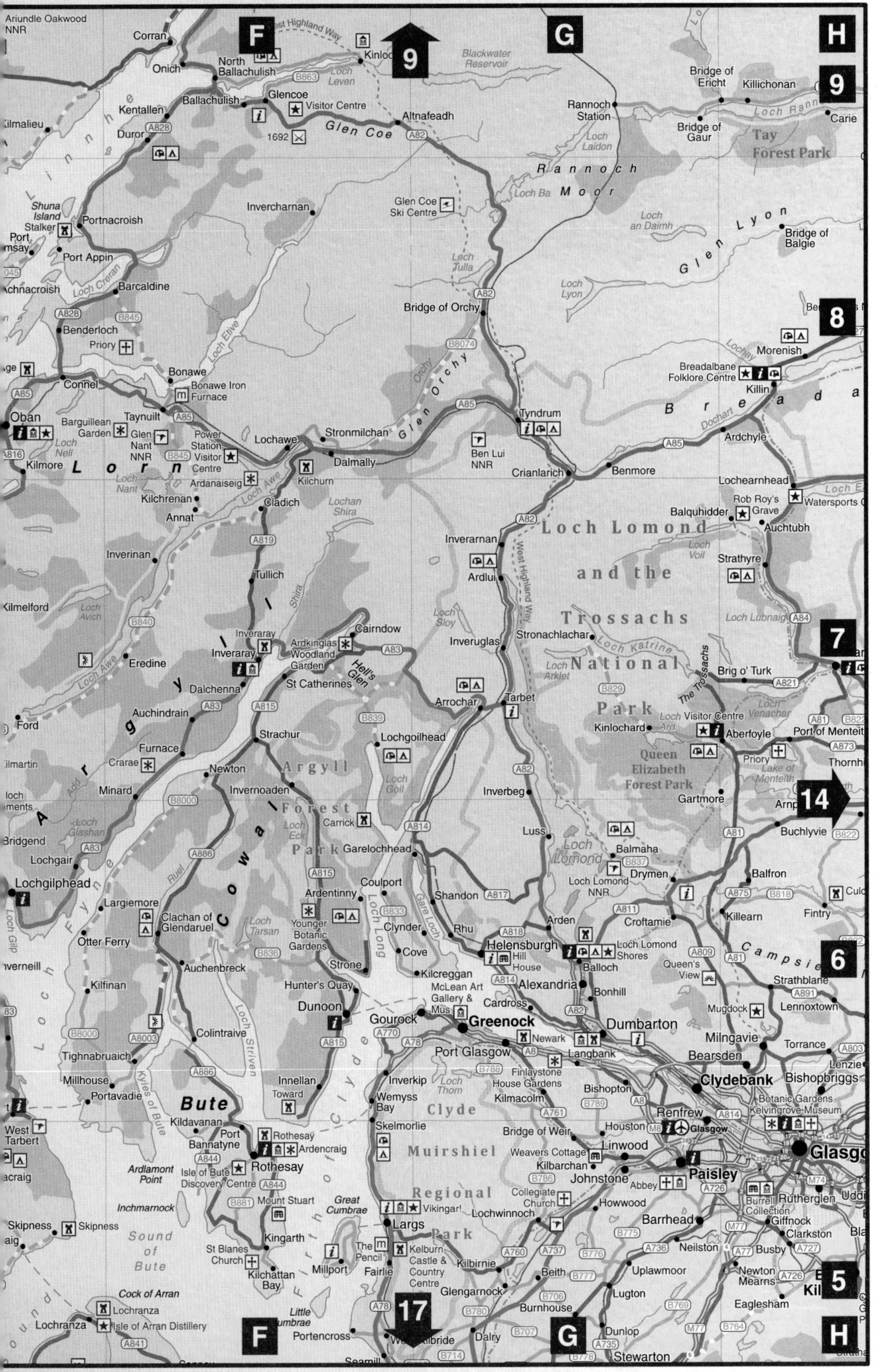
F
G
H
9
8
7
6
5
14
17
Ariundle Oakwood NNR
Corran
Onich
North Ballachulish
West Highland Way
Kinloch
Blackwater Reservoir
Loch Leven
Ballachulish
Glencoe
Visitor Centre
Kentallen
Altnafeadh
Glen Coe
1692
Duror
Loch Linnhe
Kilmalieu
Rannoch Station
Bridge of Ericht
Killichonan
Loch Rannoch
Carie
Bridge of Gaur
Tay Forest Park
Loch Laidon
Rannoch Moor
Loch Ba
Loch an Daimh
Glen Lyon
Bridge of Balgie
Loch Lyon
Shuna Island
Stalker
Portnacroish
Inverchardnan
Glen Coe Ski Centre
Port Appin
Loch Tulla
Loch Creran
Barcaldine
Achnacroish
Bridge of Orchy
Benderloch
Priory
Loch Etive
Bonawe
Bonawe Iron Furnace
Connel
Oban
Barguillean Garden
Taynuilt
Glen Nant NNR
Power Station Visitor Centre
Lochawe
Stronmilchan
Glen Orchy
Tyndrum
Ben Lui NNR
Crianlarich
Benmore
Dalmally
Kilchurn
Kilmore
Lorn
Loch Nell
Loch Nant
Ardanaiseig
Kilchrenan
Loch Awe
Annat
Cladich
Lochan Shira
Breadalbane Folklore Centre
Morenish
Loch Tay
Killin
Breadalbane
Dochart
Ardchyle
Lochearnhead
Loch Earn
Watersports Centre
Rob Roy's Grave
Balquhidder
Auchtubh
Loch Voil
Strathyre
Loch Lubnaig
Inverinan
Tullich
Inverarnan
Ardlui
Loch Lomond and the Trossachs National Park
West Highland Way
Kilmelford
Loch Avich
Loch Sloy
Cairndow
Inveraray
Ardkinglas Woodland Garden
Inveruglas
Stronachlachar
Loch Katrine
Loch Arklet
The Trossachs
Brig o' Turk
Eredine
Dalchenna
St Catherines
Hell's Glen
Arrochar
Tarbet
Argyll
Auchindrain
Ford
Strachur
Lochgoilhead
Loch Goil
Loch Venachar
Visitor Centre
Kinlochard
Loch Ard
Aberfoyle
Port of Menteith
Lake of Menteith
Priory
Queen Elizabeth Forest Park
Gartmore
Furnace
Crarae
Kilmartin
Newton
Argyll Forest Park
Invernoaden
Minard
Inverbeg
Carrick
Loch Eck
Luss
Buchlyvie
Bridgend
Loch Glashan
Lochgair
Lochgilphead
Loch Fyne
Garelochhead
Loch Lomond
Balmaha
Loch Lomond NNR
Drymen
Balfron
Coulport
Ardentinny
Shandon
Loch Long
Gare Loch
Killearn
Fintry
Largiemore
Clachan of Glendaruel
Cowal
Loch Tarsan
Younger Botanic Gardens
Clynder
Rhu
Arden
Croftamie
Otter Ferry
Loch Gilp
Helensburgh
Hill House
Loch Lomond Shores
Balloch
Queen's View
Campsie Fells
Strathblane
Inverneill
Auchenbreck
Cove
Strone
Kilcreggan
Kilfinan
Hunter's Quay
McLean Art Gallery & Mus
Alexandria
Bonhill
Cardross
Mugdock
Lennoxtown
Dunoon
Gourock
Greenock
Dumbarton
Loch Striven
Colintraive
Newark
Milngavie
Torrance
Tighnabruaich
Port Glasgow
Langbank
Bearsden
Lenzie
Kyles of Bute
Millhouse
Portavadie
Innellan
Toward
Inverkip
Loch Thom
Finlaystone House Gardens
Kilmacolm
Bishopton
Clydebank
Bishopbriggs
Botanic Gardens
Kelvingrove Museum
Bute
Wemyss Bay
Clyde Muirshiel Regional Park
Renfrew
Glasgow
West Tarbert
Kildavanan
Port Bannatyne
Rothesay
Ardencraig
Skelmorlie
Bridge of Weir
Houston
Linwood
Paisley
Ardlamont Point
Isle of Bute Discovery Centre
Weavers Cottage
Kilbarchan
Johnstone
Abbey
Rutherglen
Uddingston
Mount Stuart
Great Cumbrae
Vikingar!
Collegiate Church
Howwood
Burrell Collection
Inchmarnock
Largs
Lochwinnoch
Barrhead
Giffnock
Clarkston
Skipness
Sound of Bute
Kingarth
The Pencil
Kelburn Castle & Country Centre
Neilston
Busby
St Blanes Church
Kilchattan Bay
Millport
Fairlie
Kilbirnie
Beith
Uplawmoor
Newton Mearns
Cock of Arran
Glengarnock
Lugton
Eaglesham
Lochranza
Isle of Arran Distillery
Little Cumbrae
Burnhouse
Portencross
West Kilbride
Dalry
Dunlop
Stewarton
Seamill
A82
A828
B863
B845
B8074
A85
A816
B845
A819
B840
A83
A815
B839
A814
A821
A81
B822
A873
B8000
A886
A815
B833
B836
A817
B837
A811
A875
B818
A809
A818
A891
A803
B8000
A8003
A770
A78
A8
B786
A761
B789
M8
A737
B775
A736
M77
A726
A727
A844
B881
A760
B776
B777
B706
B780
B707
B769
B764
A735
B778
B714
A841

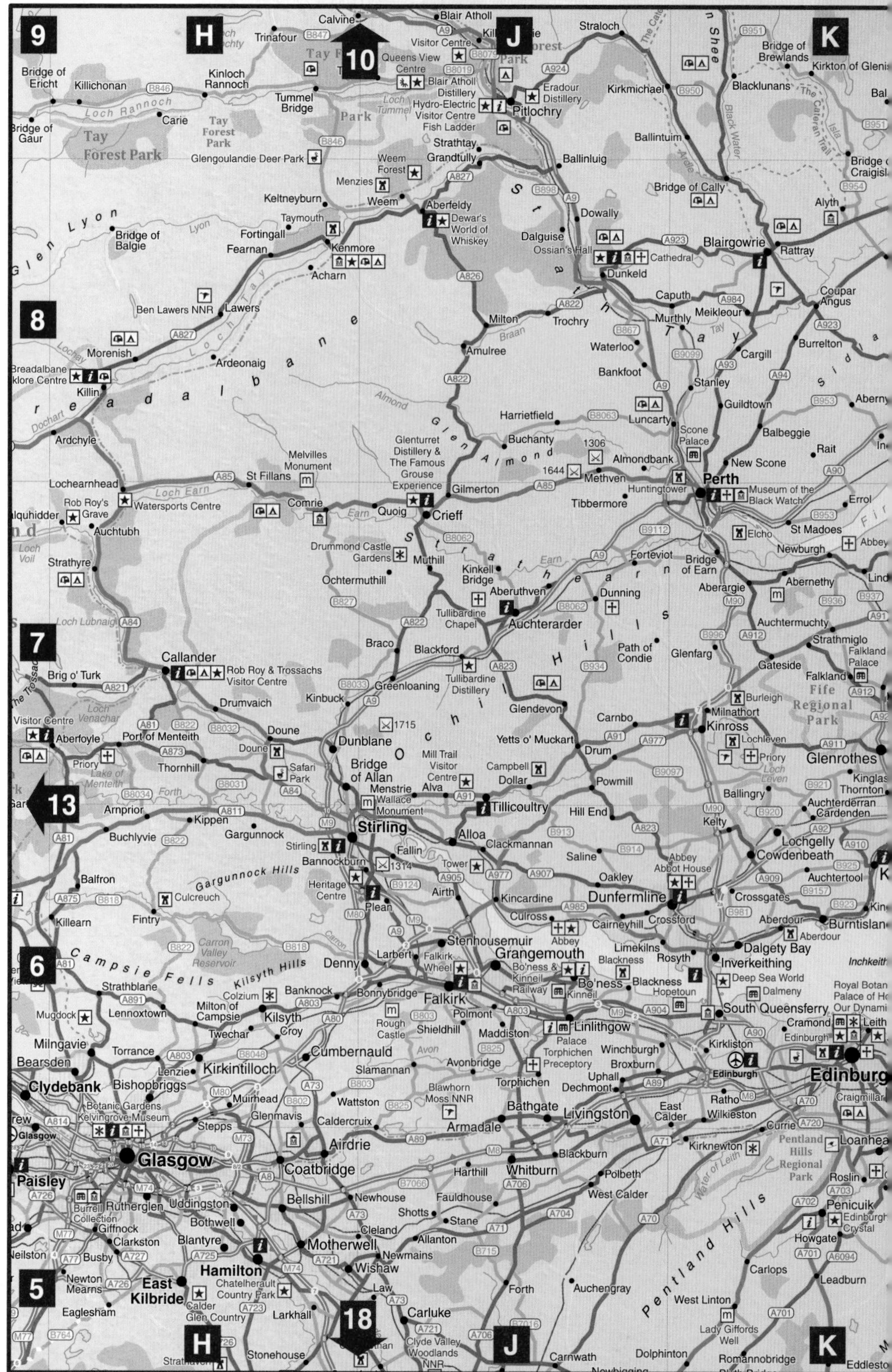

9
H
10
J
K
Calvine
Blair Atholl
Trinafour
Straloch
Bridge of Brewlands
Kirkton of Glenisla
Bridge of Ericht
Killichonan
Kinloch Rannoch
Queens View Visitor Centre
Blair Atholl Distillery
Hydro-Electric Visitor Centre Fish Ladder
Pitlochry
Eradour Distillery
Kirkmichael
Blacklunans
Loch Rannoch
Carie
Tummel Bridge
Tay Forest Park
Bridge of Gaur
Ballintuim
Glengoulandie Deer Park
Strathtay
Grandtully
Weem Forest
Ballinluig
Bridge of Craigisla
Menzies
Keltneyburn
Weem
Aberfeldy
Bridge of Cally
Alyth
Glen Lyon
Taymouth
Dewar's World of Whiskey
Dowally
Bridge of Balgie
Fortingall
Fearnan
Kenmore
Dalguise
Ossian's Hall
Blairgowrie
Rattray
Cathedral
Dunkeld
Acharn
Ben Lawers NNR
Lawers
Caputh
Coupar Angus
8
Murthly
Meikleour
Milton
Trochry
Waterloo
Cargill
Burrelton
Morenish
Ardeonaig
Amulree
Bankfoot
Breadalbane Folklore Centre
Killin
Breadalbane
Stanley
Guildtown
Abernyte
Harrietfield
Luncarty
Ardchyle
Glenturret Distillery & The Famous Grouse Experience
Buchanty
Glen Almond
Scone Palace
Balbeggie
Melvilles Monument
1306
Almondbank
Rait
1644
Methven
New Scone
Lochearnhead
St Fillans
Loch Earn
Gilmerton
Huntingtower
Perth
Museum of the Black Watch
Rob Roy's Grave
Watersports Centre
Comrie
Quoig
Crieff
Tibbermore
Errol
Balquhidder
Auchtubh
Elcho
St Madoes
Drummond Castle Gardens
Muthill
Forteviot
Bridge of Earn
Newburgh
Strathyre
Ochtermuthill
Kinkell Bridge
Aberuthven
Dunning
Aberargie
Abernethy
Strathearn
Tullibardine Chapel
Auchterarder
Auchtermuchty
Loch Lubnaig
7
Braco
Blackford
Ochil Hills
Path of Condie
Glenfarg
Strathmiglo
Falkland Palace
Callander
Rob Roy & Trossachs Visitor Centre
Tullibardine Distillery
Gateside
Falkland
Brig o' Turk
Greenloaning
Fife Regional Park
Drumvaich
Kinbuck
Burleigh
Milnathort
Glendevon
Carnbo
1715
Kinross
Visitor Centre
Aberfoyle
Port of Menteith
Doune
Dunblane
Yetts o' Muckart
Drum
Lochleven
Priory
Glenrothes
Lake of Menteith
Thornhill
Safari Park
Bridge of Allan
Mill Trail Visitor Centre
Campbell
Dollar
Powmill
Kinglassie
Thornton
13
Menstrie
Alva
Wallace Monument
Tillicoultry
Hill End
Ballingry
Auchterderran
Cardenden
Arnprior
Kippen
Stirling
Kelty
Buchlyvie
Gargunnock
Alloa
Clackmannan
Lochgelly
Cowdenbeath
Fallin
Saline
Abbey Abbot House
Balfron
Bannockburn
1314
Tower
Oakley
Auchtertool
Gargunnock Hills
Heritage Centre
Plean
Airth
Kincardine
Dunfermline
Crossgates
Culcreuch
Killearn
Fintry
Culross
Cairneyhill
Crossford
Aberdour
Burntisland
Carron Valley Reservoir
Stenhousemuir
Grangemouth
Limekilns
Dalgety Bay
Campsie Fells
Kilsyth Hills
Denny
Larbert
Falkirk Wheel
Blackness
Rosyth
Inverkeithing
Bo'ness & Kinneil Railway
Bo'ness
Deep Sea World
Strathblane
Colzium
Banknock
Bonnybridge
Falkirk
Kinneil
Hopetoun
Dalmeny
Royal Botanic
Lennoxtown
Milton of Campsie
Kilsyth
Rough Castle
Polmont
South Queensferry
Mugdock
Twechar
Croy
Shieldhill
Maddiston
Linlithgow
Cramond
Leith
Milngavie
Torrance
Cumbernauld
Palace
Torphichen
Winchburgh
Kirkliston
Edinburgh
Bearsden
Lenzie
Kirkintilloch
Slamannan
Avonbridge
Preceptory
Broxburn
Clydebank
Bishopbriggs
Blawhorn Moss NNR
Torphichen
Dechmont
Uphall
Ratho
Craigmillar
Botanic Gardens
Kelvingrove Museum
Muirhead
Wattston
Bathgate
Livingston
East Calder
Wilkieston
Glenmavis
Stepps
Caldercruix
Armadale
Currie
Glasgow
Airdrie
Pentland Hills Regional Park
Loanhead
Paisley
Coatbridge
Harthill
Whitburn
Blackburn
Kirknewton
Roslin
Burrell Collection
Rutherglen
Uddingston
Bellshill
Newhouse
Fauldhouse
Polbeth
West Calder
Penicuik
Giffnock
Bothwell
Shotts
Stane
Clarkston
Blantyre
Cleland
Motherwell
Allanton
Pentland Hills
Edinburgh Crystal
Howgate
Busby
Newmains
Wishaw
Hamilton
Carlops
Newton Mearns
East Kilbride
Chatelherault Country Park
Forth
Auchengray
Leadburn
5
Calderglen Country Park
Law
Carluke
West Linton
Eaglesham
Larkhall
18
Lady Gifford's Well
Clyde Valley Woodlands NNR
Stonehouse
Carnwath
Dolphinton
Romannobridge
Eddleston

L
M
N
9
11
Inchbare
Kirkton of Menmuir
Marykirk
St Cyrus
Fern
Trinity
House of Dun
Hillside
Brechin
Tannadice
Finavon
Caledonian Railway
Montrose
Ferryden
Doocot
Montrose Basin
Aberlemno
Priory
Red
Lunan Bay
Forfar
Letham
Friockheim
Inverkeilor
Craichie
685
Chapelton
Redford
Kirkbuddo
Carmyllie
Arbroath
Abbey
Crombie Country Park
Affleck
Monikie
8
Muirdrum
Newbigging
East Haven
Kellas
Carnoustie
Monifieth
Broughty Ferry
Broughty
Buddon Ness
Tayport
Norman Church
Leuchars
St Andrews Bay
Earlshall
St Andrews Aquarium
St Andrews
Strathkinness
Botanic Garden
Boarhills
Pitscottie
Tarvit
Kingsbarns
Dunino
Fife Ness
Peat Inn
Largoward
7
Crail
Arncroach
Kilrenny
Anstruther
Scottish Fisheries Museum
Kilconquhar
Pittenweem
St Monans
Largo Bay
Elie
Isle of May
of Forth
Bass Rock
Fidra
North Berwick
Craigleith
Eyebroughy
Tantallon
Dirleton
Gullane
Auldhame
Dirleton
Scottish Seabird Centre
Whitekirk
6
Aberlady
Luffness
Drem
Tyninghame
Dunbar
Museum of Flight
East Linton
Preston Mill
Longniddry
1296
Stenton
Pitcox
1650
Torness Power Station Visitor Centre
Haddington
Innerwick
Lennoxlove
Garvald
Fast
St Abbs Head NNR
Pencaitland
Bolton
Cockburnspath
St Abb's Head
Nunraw Abbey
Ecclaw
East Saltoun
Gifford
Lammermuir Hills
Grantshouse
St Abbs
Coldingham
Eyemouth
Longyester
Abbey St Bathans
Humbie
Reston
Ellemford
Auchencrow
Ayton
Lammermuir
Edin's Hall Broch
Preston
Chirnside
Longformacus
Foulden
1333
Berwick
Ravensdowne Barracks
Jim Clark Room
Manderston
Whiteadder Water
Oxton
Duns
Allanton
Paxton
Berwick-upon-Tweed
5
Southern Upland Way
Thirlestane
Westruther
Tweedmouth
Polwarth
Whitsome
Horncliffe
Scremerston
19
Lauder
Houndslow
Ladykirk
Norham
West Allerdean
Greenlaw
Blackadder Water
Swinton
© Nicolson Maps

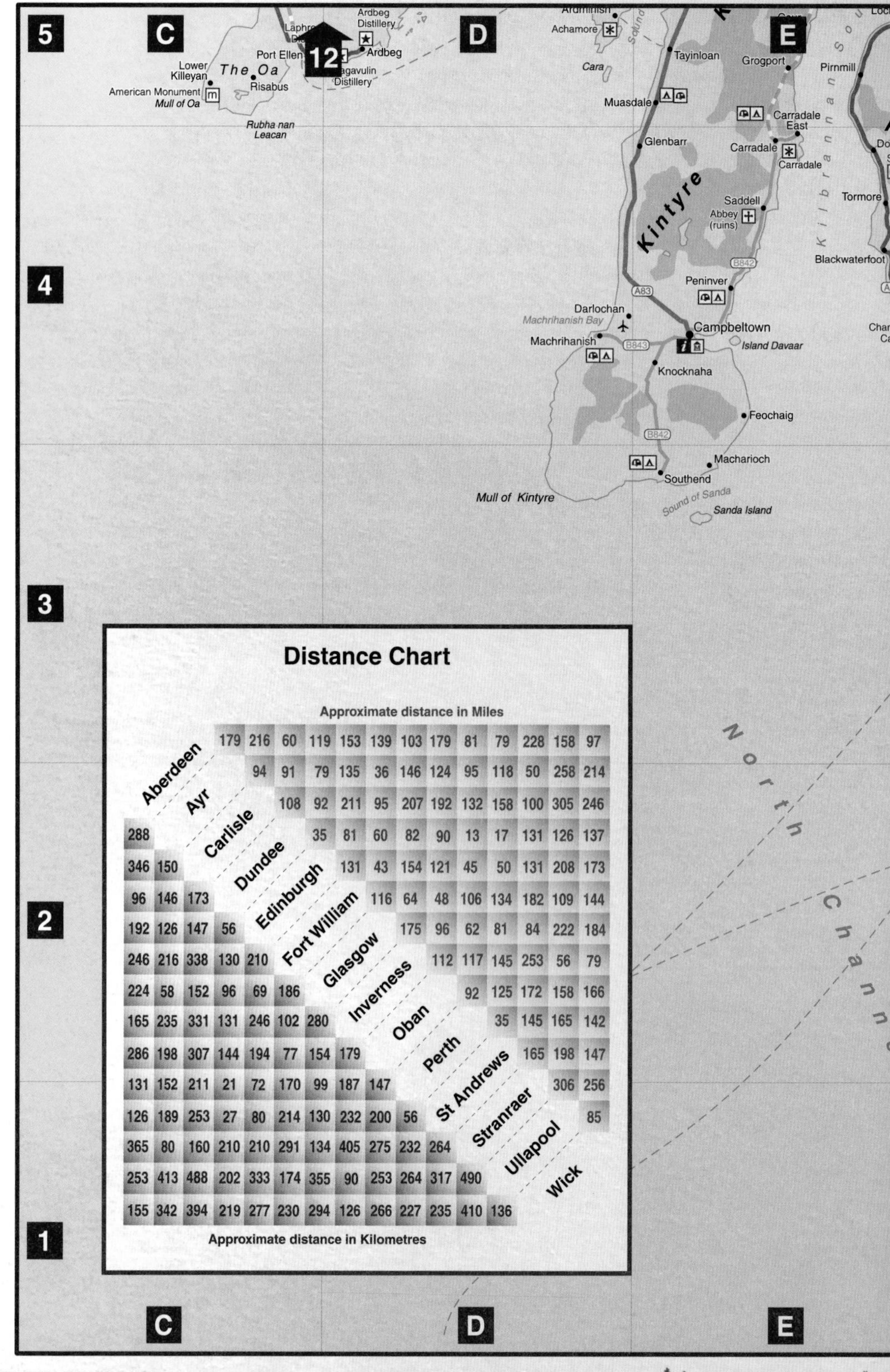

Distance Chart

Approximate distance in Miles (above the diagonal) / Approximate distance in Kilometres (below the diagonal)

	Aberdeen	Ayr	Carlisle	Dundee	Edinburgh	Fort William	Glasgow	Inverness	Oban	Perth	St Andrews	Stranraer	Ullapool	Wick
Aberdeen		179	216	60	119	153	139	103	179	81	79	228	158	97
Ayr	288		94	91	79	135	36	146	124	95	118	50	258	214
Carlisle	346	150		108	92	211	95	207	192	132	158	100	305	246
Dundee	96	146	173		35	81	60	82	90	13	17	131	126	137
Edinburgh	192	126	147	56		131	43	154	121	45	50	131	208	173
Fort William	246	216	338	130	210		116	64	48	106	134	182	109	144
Glasgow	224	58	152	96	69	186		175	96	62	81	84	222	184
Inverness	165	235	331	131	246	102	280		112	117	145	253	56	79
Oban	286	198	307	144	194	77	154	179		92	125	172	158	166
Perth	131	152	211	21	72	170	99	187	147		35	145	165	142
St Andrews	126	189	253	27	80	214	130	232	200	56		165	198	147
Stranraer	365	80	160	210	210	291	134	405	275	232	264		306	256
Ullapool	253	413	488	202	333	174	355	90	253	264	317	490		85
Wick	155	342	394	219	277	230	294	126	266	227	235	410	136	

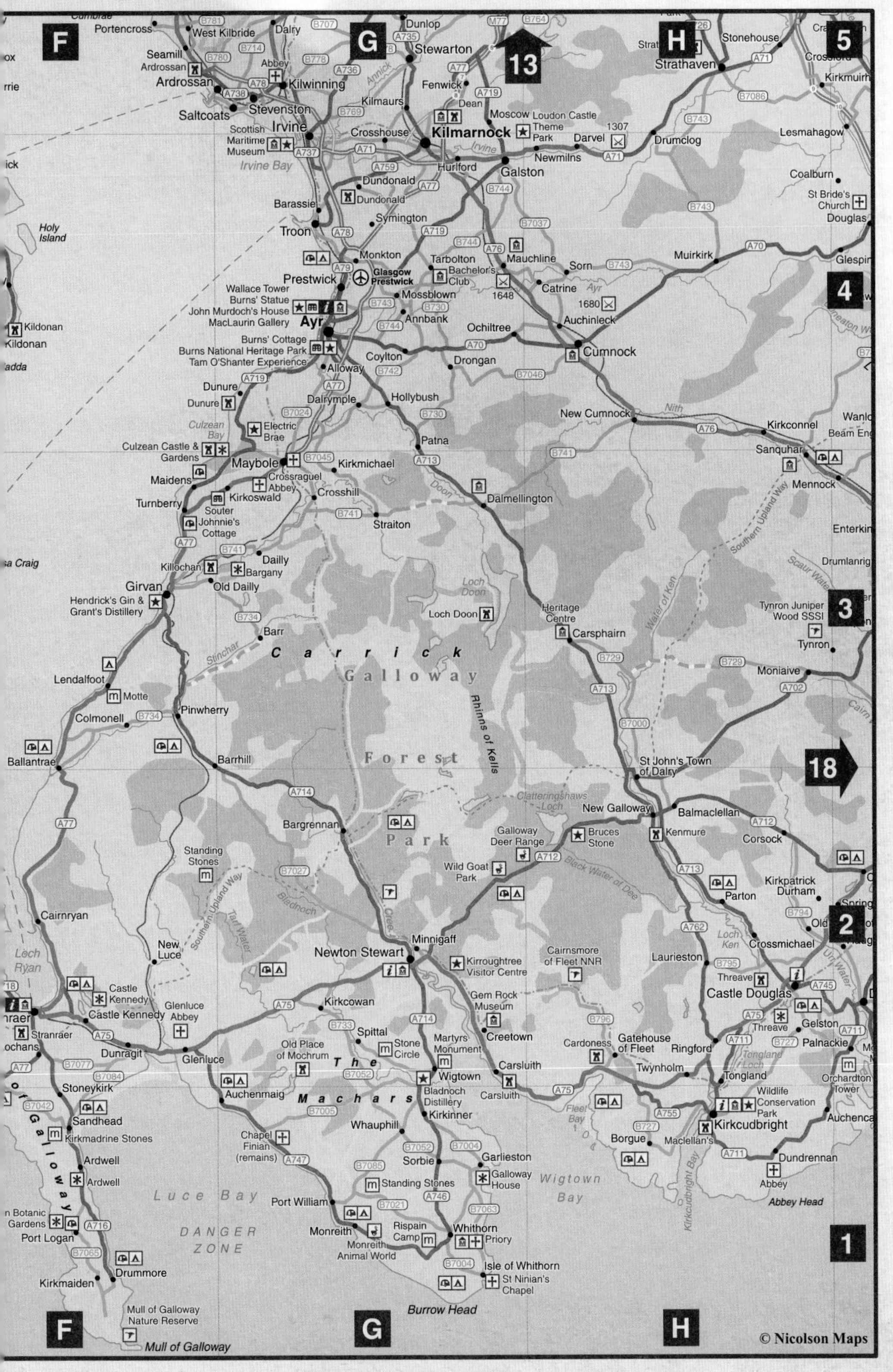
F
G
H
5
13
Portencross
West Kilbride
Dalry
Dunlop
Stewarton
Stonehouse
Strathaven
Kirkmuirhill
Seamill
Ardrossan
Abbey
Kilwinning
Fenwick
Kilmaurs
Dean
Saltcoats
Stevenston
Irvine
Scottish Maritime Museum
Crosshouse
Kilmarnock
Moscow
Loudon Castle Theme Park
Darvel
1307
Drumclog
Lesmahagow
Irvine Bay
Hurlford
Newmilns
Galston
Coalburn
Dundonald
St Bride's Church
Douglas
Barassie
Symington
Holy Island
Troon
Monkton
Tarbolton
Bachelor's Club
Mauchline
Muirkirk
Glespin
Prestwick
Glasgow Prestwick
Sorn
Catrine
Ayr
Wallace Tower
Burns' Statue
John Murdoch's House
MacLaurin Gallery
Mossblown
1648
1680
4
Kildonan
Annbank
Auchinleck
Ayr
Ochiltree
Burns' Cottage
Burns National Heritage Park
Tam O'Shanter Experience
Coylton
Cumnock
Alloway
Drongan
Dunure
Dalrymple
Hollybush
Nith
New Cumnock
Culzean Bay
Electric Brae
Kirkconnel
Wanlockhead
Beam Engine
Culzean Castle & Gardens
Patna
Sanquhar
Maybole
Kirkmichael
Crossraguel Abbey
Maidens
Mennock
Doon
Crosshill
Turnberry
Kirkoswald
Dalmellington
Souter Johnnie's Cottage
Straiton
Southern Upland Way
Enterkinfoot
Ailsa Craig
Dailly
Scaur Water
Drumlanrig
Killochan
Bargany
Loch Doon
Water of Ken
Girvan
Old Daily
Hendrick's Gin & Grant's Distillery
Heritage Centre
Loch Doon
Tynron Juniper Wood SSSI
3
Carsphairn
Barr
Tynron
Stinchar
Carrick
Galloway
Rhinns of Kells
Moniaive
Lendalfoot
Motte
Pinwherry
Colmonell
Forest
St John's Town of Dalry
18
Ballantrae
Barrhill
Clatteringshaws Loch
New Galloway
Balmaclellan
Bargrennan
Park
Galloway Deer Range
Bruces Stone
Kenmure
Corsock
Standing Stones
Wild Goat Park
Black Water of Dee
Kirkpatrick Durham
Parton
Bladnoch
Southern Upland Way
Tarf Water
Cairnryan
Cree
Minnigaff
Loch Ken
Crossmichael
2
Springholm
New Luce
Newton Stewart
Cairnsmore of Fleet NNR
Laurieston
Loch Ryan
Kirroughtree Visitor Centre
Threave
Castle Douglas
Urr Water
Castle Kennedy
Glenluce Abbey
Kirkcowan
Gem Rock Museum
Stranraer
Castle Kennedy
Spittal
Creetown
Threave
Gelston
Lochans
Dunragit
Old Place of Mochrum
Stone Circle
Martyrs' Monument
Cardoness
Gatehouse of Fleet
Ringford
Palnackie
Glenluce
The
Carsluith
Twynholm
Tongland Loch
Orchardton Tower
Stoneykirk
Auchenmaig
Machars
Wigtown
Bladnoch Distillery
Carsluith
Tongland
Wildlife Conservation Park
Sandhead
Kirkinner
Fleet Bay
Kirkcudbright
Auchencairn
Kirkmadrine Stones
Chapel Finian (remains)
Whauphill
Borgue
Maclellan's
Ardwell
Garlieston
Sorbie
Galloway House
Wigtown Bay
Kirkcudbright Bay
Dundrennan
Ardwell
Abbey
Luce Bay
Port William
Standing Stones
Abbey Head
Rhins of Galloway
Logan Botanic Gardens
Port Logan
Monreith
Rispain Camp
Whithorn
Priory
DANGER ZONE
Monreith Animal World
1
Isle of Whithorn
St Ninian's Chapel
Kirkmaiden
Drummore
Burrow Head
Mull of Galloway Nature Reserve
Mull of Galloway
© Nicolson Maps

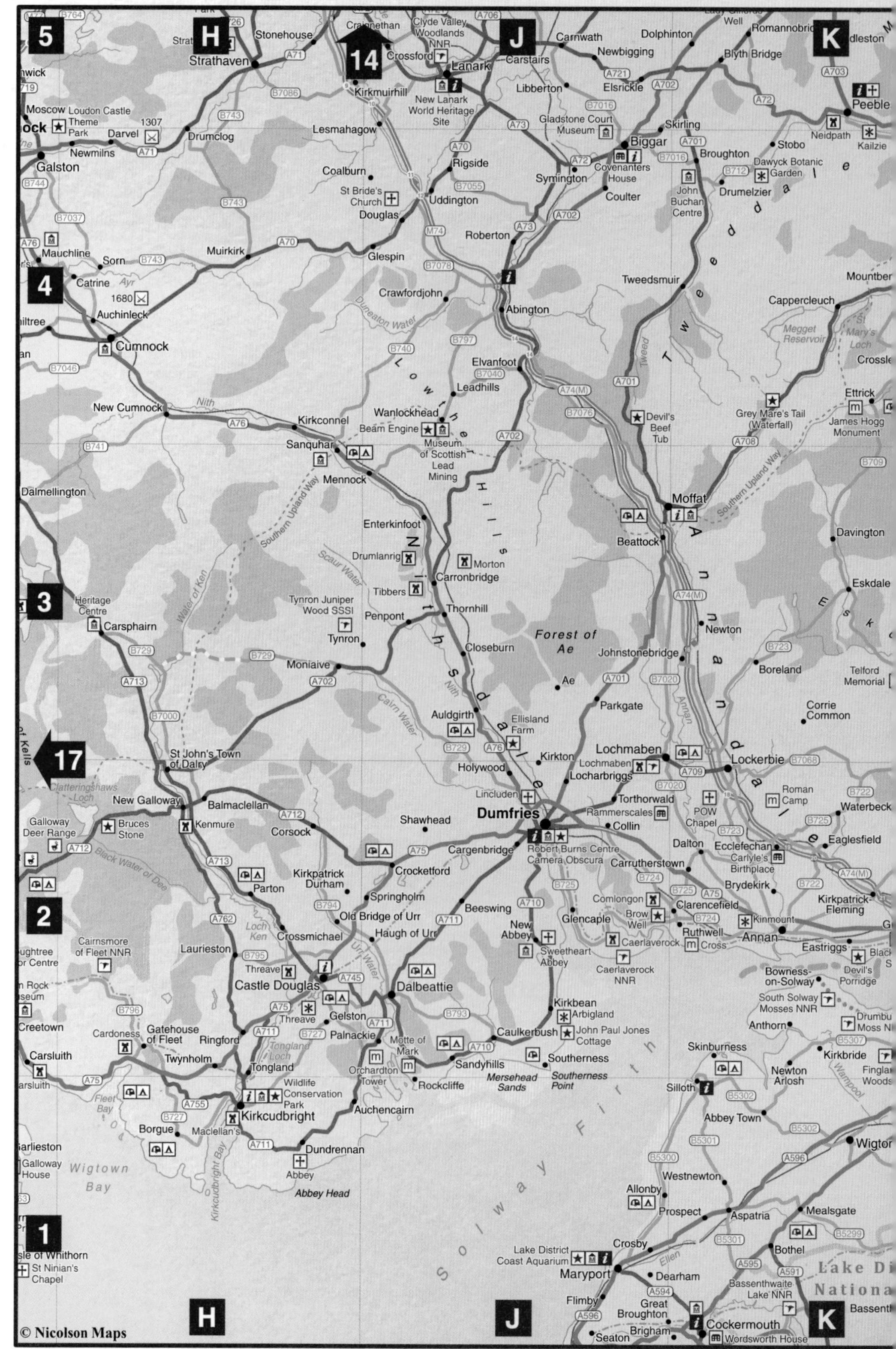

© Nicolson Maps

L
M
N
5
4
3
2
1
15
Houndslow
Greenlaw
Ladykirk
Norham
West Allerdean
Stow
Legerwood
Tower
Gordon
Hume
Leitholm
Swinton
The Hirsel
Coldstream
Cornhill-on-Tweed
Eccles
Birgham
Duddo
Ancroft
Bowsden
Lowick
Fenwick
Holy Island or Lindisfarne
Holy Island
Lindisfarne
Lindisfarne NNR
Priory
Langshaw
Torwoodlee
Earlston
Mellerstain
Sitchill
Etal
Crookham
Ford
Galashiels
Abbey
Redpath
Scotts View
Smailholm
Smailholm Tower
Grace Darling Museum
Budle Bay
Bamburgh
1513
Flodden
Caddonfoot
Abbotsford
Melrose
Priorwood
Dryburgh Abbey
Floors
Kelso
Abbey
Milfield
Doddington
Belford
Seahouses
Newtown St Boswells
St Boswells
Mertoun
Roxburgh
Heiton
Blakelaw
Kilham
Glen
1402
Adderstone
Selkirk
1645
1545
Waterloo Mon
Teviot Water Gardens
Town Yetholm
Kirk Yetholm
Akeld
Wooler
Chatton
Newham
Swinhoe
Ale Water
Nisbet
Eckford
St Cuthbert's Way
Haugh Head
Wild Cattle of Chillingham
Lilliesleaf
Belses
Ancrum
Bonjedward
Morebattle
Hepburn
North Charlton
Christon Bank
Ashkirk
Hassendean
Teviot
Mary Queen of Scots House
Jedburgh Castle Jail
Jedburgh
Abbey
Oxnam
Hownam
Wooperton
Eglingham
Rennington
Drumlanrigs Tower
Scott Gallery
Denholm
Jed Water
Powburn
Hulne Priory
Hawick
Ingram
Glanton
Bolton
Alnwick
Denwick
Bonchester Bridge
Camptown
Northumberland
Alnham
Whittingham
Edlingham
Chesters
Hass
Callaly
1575
Shilbottle
Carter Bar
National
Netherton
National Park Visitor Centre
Cragbank Wood NNR
Byrness
Harbottle
Cragside
Thropton
Rothbury
Longframlington
Felton
Park
Hepple
Coquet
Hermitage
Saughtree
Cheviot Hills
Redesdale
Pennine Way
Rede
1388
Otterburn
Elsdon
Longhorsley
Kielder
Kielder Forest
Otterburn Mill
Netherwitton
Kielder Water
Kielder Water Experience
Greenhaugh
Falstone
Newcastleton
Scots' Gap
Hartburn
Morpeth Chantry
Morpeth
Morpeth (ruin)
Kielder Forest Park
North Tyne
Bellingham
Wallington Hall
Kirkwhelpington
Wansbeck
Liddesdale
Liddel Water
Ridsdale
Whalton
Belsay
Belsay Hall
Chipchase
Wark
Catlowdy
ENGLAND
Barrasford
Humshaugh
Stamfordham
Ponteland
Newcastle
Irthing
Kirkcambeck
Lyne
Once Brewed Visitor Centre
Housesteads
Roman Army Museum
Hadrian's Wall
Chesters
Fourstones
Wall
Heddon-on-the-Wall
Birdoswald
Acomb
Aydon
Smithfield
Walton
Priory
Gilsland
Greenhead
Bardon Mill
Haydon Bridge
Corstopitum
Corbridge
Newcastle upon Tyne
Newtown
Haltwhistle
South Tyne
Hexham
Tyne
Ryton
Metro Cen
Low Row
Dilston
Prudhoe
Blaydon
Bede's World
Brampton
Allen Banks (Woodland Walks)
Riding Mill
Hallbankgate
1464
Painshawfield
Whickham
Rowlands Gill
Lambley
Halton-Lea-Gate
Catton
Slaley
Bearsbridge
Dalton
Burnopfield
Warwick Bridge
Castle Carrock
Wetheral
Allendale Town
Derwent Reservoir
Ebchester
Stanley
Eden
Consett
Pennine Way
Slaggyford
South Tyne
Blanchland
Edmundbyers
Newbiggin
South Tynedale Railway
Castleside
Lanchester
Alston
The Hub
Allenheads
Rookhope Nurseries & Gardens
Croglin
High Hesket
Langley Park
Nenthead
Rookhope
Satley
Renwick
Esh Winning
Pennines
Garrigill
Cowshill
Killhope Lead Mining Museum
Kirkoswald
Stanhope
Tow Law
Lazonby
Westgate
Weardale
Durham Dales Centre
Wolsingham
Crook
Willington
Melmerby
Pennine Ski Area
Weardale Railway
Eden Ostrich World
Langwathby
Skirwith
Langdon Beck
Moor House Upper Teesdale NNR
Hamsterley
Auckland
Penrith
Culgaith
Bishop Auckland
A697
A6089
A68
A6105
B6364
A6112
A698
A1
B6525
A6089
B6397
B6461
B6350
B6353
A698
B6396
B6352
B6525
B6356
B6404
A699
A697
B6349
A707
A699
A698
B6352
B6351
B6436
B6348
A68
B6400
B6401
A1
A7
B6359
B6346
B6347
A698
B6357
A697
A68
A6088
B6341
B6399
A1
B6357
A68
B6341
B6345
B6342
A697
A696
A68
B6343
B6524
B6357
B6320
B6342
B6318
A1
B6309
A696
A6079
B6318
A68
B6318
B6319
A69
A6071
A69
A695
B6305
A689
A69
B6309
A692
A686
B6306
A68
B6310
A694
B6413
B6295
A689
A6076
B6278
A691
B6296
A689
B6302
A6
B6301
M6
A686
B6299
B6413
B6412
A689
B6277
B6278
A68
A689
B6412
B6295

INDEX OF PLACE NAMES

N

The Broons' Days Oot!
Great money-saving offers from
The National Trust for Scotland and Historic Scotland

the National Trust for Scotland

a place for everyone

SPECIAL MEMBERSHIP OFFER

Discover Scotland's heritage with membership of the National Trust for Scotland.

Joining the Trust gives you a year's unlimited access to the castles, gardens, houses, historic sites, visitor centres, nature reserves and museums in the Trust's care.

Since the Trust is a charity, your membership supports its vital conservation work in protecting these unique places for future generations.

Membership is great value – for instance, just £6.50 per month for a family!

You can enjoy 18 months for the price of 12 by calling our Customer Service Centre on 0844 493 2100 and quoting :

"***The Broons' Days Oot***."

This special offer applies to new members joining by direct debit.

KIDS GO FREE

AT HISTORIC SCOTLAND SITES

For one-time use at Historic Scotland sites with a copy of The Broons' Days Oot!

- Kids go free (to a maximum of four) when accompanied by two adults to Historic Scotland sites.
- To check seasonal opening times of sites, go to Historic Scotland's website at www.historic-scotland.gov.uk/places
- Take a copy of ***The Broons' Days Oot*** when you visit, and get the voucher stamped on entry.

Terms and conditions:
The 'Kids Go Free' offer is valid for children under 16. A maximum of two free child tickets per paying adult is permitted, but cannot be used in conjunction with any other offer.
Process under PLU code 619.

See www.historic-scotland.gov.uk for further information.

STAMP HERE